LIVING IN BLACK HOLES

Works by Bill Reed

Printed/ebook plays
Living in Black Holes (ISBNs 9780994531100/9780994531117)
Living on Mars (ISBNs 9780994327784/9780994322791)
Burke's Company (ISBNs 9780994280565/9780994280572)
Bullsh   (ISBNs 9780994322746/9780994322753)
Cass Butcher Bunting (ISBNs 9780994327722/9780994322739)
Mr Siggie Morrison with his Comb and Paper (ISBNs 9780994322760/9780994322777)
Truganinni   (ISBNs 9780994280596/9780994322708)

Printed/ebook novels
The Pipwink Papers\
Me, the Old Man
Stigmata
Ihe
Dogod
Crooks
Tusk
Throw her back
Are You Human?
Tasker Tusker Tasker
Awash
1001 Lankan Nights book 1
1001 Lankan Nights book 2
Water Workout (Nonfiction)

Professionally-staged plays
Burke's Company
Truganinni
The Pecking Order
Mr Siggie Morrison with his Comb and Paper*
Jack Charles is Up and Fighting
Just Out of Your Ground
You Want It, Don't You, Billy?
I Don't Know What to Do with You!
Paddlesteamer
Cass Butcher Bunting
More Bullsh
Talking to a Mirror
Auntie and the Girl
(plus the work-shopped plays in this collection)

award-winning short stories (see title 'Passing Strange')
Messman on the C.E. Altar
English Expression
The 200-year Old Feet
The Case Inside
Blind Freddie Among the Pickle Jars
The Old Ex-serviceman
Mahood on the Thin Beach
The Shades of You my Dandenong

LIVING IN BLACK HOLES

Five Plays

BILL REED

R

First published in 2016 by Reed Independent, Victoria, Australia.

Printed by Createspace.com, a division of Amazon.com.

This first edition is available from most major book retail chains and online retail outlets worldwide as:
paperback: ISBN 9780994531100
ebook: ISBN 9780994531117

Front cover: Dilani Priyangika Ranaweera, Dart Lanka Productions, Sri Lanka

National Library of Australia Cataloguing-in-Publication entry:
Creator: Reed, Bill, 1939 -- author.
Title: Living in Black Holes/ Bill Reed
Edition: first
ISBN: 9780994531100 (paperback)
ISBN: 9780994531117 (ebook)
Notes: includes bibliographical reference.
Subjects: Drama/drama collection/Australian drama/Indigenous theatre.
Dewey Number: A822.3

CONTENTS

To my dearest E.
The things she is naturally graced in seeing are far greater than these few things she hasn't seen.

MR SIGGIE MORRISON WITH HIS COMB AND PAPER

Introduction

At a time when our playwrights are concerning themselves more with our history than its heritage, it is a startling and exciting experience to be confronted by a new play which is far from the current mainstream in its individuality and perception.

As a director, I was immediately impressed, on the first reading, by the inherent theatricality of the play - the knowledge and understanding of the special requirements that constitute a theatrical event. In this work the combination of knowledge and enquiry gives us not just a play but an experience of the struggle for creation.

The playwright takes us on a journey in search of reality. At times we arc totally convinced, (often by use of the unreal theatrical device) at other times we withdraw from these convictions. But our total involvement is governed by the emotions experienced, whether by fake stage characters or real people, so that we are concerned, not just by the search for truth but by man's inhumanity to man. I believe this play has a great deal to say about mankind. Our treatment of each other, whether it be at the humanitarian level of simply helping our fellow man or on the personal level of using and destroying someone for our own gain. Then again it questions our inheritance. Is this the land of milk and honey where the sun continually shines - the land of our fathers where life is wonderful for all men? Is this a great Australian myth?

The Australian theatre is concerning itself with Australian ideas and problems. For me MR SIGGIE MORRISON with his comb and paper is a definite acquisition to this growth, but better still I believe Bill Reed has provided us with a play that is not for our eyes and ears alone but speaks a universal language for all theatres.

Peter Batey,
Artistic Director,
South Australian State Theatre Company

2

The Premiere

First performed at Scotch College open-air amphitheatre, Adelaide, by the South Australian Theatre Company as part of the Adelaide Festival of Arts, February 29 1972, with the following cast:

SIGGIE   Neil Curnow
PARSONS   Shawn Gurton
BIG JULIE   Daphne Grey
MISS GLAMORGAN   Rona Coleman
'BOY'   Tony Porter
JARVIS   Brian Wenzel
MISS HOLLAND   Barbara West
MRS PRUFROCK   Julie Hamilton

Directed and designed by Peter Batey

The Cast

If the cast needs to be reduced for practical purposes, the playwright suggests that:

1. JARVIS could very ill-humouredly double up as 'BOY'
2. BIG JULIE could very disgustedly double up as MISS GLAMORGAN
3. MISS HOLLAND could very fumblingly double up as MRS PRUFROCK.

One production simply had MISS GLAMORGAN represented by a spotlight on the stage with voice over.

Any character changes should be swift and out in the open and with the minimum of change of pace… eg, JARVIS could simply roll up a trouser leg and change voices to take the part of 'BOY'.

The Monologue

The Monologue should be on a continuous tape and run without break from the opening of the doors of the theatre to the closing of the doors of the theatre. It should be piped into both the auditorium and the foyer.

It should be the continuing, organic backdrop to the performance. It is never shut off, but only lowered to an inarticulate, yet still audible level whenever necessary. It is the 'consciousness' of the play, although its effect shouldn't be more than the background 'hum' of, say, other people at an animated gathering

The full text can be used or those parts of it given in this playscript can simply be used repetitiously.

When the Monologue 'breaks through' it is as disruptive and is of a source just as unknown to the actors as it is to the audience.

Monologue Text

You ought to shine through down here. You ought to shine through a little bit more down here. That's what you ought to do. Peek through. There's a hole up there. You could shine through the hole up there a little bit. For a bit. Just for a bit. Let me know you know I'm down here. You ought to know that. You ought to shine through down here just a peek. Now. Please.

I'm cold. I'm wet. I'm cold and wet. I don't want to be cold and wet. I didn't come home to be cold and wet. Don't turn away from me. You oughtn't to turn away from me. Please. Why have you turned away from me? There is a hole up there. You could shine through. There's a hole. You ought to shine through. Why don't you shine through just a little bit? A peek. A little peek There's a hole there. I don't want to die down here. Why should I die down here?
   (coughs)
Smell. Smell. Is it me? It's not me. It's me a little bit. Not all me. You know it's not all me You know I couldn't hold my bowels for days and days. If you shine through a little, just a peek a little bit, you could dry it all up. You could dry it all up. You could dry me up. Bum me. Bum me again. That's what I want. You know that Bum me. That's what I want. It's me. Don't you see? It's me. It's my face. Look at me. It's my face. Don't I shine through it anymore? Don't I? I've come home. It's me, Siggie, and I've come home. I'm home. I didn't come home to die down here. I've come home to you. I came home to you, you know that. You don't shine much in England. You don't shine through much in England, do you?

It's so dark down here. I can't live down here It's too dark for me to live down here. You know that. Why don't you shine through? You could shine through if you wanted to. If you really wanted to, you could shine through just a little bit down here. You should know I've been trying to get back for years. I shouldn't have to be down hem if you're angry with me not coming back. You should have been there and seen what it was like. Not very nice. All that yellow water and all that. Not to mention my arthritis. Which I haven't because I don't want to gripe. What's the use of griping? Griping gets you nowhere

6

because nobody ever listens to you when you're griping. About arthritis in particular. About yellow water in your... in...

(cannot hold back coughing fit any longer)

Nobody wants to know if you've got yellow water in your lungs. Or if you've got arthritis like I've got arthritis. But what can a bloke say? There's nothing a bloke can say about it because nobody even bothers to listen. All they say is stiff. Stiff. That's all you get. Really. Really and truly deep down where it all matters in your mind. That's all you get. Or they've got troubles of their own. When they haven't really because if they had yellow water in their lungs and arthritis of the fingers like I've got and sitting here rotting because I reckon I'm going to rot pretty soon and all itchy and peeing in their trousers like I am, they'd know what trouble really is. I can tell you. I can't even move and it's smelly down here. I can't even turn away from the pong. I know I pong. Nobody has to tell me I pong. Anybody would pong if they were stuck down here like I'm stuck down here not able to even turn away from the pong and it not doing my lungs any good…

Oh, my God Jesus dear sweet Jesus God, help me Please get me out. Please get me out. I don't want to die. Why should I die? Why should I die? I don't want to die. I shouldn't have to die. Why should it be me down here ponging and dying. I've never ever thought about death so why should it be me down here dying when I haven't given death a second thought. Oh, God. Help me. Please help me because I don't want to die. What would the world be like without me? How can I think about dying when the world would be something that didn't have me in it? Something that wouldn't have me in it oh God Jesus sweet dear Jesus. It's blank when I think of death. There's nothing there when I think of death. Why should I be born if all I can do is die because what is the use of living if you're going to die all over the place from the time that you are born. It's not fair. It's not something I asked for. I didn't ask to be down here. I didn't ask to be put down here and to die like this what with all that horrible yellow water in my lungs and Miss Glamorgan.

Miss Glamorgan? Who's Miss Glamorgan? Oh, yeah. Yeah. Anyway, as I was saying, they say nothing if you try to tell them. What you've got that'd kill anybody else. Nothing. Not a thing. It doesn't matter a thing if I suddenly up with... like that saying; it flows,

Siggie, honestly Siggie, it really flows, y'know? if I come up with…
just let's say for the sake of, up with…

(outcry; a theatre-wide conversation-stopper)

HELP! HELP! PLEASE… HELP!

What I mean is if I came out with a blood curdler, they wouldn't
even… even… they wouldn't even… What's that? Listen! What's that?
Ssh. What's that? Let's have a bit of shush…

(but coughs while trying to keep silent.)

Please let the kids come back. I'd be all right if the kids came back.
No sweat if the kids came back. I'll play fox. Right, I'll play fox and
when they come back they'll think they've done me damage and. I'm
not saying they haven't done me a damage. They've certainly done me
a damage all right. But when they come back I'll lay down and play
possum and they'll think they've done me more damage than even the
little bloody… sorry… horrors think they have and they'll have to go
and get their daddies or mums or go and get me a policeman. I
wonder whether they'll send around the fire brigade. You hear about
the fire brigade going and hauling people out of places in the nick of
time so it could well be the fire brigade gets around here first. That's
if those kids tell them. Even if those kids tell their daddies or their
mums or a policeman or anybody. They can tell anybody. I must
remember to tell them that. Might make them feel better if they know
I don't care whether they tell anybody just as long as they tell
someone. After all, it doesn't matter who they tell as long as they tell.
That's the main thing. As long as they tell. Not all of them have to tell
either. Only one of them has to tell really. Only one of them has to
open his mouth. It could be her mouth. Its mouth. That's better. I don't
want to be caught being rotten to kids but any kids that do what those
kids are doing to me don't deserve proper parents. Things. Things at
Christmas time. Books. Though I never had books. But you know
what I mean. Any kids who do what they've done to me don't deserve
the basic courtesies… good word. Gee, I've got them floating all
around my mind. It's incredible… there I go again… how it just comes
and goes. All those lovely words. I've always loved all those lovely
words. All those lovely words just floating around in your mind just
like it's a nice cool pond in a park and all those lovely nice words are
swans drifting along and popping out now and again when you last
expect it. Don't deserve basic courtesies of common decency… lovely
words, those… of a normal society and good friendship and common
decencies and nice manners and good behaviour and doing the right

8

things by others when it comes down to it all. Or something or other. You know what I mean.

It's just the stink. It's just the pong. It's just my legs. It's just my leg aching so much and my fingers aching so much and swelling up like they are. Look at them. It's just that all that bubbling in my... you know... lots of places in me really...

    (coughs gently by auto suggestion.)

I think I've wet my strides. I think I've done it. I can't help it. I've done it. That's all there. Is to it. I've done it. Not the first time. I've done it. Down there. Oh God, I smell. I smell. Gee, I smell. It smells down. Here and. I've done it in. In my pants. Damn. Damn. Damn. Please. Please. I'm not complaining. No. Not. Complaining. But I. But I think I've done it in my pants. Yes. I think I've done it in my pants. I think I've done it in my pants. What have I done? What is going... to happen...? What's going to happen to me, please? Please?

Mustn't think about it. Mustn't. You mustn't think I'm complaining. It's just that I'm so cold and wet and aching. Well, I was aching and smelly. I just don't like to think I'm doing something down there that I'd be... yes, embarrassed about. Yes, all embarrassed when somebody finds me. When somebody finds me and says what have you been doing down there and then sniffing like they do or me trying to cover up something embarrassing that I've been doing because they wouldn't believe that I've had to do it and there was nowhere else to do it. They don't believe you. That sour looking man. I think it was a man. That sour looking man who was sitting next to me on the plane when I was coming home and asking the nice young air hostess for another seat, he wouldn't believe that I had to do it in one of those lovely brand new brown paper bags. I could tell he wouldn't. Oh, yes. I could tell all right. When I tried to get out excuse me to him each time, he just turned away. He turned away and put his head up in the air. He turned away and put his head up in the air and his nose under one of those funny old nozzles they had in there where air came through.

I didn't care. I was on my way home. I had my ticket in my hand. I would have had my ticket in my hand if they hadn't taken it off me before we got on. That's not the point though. It's as good as having your ticket in your hand when you're sitting in the plane and they haven't turfed you off because if they haven't turfed you off then that

9

means you must have had a ticket in your hand to be able to get on in the first place. Stands to reason. And if you had your ticket in your hand that means you must have been able to buy it. And if they haven't turfed you off and you've been able to buy a ticket then that means you were able to afford to buy the ticket in the first place. That's fair enough. That's logical. Gee, where do I get all these words from? What was it? Never mind.

You would not have thought dear little children could be like that. I was always nice and kind and helpful to dear little children and you wouldn't have thought that dear little children would do a thing like this to me. You'd think they'd care. You'd think they'd say sorry. You'd think they'd go home right away and say: Dad, there's a poor old man stuck down there and what can you do about it. But what can you do about it? There's some little kids who are not dear little children and they're never going to grow up to be nice and kind to old people like me stuck down here like me. Even if they're not stuck down here like me. Dying for all I know. I'm not saying that to scare myself. I don't want to die down here and I know you won't let me die down here but there could be cases of poor old people like me stuck down here or some other place just like this who would die down here if they came across some rotten little kids who didn't care whether they were stuck down here and wouldn't go and tell their daddies or a policeman or get an ambulance or help you out, like. That's what I mean. What I mean is that there are some poor old people who might die down here if they 'were stuck down here like me and they were cold and wet and aching or was aching but now not being able to feel a thing down there which is. Which is just as worse when you think about it because it could be anything. It could be a disease down there in my legs and with a disease down there in their legs like I think there's something wrong with my legs then they mightn't be able to pull out of it if some kids didn't bring them enough to eat even or even go and tell their daddies or mummies. Mummies would be better, because they'd understand...

(*Ed*: *plus see other monologue bursts given in the play... and on continuous loop*)

Act I

(Stage dark, except for SIGGIE back stage. He seems to be lying beneath some weight that he has given up trying to shift off him.

He lies statically for a long time, staring up into the spotlight, as though it was the sun. When he speaks it is equally as flatly.

In the meantime, however, the MONOLOGUE continues to dominate the theatre until it gradually decreases into an underlying 'hum'.

Finally, SIGGIE finds himself able to be heard... somehow knowing that, and:)

SIGGIE: Who's out there?

(It comes back as an empty echo. In the distance y a dog howls faintly. There is a disturbing and indistinct human cry for attention. An ambulance siren rises then fades again. All this is far off. Nothing more. SIGGIE falls back. The MONOLOGUE bursts through again... quickly, aggressive to him, before receding again suddenly.

The 'sunlight' comes across the old man until it falls directly onto him. He basks in it, until...)

SIGGIE (outcry) *Why've you turned off me?*

(Instantly a blackout, during which the MONOLOGUE hums along with the added background of the ambulance siren receding too.

When the spot returns upon him, he is calm again:)

SIGGIE: I was dreaming... silly... I was here, but it wasn't hurting though and there was a big hall with bouquets of flowers all around me. The sun was shining through the rafters and then this funny shape came in and walked up the aisle towards me. When he came close I saw he was wearing my face and his eyes were closed and I knew he

11

was dreaming and dreaming about me up here and when he woke up I knew, listen, I knew, I would no longer be...
  (shudders, then)
Listen, please go and tell your...

  (Lighting up.

  The 'main stage' set shows half-completed scenery of an airport lounge. At back is a large plate-glass observation window. It is dark outside; only the lights from the control tower shine dimly through.

  The actors, except PARSONS, are back stage with SIGGIE being a very loose focal point. MISS GLAMORGAN sits apart from them. They are all carrying scripts to which they will refer occasionally as at an advanced rehearsal. Whenever they do consult these, they speak unmistakably theatrically. Otherwise, they are evidently not 'within' the play.

  PARSONS himself is front stage, trouncing up and down, creating 'mentally'.)

MISS HOLLAND: That's all very well.

JARVIS: Why follow anything but your worst nature?

MISS HOLLAND: No, I've arrived where I've got to face my obligations.

JARVIS: You're single.

MRS PRUFROCK: (hotly) So am I. But that doesn't mean to say all single women only have nursed waiters. Worst natures.

JARVIS: Don't you start. I've been through it all myself.

PARSONS: (shout upwards meaning MONOLOGUE) Turn that annoying thing off!

MISS HOLLAND: You haven't got an eighty-year-old mother at home who you've been neglecting for years precisely because your feet have taken you in your own selfish direction.

MRS PRUFROCK: (sententiously) I know. I've been through it all.

MISS HOLLAND: What one's got to be sure of is whether your own thing is a thing worth doing. Oh God, two months and I ache to leave again. Rothenburg, the Tauber, Stuttgart, Konigsberg Klops and strudel and wurst, Berlin. Lieder in the snow on tipsy nights, hic. Mothers… honestly.

MRS PRUFROCK: I was exactly the same.

JARVIS: Ptochocracy!

MISS HOLLAND: What?

JARVIS: Government by beggars. Ptochocratic. This country, this
    (waves script)
archaeological-dig script. It's all so shagging pauce. Tell you what, the best you can hope for back here is to become that single black jelly bean everybody wants in a bag of sucked-out jujubes.

MISS HOLLAND: What worries me is I feel so unreal. Staying imperial somehow when everybody else has... gone metric.

JARVIS: (snorts) Moral émigrés, aren't we all?

MISS HOLLAND: Faites rien. 'Tomorrow's troubles to the windes resolve'.

PARSONS: (flourish at them) Use the time to consolidate, mes enfants. Animate. Behave. Assimilate. Assumizate. Enmesh. Adjunct together.

MISS HOLLAND: (sotto voce, indicating PARSONS) When I told them I was going to work for him, they said he was around the bend. Even in London.

JARVIS: Wagner himself. Raving dead ringer.

13

MRS PRUFROCK: Oh, let's get on with it. I'd like to go abode wise moi, just for a change.

JARVIS: (joke sniff) I smell the change you mean.

PARSONS: (still acting the creative director) Imbiba mugga fermented mare's milka morning.
        (stops, starts again)
Co-actate into coagulates. Make more intimated moments magical. Say, a bird flies across the Arctic waste, turns left at the first pole returns across the steppes with a glorious landslide right back to the equator, turns to his mate getting high on monkey juice and says, 'Jesus, that's the real stuff. Have I just been on a freak freeze-out'.
        (self-rebuke)
Merde, not quite there. Try this:
        (then)
You are standing on your head looking up at the heavens above you and see the clouds sweeping towards some distant and mysterious white tower. The illusion is that the whole sky is moving and carrying you along with it. But you know it is supposed to the Earth which is moving, so all that empty sky out there can't be moving per se. But supposing it is just as you think you might be. Are you going to dissolve into it, or it into you? And dissolve how? Into some pinpoint of super-heavy mayhems, or into a vast lighthearted dissipation? What we are posing here is: is imagination real thought or visitation?

        (The actors are still gathered around themselves with their scripts, though, and:)

MISS HOLLAND: (looks at script) Where were we?

JARVIS: (reads) 'Night'.

MRS PRUFROCK: (ditto) Day.

JARVIS: Night.

MRS PRUFROCK: Pardon poke, day.

JARVIS: It says night, you scarecrow.

14

MRS PRUFROCK: It says day.

JARVIS: Christ. Night, night.

MRS PRUFROCK: Tell him, dear.

MISS HOLLAND: Well... dayish. I suppose. It varies at the turnarounds, you know.

> *(By now, PARSONS has regathered his creative juices. He looks down, then around, then with right theatrical mood caught, drops to his knees and knocks on the floor boards.)*

PARSONS: We know you're there, Siggie. Somewhere down there among the... not to put too much of a pretty picture on it... the rats. Slugs. Earwigs. What have you. Backing your skinny arms against the slimy wet walls.

> *(BIG JULIE strides in behind PARSONS and cuts them all off. She goes up to the others and points to where, back stage, SIGGIE in his technicolour Sunday-best outfit -- but trousers too big and coat shroudish -- staggers under the weight of a cheap cardboard suitcase from left and eventually off right. PARSONS doesn't notice him, nor the actors being led off in disgust by BIG JULIE.)*

PARSONS: Siggie? Come on, Siggie. Stale urine raising steam. Smelling yourself. Alas, Siggie, mate, who hasn't piddled in his pants some time in his life? Keeps you from drying up. Know what I mean?
   (pause)
What're you thinking, Siggie? Oysters for breakfast? Out of bed, p.m. The old one-two shuffle with cane and monocle, Astaire twirl of the old duke and away he goes... Siggie Morrison, bon viveur, life's traveller... England, Europe, Siam, Warrnambool... Siggie Himself swanking down Castlereagh Street. We're all turning our heads. Who's the pop Pop? Who's the dandy Daddy? The cry goes up. Siggie Morrison, who else, you dead ignoramuses. Or ignorami. Siggie's arrived back in Australia at last. Honky tonk. The harbour bridge falls into the sea. Members of all parliaments confess to being boy scouts. Come on, Siggie. Relent.

15

(BIG JULIE re-enters, stands looking down at PARSONS with contempt. He senses her presence, looks up, laughs nervously.)

BIG JULIE: Now I've seen it all.

PARSONS: (knocks on the stage boards) Sydney. Down here.

BIG JULIE: Oh, yes.

PARSONS: Why not? I make it Sydney. I dub thee Sydney of the Southern Cistern Seas.

BIG JULIE: You need dubbing on your deadwood.

PARSONS: I was using the divine human attribute of abstract reconstruction.

BIG JULIE: (eyes upward) Good God.

PARSONS: I will ignore that by pointing out that if mere prop men, at a few right-hand turns of a few countersunk screws, are able to string a few bits of wood together and say, right, this is an airport lounge. No, more. London airport. And if you don't believe it, then up yours. Now if yer actual tradesmen can shove that down yer gullet, I say: All right, I, being the leading creative light around here... I say it modestly... I wish to add to all this: fine, and Sydney's down here and old Siggie's down here and if you laugh at that, and don't give me any of your sneering hiccoughs, you're in the wrong game. That's all. Signing off.

BIG JULIE: Ha. Ha.

PARSONS: I'll ignore that too. Visions sharpened by the fourth dimension. I, an actor... an ancient craftsman looming away at his dying art... adding for my own amusement... although admitting that that need not negate the inherent flair of it all... a bird, for example, with its wings clipped is still inherently capable of flying... I may be quoted... as I, an actor without spectators am still capable of shooting a certain style, shall we say, at blank spaces... adding, to re-iterate, a qualm of a soupcon, a pinch of imagination's adumbration… look it up in the online Oxford... to the dreary and unchanging three dimensions of wood and plaster board...

(BIG JULIE burps loudly.)

PARSONS: (pained) That is extremely rude. Still, I say again. This is the northern airport from which Siggie Morrison, hero of our play, journeys home after forty years. Creative statement. Siggie Morrison after forty years is travelling Down Under. Ergo.
(knocks on floor boards)
This way in the mind's eye. Down here, therefore, is Sydney. There. You may not realize it, but I have just retrieved your sense of logic through illusion. You needn't thank me. I shall go even further.
(knocks on the floor boards again)
Listen. If you tap Sydney, it's hollow too.

BIG JULIE: Like your head.

PARSONS: (calls out) Take five.

BIG JULIE: We're taking more than five. We've gone on strike, tinkerbell.

(And turns to go off.)

PARSONS: No, seriously. Imagine if Siggie Morrison was a real person, renamed only for the exigencies of drama. Imagine him stepping arthritically out of some room-and- board right now in his yellow corduroy pants and his pink shirt and his white straw hat, carrying that ridiculous lady's mauve umbrella... started out on his daily circuit with the snot drop hanging from the end of his nose and his little reptilian eyes filling up with decrepit pools while, behind, the landlord tries to think of ways he can get the little drip out of the room... and some hairy labourer right now is pointing out that little technicolour poof to his mates... If that's what a flesh-and-slosh Siggie Morrison was probably doing right now... actual, breathing, material and murmuring his idiotic little 'my, my's' and 'geez's' to all the retrorockets in women's ears... then for the sake of argument, this...
(taps boards)

17

'ere be Sydney. And down there, Siggie Morrison crawls away into his sad, pathetic tear-jerking existence just as really as if he was up on the stage here with us right now...

> *(Before huffing off, BIG JULIE disgustedly turns PARSONS' head around so that he can see SIGGIE back onto stage dragging his suitcase along the ground, sighing, letting the suitcase drop, catching his breathy then speaking back to the wings)*

SIGGIE: Crikey me, of course I will. I'll just wait here. Don't you all go worrying about little old me.

> *(He smiles warily at PARSONS. Then notices the couch and, dragging his suitcase after, goes over to it, lies back with eyes closed.*
>
> *PARSONS turns away when he recovers his senses, tries to ignore SIGGIE's presence... whistles, sits, examines a bit of prop, calls for coffee -- nobody answers -- examines his fingernails until he cannot stand it anymore. Whips around to SIGGIE)*

PARSONS: What's the game?

SIGGIE: Sorry, this your seat?

PARSONS: Never mind about the seat.

SIGGIE: I didn't mean to take your seat.

PARSONS: I don't care about the seat.

SIGGIE: I wouldn't like to have taken your seat.

PARSONS: Forget the seat!

SIGGIE: You don't come across somebody nice enough to give an old man like me his seat often. Not these days.

PARSONS: (into air) Big Julie!

18

BIG JULIE: (head appears) Don't call me Big.

PARSONS: Julie!

BIG JULIE: (reappears, indicates SIGGIE) Answer that then, divine re-creator.

(She retracts her head again)

PARSONS: Big Julie! Julie!

(He gets no reply)

SIGGIE: My, my. I'm all so excited.
    (giggles)
It's the first time I've ever flown. It's the first time I've ever flown through clouds, too. I've always wanted to fly through those lovely clouds. They say it's like snow. But it's vapour really. That's where we get the word vapourized from. From flying through clouds that we think are like snow. Excuse me.

(He closes his eyes again.)

PARSONS: You!

SIGGIE: Oh dear. My friends said it'd be all right for me to wait here on this seat.

PARSONS: (suspiciously) What friends?

SIGGIE: They came all the way up to see me off. Isn't that nice? I'm going home.
    (giggles)
I've been away forty years give or take. I'm an Australian.

PARSONS: All the world's a stage Australian.

SIGGIE: Forty years, two months and three days.
    (giggles)
Stayed Aussie all that time even if I say so meself.

(And closes his eyes again.

PARSONS hurries over to the wings.)

PARSONS: (off) How did he get here?

BIG JULIE: (head on) I found him in the Mens, if you must know.

PARSONS: In the Men's can?

BIG JULIE: (defiantly) I've got nothing to hide.

PARSONS: Don't you know who he's trying to impersonate?

BIG JULIE: Give over. Who else could look like that? Bit of luck the poor old bugger has brought his lawyer along to sort you out too.

PARSONS: (reverting to style) Mere bagatelle of an imbroglio. Main street, rush hour, two people suddenly dash into each other's arms, make violent love by the fire hydrant. They don't know each other's name. It's just that for the last twenty years they've just bumped into each other on the way from work and had it away by the fire hydrant. That's imbroglio. Who's to blame?
    (to 'off')
Did someone take that down? We might be able to use it later.
    (back to BIG JULIE)
However, imbroglio must be in good taste before I'll go along with it.
    (indicating SIGGIE)
That ain't good taste.

SIGGIE: (looking up) If you see my friends, would you tell them I'm here? Case I go the nod off, you see.

(They stop. But SIGGIE says no more. Finally...)

PARSONS: I warn you. I shall maintain my aloof stance against ridiculous imported possibilities.

BIG JULIE: You should have seen your slack gob when old Siggie walked on, big man.

PARSONS: (carefully) Who said it's Siggie?

BIG JULIE: I asked him, you squashed dung.

PARSONS: (uncomfortable nonchalance) How can it be Siggie? There's no Siggie up here. He lives with Charon in men's minds down beneath the aspidistra roots.

BIG JULIE: Like hell there ain't no Siggie, you shiver of shot.

PARSONS: I wouldn't pull a thing like that on an old man who was real.

BIG JULIE: Yeah, you'll kick yourself all the way to the bank.

PARSONS: Art and association.

BIG JULIE: Bad art and bank accounts, you mean. You conned your way around him. They give them free legal aid these days.

PARSONS: (shivers) Don't say things like that.

BIG JULIE: I always knew about you. But this is where you really strained your striber with me.

PARSONS: (whisper) Is he asleep?

BIG JULIE: No, he's just working up the energy to get at your jugular. And that's in your damn pocket, too...

PARSONS: (generally) Everybody hold everything! Hold it! We'll start again. And this time let's work together to arrive at something, given that the moment of infant rift from the mother has come to us all.
    (clicks finger at SIGGIE)
Go away.

    (He waits but nothing happens.)

BIG JULIE: You stand to make a bomb out of this damn play.

PARSONS: (evasively) Where's the others?

BIG JULIE: Looking at you, thinking what a tic you are. We didn't know he even existed. You're just psycho enough to make up something like him. You didn't even bother to change his name. Mongrel.

PARSONS: Typical feminine reaction.

BIG JULIE: You... crossbreed.

PARSONS: I deny that. Anyway, assume with great assumption that this really is Siggie. I would have done him a favour by using his name. I nestled him within the diphthongs of my art... pupated him... gave him a cocoon to you... Siggie Morrison, the pupa Poppa. Dozing in a nice quiet sunny corner of the theatrical garden. What's wrong with that?

(BIG JULIE burps at him again. PARSONS indicates SIGGIE.)

PARSONS: I ask you: who is this... screw-on screwdriver anyway? Another secret of your whoreabouts?

BIG JULIE: (shrugs) Use the spare flair of your imagination. Your two backs are showing.

(She goes off.)

PARSONS: (after her) And you need a lifesaver to take up the slack.

BIG JULIE: (comes back on, grabs him by shirt front) Look, you...

PARSONS: Beat me. I'm suffering already.

(BIG JULIE releases him in disgust, goes off. PARSONS turns to SIGGIE, watches as the sunlight from outside slowly pans across to fall across SIGGIE. As it strikes him, he comes awake with a delighted cry, gets up to stand in its warmth. Tries to 'dry out'.

SIGGIE and the MONOLOGUE start up saying the same thing together as he does so. At first his ululating of the sunshine has him audible with the MONOLOGUE but he is soon merely mouthing what it is saying, and even sooner not bothering to try to keep up with it anyway)

MONOLOGUE and SIGGIE initially: (all around) I was born in the sun. I don't like not being in the sun. I always said to myself, I said: it's not right not being in my sun.

PARSONS: (to wings) What about a bit of help back there?

MONOLOGUE and fading SIGGIE: (all around) Come over here, Siggie, they said. Come back home. We know a place where your sun, where you, where your sun shines through all day every day. Where you never miss a beat, they said. They said a place where you shine through all the time, summer, winter, autumn and that other time. Spring, that's it. Spring. Fancy me forgetting Spring. They said it made no diff. Summer, autumn, winter or spring. They said. Because you shine through all day every day, see, Siggie. Even all night if you want, every night. Although I didn't believe that ... I mean fancy expecting a man to believe that. Every day and all day. My sun. Well, why not? Where there's a lemon-scented hum and a salmon gum and there's a poplar popping up all over the place and a bloom, like, and there's...

PARSONS: (above fading MONOLOGUE) Anyway, let's not jump to conclusions. It might be him, then again it mightn't be him. Let's put it this way: it could be him but it ought not to be him. All I can do is grant you a certain ambience, that's all. And to be perfectly crude, ambience sucks.

(The MONOLOGUE resides to its normal background humming.

PARSONS stares daggers up at the control room.)

SIGGIE: (up at sunlight) You don't shine through much anymore. I'm cold and wet. I'm in pain... somewhere...
   (confused)
it's wet and slimy in here... pain somewhere...

PARSONS: I'm in pain. We're all in bloody pain. Go on, get it off your convex chest. Say you remember me. Say I remind you of someone. I can't stand people... standing around.

SIGGIE: (sweetly) Are you from the airline? How nice.
   (giggles)
I had to take all sorts of odd jobs to save up my fare. But I finally made it. Heavens, I'm not boring you, am I? You will say if I'm boring you, won't you? Don't feel you've got to keep me company just because you're from the airline people, because I always bore people like airline people.

PARSONS: You won't bore me.

SIGGIE: But you will tell me if I bore you, won't you? Promise?

PARSONS: (bored) I'll tell you if you bore me.

SIGGIE: The awful thing is I know I'll bore you sooner or later. My, everybody's being so nice to me. Last year, I cleaned up a bank for a bit. The back manager left me a note one night. ... Have I told you this?

PARSONS: (still bored) His note read: 'Dear Mr Morrison, you don't seem to be able to remember any of the little notes I leave behind for you, so I'm afraid we'll have to let you go'...
   (as much as he can round on the old man)
1 know all about it but where did you get it from?

SIGGIE: I think it was under his Dictaphone thingo.
   (giggles)
Knock, knock.

PARSONS: Who's there?

SIGGIE: Dictaphone.

PARSONS: Dictaphone who?

SIGGIE: (giggles) Dictaphone up your...

(stops, shivers.)
Why is it so cold and wet and slimy here...? It's getting at... my pain... somewhere.

PARSONS: You're not cold and wet and slimy.

SIGGIE: I feel cold and wet and slimy. My old legs feel heavy.
 (sits)
It's not right never to have my sun, is it? White things without blood crawl around under tin when the sun doesn't shine...
    (he stops, convulsively brushes revolting things off his legs.)
Uh.

PARSONS: For shit's sake, don't have a fit on me.

SIGGIE: Mushrooms growing. Yellow thingmebobs when I cough. Yellow water in my lungs. I'd never eat mushrooms...
    (then directly up at PARSONS)
Would you eat mushrooms?

PARSONS: I'd eat off an overcrowded fly screen. Now please go. Leave the snothouse without leaving too much snot.

SIGGIE: Without the sun, I wouldn't have grown. Truly. Not that silly old me is anything. Blood oath, no. But what sort of world would it be without me? Gee, I'd be something that *wouldn't be in it.*
    (shudders)
I was born in the sun. In the back of my dad's ute on the way to hospital. I think. That was in Australia. I am Australian. You mightn't wear that, but I am. They wouldn't believe me.

MONOLOGUE: (sudden burst) They said, Siggie come with us. I said why I don't mind telling you. I said why all suspicious like. But I didn't like to let somebody know you're all suspicious. It doesn't help relationships if you let somebody know you're all suspicious. They go and get all suspicious if they think you are being suspicious. They think hello what's he or she been doing to make me feel suspicious that he's feeling suspicious about me. It's the insinuation. Beaut word that. I say again. What was that...

    (stops as suddenly as it begun but it has been enough to have

25

SIGGIE covering his ears and rebelling against it)

SIGGIE: (trying to get above it) *They wouldn't believe a man!*

PARSONS: (shouting too) Who?

SIGGIE: (agitated) Kids... jumping about on the tin sheets on me...!

(Long pause, until:)

PARSONS: You would turn up sooner or later, wouldn't you?

SIGGIE: I'll just rest here until my friends come back.

(PARSONS indicates his annoyance by coming forward and yelling up at the theatre's control room at the back of the auditorium)

PARSONS: Testing, testing. One, two, three...

(Listens, gets no acknowledgment, shrugs, turns away.)

SIGGIE: (conversationally) Are you going on the same plane? I hope you won't give me tomato sandwiches. I wouldn't even dare go in a lift with a tomato sandwich under my belt.
   (giggles)
Who wants more wind up there?
   (then)
Are you going home too?

PARSONS: Strike me lucky.

SIGGIE: (delighted) Old Roy Rene Mo.

PARSONS: (mimic of Mo) No, no. So help me, I'm a dirty great spud on top of a lot of flaming matchsticks... call a mug mash-head.

SIGGIE: I could tell you were Australian too. What've you been doing over here?

PARSONS: (now pretty much looking for help) I'll bite... where?

SIGGIE: London. Gawd. Whatareya?

PARSONS: (stops, looking about) Oh... London.

SIGGIE: London.

PARSONS: London... oh, sure.
   (looks at him closely, then runs excitedly to wings, speaks off.)
He really thinks he's still in London!

BIG JULIE: We could have told you that half an hour ago.

PARSONS: (accusingly) Put-up job.

BIG JULIE: Sure, sure.

PARSONS: (decision) Nobody do anything. I've got to think.

BIG JULIE: Yeah and that way, *you* get to do nothing.

PARSONS: (to wings) As I see it there are three alternatives. All of
which aren't worth a pig's arse, I admit. However...
   (back to SIGGIE)
Actually, it was dictaphone up your directory. Or dictionary.
   (then back to wings)
Okay, so we shut down. We shall inertia-ize rather than
anathematize... look that up in your English aids to Australian
actors... him out. We shall sit around him and *stare*. Bodily.
Sedentary as the seasons in slide shows. Note the attachment of words
to the various alloyed anodes around which art bubbles. He will then
fidget; we will do nothing. He will ask perhaps for a script; we will do
nothing. Eventually he will ask for the bus fare. I myself am broke,
but one of you will...

   *(MISS GLAMORGAN skips onto the stage from the other side
   to the accompaniment of an extract from 'Swan Lake'. She is
   dressed in a long white robe, with a white rose in her hair, and
   is bathed in a sweet and pure light.)*

MISS GLAMORGAN:

Awake! for Morning in the Bowl of Night
Has flung the Stone that puts the Stars to Flight
And Lo!...

PARSONS: Abort, abort!

(PARSONS grabs MISS GLAMORGAN, tries to muffle her. She struggles, strangely trying to make it over to SIGGIE)

PARSONS: What the... Miss Glamorgan!

SIGGIE: (sits bolt upright, into air) Miss Glamorgan?

MISS GLAMORGAN: (directed at SIGGIE) Yes!

(But is shoved off, muffled.)

SIGGIE: Did somebody say Miss Glamorgan?

PARSONS: (innocently) Miss Glamorgan?

SIGGIE: Somebody said Miss Glamorgan.

PARSONS: You said Miss Glamorgan.

SIGGIE: (really distressed) I thought somebody was saying Miss Glamorgan.

PARSONS: Oh, her.

SIGGIE: Who?

PARSONS: Her.

SIGGIE: What 'her', please?

PARSONS: (viciously) Miss Glamorgan.

SIGGIE: (thinks, then giggles) Leg puller, you.

28

PARSONS: (testing him out) Granted later in life than most but your cart-horse of love. That Strabo of your purse-strings. Miss Glamorgan. Right?

SIGGIE: (laughs weakly) I don't think it could have been. Poor Miss Glamorgan died years ago. How did you know about Miss Glamorgan?

PARSONS: (testing again) All right, I'll come clean. It was an actress playing Miss Glamorgan.

SIGGIE: (distressed) Oh dear, have I done something wrong? Why would anyone want to do that to poor Miss Glamorgan?

PARSONS: Nothing's hidden from the director's script, dad.

SIGGIE: Is that like a print-out?

PARSONS: Exactly.

SIGGIE: (nodding sadly) Nothing.

PARSONS: Ah yes, inevitably, the hot breath of the great blanking-off beginning to warm the back of your neck, old chum, a believer in the ancient occult. 'On occult of my old age'. In all the heavenly ladies' bodies, eh?

> *(SIGGIE giggles.)*

PARSONS: Well now, shall we prophesy where you are now, or tell you where you were or conflute... conflute?... conflute, of my own manufacture, where you're going to. And to what, of your own manufacture.

SIGGIE: (impressed) Geez…

PARSONS: Service, service. To the great meeting hall of life and its ha-ha sick joke pitfalls.
    (grabs SIGGIE's hand)
Aha.

SIGGIE: Aha?

PARSONS: What we in the art-of-magic trade call the inside itch. This dandy Rio Grande of a handy is the cosmic arrival-at of *(a)* a musician, *(b)* an effeminized actor, *(c)* an action painter, *(d)* a beautician... or *(e)* a compassionate dog-catcher. You are neither. So much for theory.

SIGGIE: (wonder at one hand) Is that all down on there?

PARSONS: Lithographically etched. Call me the gypsy who doesn't palms empty as the Sahara, Blue.

> *('PARSONS turns away but with hand out for coin, busker-wise. While SIGGIE fumbles for some money and finally holds it pleadingly out, the actors, dressed for the street, walk across back stage.*
>
> *They catch PARSONS out trying to get money from SIGGIE and their conversation is a la behind-the-arras, although, apart from BIG JULIE, they don't care all that much. Their conversations are 'under' the attempted fleecing of SIGGIE by PARSONS and are:)*

BIG JULIE (at PARSONS) Hey!
    (to others)
He's even fleecing him now. What a bozo!

MISS HOLLAND: He's all woolly and greasy?

BIG JULIE: Lifting his money off him.

MISS HOLLAND: He wouldn't.

BIG JULIE: Wouldn't he?

MISS HOLLAND: He's doing it again.

JARVIS: The dog bit me for five just now too. Can you beat it?

MRS PRUFROCK: I don't know about you lot. Me, I'm going back to flamish my new flurt. Flat. Furnish it.

(Meanwhile)

SIGGIE What else do you see, Mr Gypsy?

PARSONS (finding a few more coins) I really shouldn't.

SIGGIE C'arn.

PARSONS You insist on twisting my arm?
  (grabs the old man's palm again)
Well, so happens I do see the mount on Queen Moon if you insist on being a believer. The small lines leading to her, here and here. They signpost vast journeys of the mind. Real rambles among the brambles, like.

SIGGIE: (giggles) I forget things.

PARSONS: The pronounced volcano of the Great Sun God.

SIGGIE: I think that's my old boil.

PARSONS: I see a journey of the mind.

SIGGIE: (wonder) That right?

PARSONS: Great eruptions of the orb of day.
  (at 'BOY' who is with the others)
Get ready, kid!

MISS HOLLAND: (at 'BOY'; Don't you dare.

> *(PARSONS conducts behind SIGGIE's back. Sun music rises, takes over even from the MONOLOGUE, lights dim allowing a sort of sunlight down a storm water drain to fall on SIGGIE. He rises adoringly to it. 'BOY' throws himself into a mime.*
>
> *The actors watch as the 'BOY' goes through his rehearsed paces.)*

31

PARSONS: Now, listen to the past's metaphysical stirring as though you were lying next to some drunken old lover... Yesterday is alive and well, caught forever in the slipstream of rumour and percussion.

SIGGIE: (hissing) I didn't think they'd find me in time.

PARSONS: Well, if you must be prosaic about it.

SIGGIE: I didn't think they'd ever find me.

PARSONS: (shrugs) Okay.
    (then)
The boy thinks the old man he's discovered down the storm water drain is going to die. The sun scorching down on his piebald prebald pate.

SIGGIE: On the back of my neck, really.

PARSONS: Lost in a hot and open land. Crying out, before he learnt how to swear...

SIGGIE: Cripes!

'BOY': Hey, hey, oldie!

PARSONS: A million suns dancing milleniumously... my word so we'll let it stand... behind his awful oozing orbs.

'BOY': Howsitgoin'?

PARSONS: Up there where the boy is, it looks to Siggie like leaves are autocombusting by his young face. The great fire god exploding triumphs in the swirls of his imagination.

SIGGIE: (outcry to sunlight) My life!

(Drain sunlight immediately off SIGGIE. Sun music fades.)

PARSONS: The heat, the sun, the whole gamma ray bit, obliterating everything. Memory, inquiry, passions, ambition, common dee-eff,

32

verve. Everything. All so much evaporation for the unquenchable furnace of the sun.
(viciously)
And you left with a few wits and a few gristly sinews to embroider the few dry mind grains left behind. Siggie Morrison, dimmed dim wit. And all because the sun, your sun, chose you out of something like the six billion inhabitants of the world to alight upon. Right?

SIGGIE: (hiss) Yes.

PARSONS: (pulls out a paper party horn and blows it) What a crapload of excrescence.

SIGGIE: (heedless) My father said, I was never the same again after the sun got at me when I was knee-high to a grasshopper. That's why I couldn't remember things anymore and I know it made me a bit funny.
(then)
Hailey's Comet caused it all, you know.

PARSONS: Go on.

SIGGIE: Nineteen hundred and ten. Not only me. It got at Paris, too. It flooded Paris. King Edward the Seventh was lying in state in Westminster. That's what it did. People said something would happen after Edward the Seventh died. It was just unfortunate it happened to me.
(giggles)
Did you see that dopey little kid mucking around me just then?

PARSONS (coyly) What dopey little kid?

SIGGIE Cheeky little b.

MISS HOLLAND (back still with the rest of the cast) He's a little doll really, don't you think? Pity about the baldness.

BIG JULIE What's bald got to do with it. I've had baldies who'd put the rest of them to shame. Take Jarvis here.

JARVIS (outraged) No going on about baldies when a man's got a wig on! What's the bloody theatre coming to.

BIG JULIE What're you on about? *Christ.*

> *(But real chimes for an airport announcement stop them short, bring their attention back to the real presence of SIGGIE)*

ANNOUNCEMENT: 'British Airways announces the departure of Flight 375 to the Bahamas, stopping at New York. Would passengers kindly proceed to Gate number five for their boarding passes…

> *(Announcement fades.)*

SIGGIE: Where did they say?

PARSONS: (genuinely) Who?

MISS HOLLAND: (quite irreverently) I didn't mean baldies can't be funny, you know.

> *(But the others are concentrating on PARSONS and SIGGIE now)*

SIGGIE: They said British Airways, didn't they?
  (searching)
I think I'm Qantas. They didn't say anything about Qantas, did they? Cripes nobody said anything about the Bahamas? Where's the Bahamas? Geez, I don't know where my ticket's gone. They said it's all on my ticket. Now I've lost my ticket.
  (at PARSONS)
Hey, mister, you seen my ticket lying about? Have you seen any of my friends asking for a bloke?

PARSONS: (daggers at actors) Don't count on friends. They've got tickets on themselves.

SIGGIE: (looking off) They should've come back by now. I think one of them has my ticket. How can I go if I haven't got my ticket?

PARSONS: You haven't got any ticket.

SIGGIE: I can't go without my ticket. Help me please? I think I've lost my ticket.

PARSONS: (angrily) No ticket.

SIGGIE: (appalled) Don't tell me I've lost my ticket now.

PARSONS: You won't believe me when I tell you no ticket?

SIGGIE: Where'd a man be without his ticket?

PARSONS: Okay have it your way. Look again. Strip search yourself. While the world edges towards its inevitable calamity, stay here rooted to the spot looking for a ticket.

> (SIGGIE starts all over again looking for his ticket, while the cast have another of their side-conversations again:)

MISS HOLLAND: Aw, look at the poor little thing.

JARVIS (but not moving) They won't let him on any plane. I can smell him from here. Me, I'm taking off.

MISS HOLLAND: Do you think we should leave him here just like that? He's getting a bit het up, poor old man.

JARVIS: He'll be all right.

MISS GLAMORGAN: He won't be all right. That Parsons keeps shouting at him.

JARVIS: Here she's going to go again.

MISS GLAMORGAN: (calls) Mr Morrison.

JARVIS: So go and mother him.

MISS GLAMORGAN: (rebuked, hotly) You had a mother! Mr Morrison probably never had a mother!

35

(MISS GLAMORGAN runs off, but soon sheepishly returns.)

JARVIS: (after her) He probably came out of your body too.

BIG JULIE: The best thing for us to do is get the hell out of here and leave Parsons holding the baby.

(They go to leave.)

PARSONS: (but short-circuits them) Excuse me, but before you desert, scuttle over here and listen to this.

(The actors draw near)

PARSONS: Right, ladies and luggers, I have called you together to hear this.
   (turns to SIGGIE.)
Old man, for the tenth time, no ticket. You've just stumbled into the right place, old cock. See, the trouble is, they've bounced you around so much in your sorry existence that you obviously don't know whether you're Billy or Martha Graham. Sydney here and now. London you left years ago. If you ever left, which I will grant was most likely. So listen carefully old sonofagun…
   (into SIGGIE's ear)
no ticket!

SIGGIE: (panic) Please… is there somewhere to go to when you've lost your ticket? It's just that I seem to have lost my ticket, see.

PARSONS: No damn ticket!

SIGGIE: I know it was in my wallet. I had it in my wallet. Now I can't find my ticket.

PARSONS: No wallet!

(But SIGGIE pulls out a wallet.

PARSONS grabs SIGGIE's wallet. A ticket flutters to the ground. SIGGIE swoops delightedly.)

SIGGIE: I knew I'd put it in my wallet. Geez, don't I ever get het up over nothing sometimes.

PARSONS: (looking at ticket) Cheap forgery.

SIGGIE: (grabs it, to it) Where're you been you little buggerlugs?

MISS HOLLAND (aside to actors) I told you we shouldn't just leave him here, all het up like that.

JARVIS: He'll outsurvive the cockroaches, this one.

MISS GLAMORGAN: (hotly returning) I heard that. You shouldn't talk to him like that.
    (mainly at PARSONS)
Shouting at him all the time like that.

JARVIS: (re MISS GLAMORGAN) I told you she'd go off again. Somebody get a good leg thrown over her.

MISS GLAMORGAN: (calls) Mr Morrison.

JARVIS: So go and mother him.

MISS GLAMORGAN: (rebuked, hotly) You had a mother! Mr Morrison probably never had a mother!

> *(MISS GLAMORGAN runs off yet again only to sheepishly return as before and probably for the thousandth time.)*

JARVIS: (after her) He probably came out of your body too.

BIG JULIE: You've said that. Now just shut it!

PARSONS: So, old fellah, whatcha reckon? You see where we are here

SIGGIE: Pardon?

PARSONS: No London. No Bahamas. Find any money when you found that wallet, did you?

SIGGIE: Eh?

BIG JULIE: (at PARSONS) Big shot. You couldn't flash your way out of a nudist colony.

PARSONS: (ignoring her) To put it bluntly, Siggie old sausage, your providing brain and your sustaining nerves, as they say, are out of whack. So you stumble into an abstraction...
   (waves arm generally)
this... and cuddle it longingly, nostalgically, to your negative nipples. I don't know, perhaps you think you're halfway through your second bottle of metho. I purely surmise that, so never mind. All of us here have known the quiet madness and sadness and badness. No pubescence without the pubes. But go back, old man. Go back to your YMCA cubicle or whatever and dream. There's no law against dreams. Dreams are stuffs; be satisfied with that. We'll see you right. Who knows, if the box office rolls its lovely rolls, you might be able to go back to England. Now can I be fairer?
   (silence)
In short, old gutzer, leave it to the professionals, what say? See, right now, we're supposed to be working. You'll just hate yourself in the morning if you cause an industrial dispute.

   (He sits back. They all do. Long fidgety pause, during which SIGGIE keeps glancing at the lounge 'entrance' and they at him.

   Finally, to break the impasse, PARSONS takes charge again...)

PARSONS: All right, for the sake of a tear drop on a burnt leaf, we'll call him Sigmund Morrison.

SIGGIE: (giggles) Make it Siggie among friends.

BIG JULIE: (at PARSONS) And?

PARSONS: Admitting playfully that this play might then be based, like a pub is on a bar, sloppily on him. What does it matter? He could have been dead and buried by now for all I knew... he ought to be; by God, he'll be biblical soon... Anyway, what's a little inhale-exhale got

38

to do with it? We inhale, we're momentarily alive. We exhale, we're momentarily dying. The brain gets its oxygen, the mind stays rarified. What about it?

BIG JULIE: You just recognize what we think about you.

PARSONS: I'm a skunk. I'm the sneaky wombat from The Magic Pudding.

MRS PRUFROCK: Hear, hear.

PARSONS: All right, I'll lay it on the line to him. If he's got any objections, we'll call the whole thing off. Well, we'll think about it. Okay?

> *(Grudging acceptance. SIGGIE innocently provokes him by bending over and tying up a shoelace. To SIGGIE.;*

PARSONS: Facts. First, you were born sometime in the early morning on February 29, 1831. A dead common little ugly potential, except that that year wasn't supposed to be a leap year, only your birth certificate recorded it as such.

SIGGIE: (stopping) I didn't know that.

PARSONS: Journeyed through life with your dunce's performance turned towards the wall until you left Australia January 5th, 1975.

SIGGIE: (giggles) I wanted to see...

PARSONS: (taking over) '... what the other side of the world was like'.
    (SIGGIE giggles.)
'But then the war came upon me'.
    (SIGGIE looks at him sharply.)
We know you've been getting quaint little nun's titters over those two dog-eared dribbles outa your mouth for years.
    (pause)
And what 'war' would have that been, hmmm? Anyway, after the war you got caught up in that no one else in the world get caught up

in, you ploughed over dung in a Sussex pigsty until, twenty-five years later, you were caught kissing the sow's ear.

(SIGGIE giggles again.)

Next day you were fired after calling the cows in and then forgetting to milk them.

SIGGIE: I told you I forget things.

PARSONS: (over him) So you pensioned yourself off in London and bronchitis and those foul little economies that turn all men mean. A room with grease on the walls. Crab down the stairs, jerk along London streets like an unoiled clockwork toy. Hail or sunshine, every day, you went on your round. At ten, standing in at the fruit stall, while the woman went to do her morning plough-back. She gave you fruit. At ten thirty, at the back door of the Athene restaurant. They gave you coffee. At eleven, into the newspaper office. They gave you a free paper. Read that, then over to the bakery. They gave you the leftovers which you wrapped in the newspaper. Then up to the Old People's Welfare; they gave you first scrounge over the bundles of clothing. You took something every day whether you wanted it or not. Into the library; 'Poor Mr Morrison, let him perc. on the radiator'. Counted your pennies, sniffed, simpered, faintly impertinent, sucked your teeth, until it was time for the fish shop, then the restaurant again, then to the newspaper office, back to the fruit stall... Need I go on?

SIGGIE: (sweetly) Go on; crossed paths have we?

(The MONOLOGUE gradually rises in volume again until eventually it fills the auditorium. The others get to their feet in somewhat alarm.)

PARSONS: (trying to keep above it) Back to the greasy room with your day's booty. When you thought nobody was looking, you used to gorby on the footpath. You crossed the road to follow a mini skirt, pretending to be looking up at the skyline while perving out of the corner of your crinkles. You wiped your hands on the wallpaper. You used to pee in the washbasin. You used to secretly fluff and secretly laugh.

(now struggling against MONOLOGUE)

I happen to know you played with your derring-do. Really and truly you were not a very nice little man. Were you?

MONOLOGUE: (drowning him) I wish I could stare people down with my eyes. I wish I could look at people with my eyes. I wish I could look people in the eyes. Just look up and look at them. That's not much to ask. It doesn't sound much to do. Just look up and look at them in the eye. When I'm buying a chop or something and I know perhaps he's selling me a brumby and a good look in the eye would stop him from selling me a brumby, I can't give...

PARSONS: (sudden shout) Siggie Morrison, don't go back to Australia! Your sun won't shine on you again down there!

> *(Sudden cutback in sound. SIGGIE drops back onto lounge, mumbles, shivers. The others stare at each other in amazed silence.*
>
> *PARSONS is amazed with himself...)*

PARSONS: What did I just say?

JARVIS: You tell us.

PARSONS: (shouts up at control room) Testing. Testing...
    (nothing, listens)
Somebody must've left the bauble of a babble running.
    (at JARVIS)
 Go up and tell the idjits to cut it out…

> *(As a show-stoppers, MISS GLAMORGAN appears suddenly to wander Ophelia-like, across the stage, accompanied by tragic music. She exalts the white rose she is carrying.)*

MISS GLAMORGAN:
Ah, Love! Could Thou and I with Fate conspire
To grasp this Sorry Scheme of Things entire,
Would not we shatter it to bits - and then
Remould it nearer to the Heart's Desire...?
    (heavy sigh)
Oh, Sigmund...

(As she goes to float past PARSONS, he grabs her, shoves her down. She 'moons' at SIGGIE.)

MRS PRUFROCK: I wish to speak.

PARSONS: Not now.

BIG JULIE: Okay, so pay us for nothing.

(They wait again in awkward silence.)

PARSONS: (tries again, to SIGGIE) A one-armed organ-grinder, say, comes in, looks around, sees no organ-grinder and might be led to think that if there's no organ-grinder here then there might be room for a one-armed organ-grinder, even turned sideways. Not so.
   (at others)
Right?

(They look vacuously back at him. He returns to SIGGIE)

PARSONS: Not being a professional that one-armed organ-grinder would be wrong. He'd be better off yanking his handle. Consider the following effect and you'll recognoitre... my amalgam and so allowed to stand... what is possible in absentia. Pavlova's dead. Brussels her next scheduled performance, but they refuse to cancel. Lights dim, last act, the dying of the swan, music up and spotlights trace the dying movements she would have made.

(Lights, music follow this. He holds up an arm to cease.)

PARSONS: If there's no art, there's no portent of immortality, old man. So go away and leave us professionals to render up, wafting like chantilly, whatever slight quiver-quaver might be quoited from the semiquaver from your reductible regions.

(Long pause, before.)

SIGGIE: I... think I'll have a little lie down.

(He lies back on couch, eyes closed.)

42

PARSONS: A damned impertinence, but an all too frequent occurrence within the confines of prosceniums, that someone walks in on the assumption that, by walking on, certain conspiracies must deliver themselves up, like rats up a drainpipe, to his requirements. Fair Muse, we can keep thee chaste, but not from being hounded.
   (pause for applause, but gets none and is hurt)
All right. He's yours. I wash my hands of him.

    (Turns away.)

BIG JULIE: You've washed'n'wiped them on him. You couldn't bully a hockey ball.

PARSONS: Sitting around at a party with a zonked-out Manchester United squad sitting around you, you don't sit around looking at the wine bottle sitting there. Suggested compromise. We carry on as per schedule, and...

MRS PRUFROCK: (primly) Just a mini moment, thank you. I was trying to say before your drude indruption that either we are not wanted as yet or not wanted at all or not just plainly wanted. Not. Also, it is clear that is quite immaterial how we feel we want to be wanted or are twinned to be twanted.

PARSONS: (pained) Let's carry on rehearsing taking it from where I just left off, and if he objects just once then recuperations and aspirins on the drawing board. There he is. Scratching the surface of his mind with his pinprick of a mentality. An ideal opportunity, keeping the rag trade in mind, for us to globulize. My word and so eligible. See what happens, to you.

MRS PRUFROCK: Well, we certainly can't stand around here all night.

    (They take off their coats, prepare for rehearsing, while...)

JARVIS: Day.

MRS PRUFROCK: I beg your togal ingorance.

JARVIS: Day
.

MRS PRUFROCK: Night.

BIG JULIE: Day, you scarecrow.

JARVIS: (indicates SIGGIE) Ask him. That twerp was the last one in.

(JARVIS goes to move towards him.)

PARSONS: I wouldn't disturb him if I was you.

JARVIS: Who's disturbing who? He's disturbing me more than I'm disturbing him. I'll stinking disturb him if I want.

PARSONS: Let's not disturb him.

JARVIS: Why can't I disturb him? You wanted to disturb him a minute ago.

PARSONS: Put it this way. If he's disturbed enough to think he's still in England, disturbing him won't get you even the time of day. Or night.

MISS GLAMORGAN: Please don't disturb him.

JARVIS: I'll disturb the old fugger if I want to.

BIG JULIE: Let him sleep.

JARVIS: What's he afraid of disturbing him for?

PARSONS: Me? Afraid of disturbing that there?

JARVIS: Then what're you wetting your wraparound for?

PARSONS: Order. 'If you can't have order, you don't get served'. Practically though, he might have dropped in to die like an old bull elephant, for all I know. We've got to think of the publicity. First things: keep out hands well out of contamination range.

JARVIS: (surly) I don't like him just hanging around.

PARSONS: You're not supposed to. Scriptwise, you're supposed to despise the little shit.

JARVIS: And he looks like a little shit.

PARSONS: Of course.

JARVIS: Picking his nose, smelling it, and putting it in his mouth is enough for me.

BIG JULIE: You're nothing out of the Good Manners Guide yourself.

MISS GLAMORGAN: (blurting out) Now, you're all being rotten to him!

(She blushes, then sulks.)

PARSONS: What's up with her?

BIG JULIE: (thumping-heart gesture) Three guesses.

MISS HOLLAND: This isn't getting us anywhere.

JARVIS: I'm going to get me somewhere. Home. Pedimobility.
   (at PARSONS)
Ever heard of that, professor? Home by pedimobility. Away from the smell of a bladder dripping out of its spout.

PARSONS: Is my suggested compromise acceptable on compromise? Yes? No?

(JARVIS and 'BOY' vote. PARSONS slaps 'BOY's hand down)

PARSONS: You're under voting age.
   (at JARVIS)
What you can't do is simply walk away and forget him.

JARVIS: Who? Funny, I can't seem to remember who you're talking about. Bysee.

(He goes to stride off, but, arriving at the wings, unaccountably stops, unable to go further.)

PARSONS: Think of our commitments to the ghosts.

JARVIS: (sneers) Ghosts have no fannies, therefore no commitment.

PARSONS: In nineteen-o-five a John Jenkins Esquire threw himself bodily off the old balcony in The Gods, emotionally swept up in a finely-wrought melodramatic net. Mr Jenkins is just one of the many ecstatic ectoplasmics wandering hollow-eyed about us all the time. Every critic who has ever waltzed through these portals has been died in the wool. You can hear them lamenting in the wee small hours about where they spumed wrong. Suppose we left him sitting here when these our siren ghosts are stirring? We turn out the lights, leaving only a 25-watter glowing feebly off in a comer, playing giantishly with his shadow against the back projection. There are three possibilities, as I see it. One, tomorrow morning...

MRS PRUFROCK: Pardonnez-me. Tonight.

JARVIS: (now staying) Gawd. Today, today.

PARSONS: (again) One, in the hollow morrow of today, we return to find the ghost of an applause on absent ghostly pale lips and also he's defecated all over the platform of our art.

BIG JULIE: Who cares?

PARSONS: The ghosts would! Oh, let me have about me live fleshy Tribals not lean mean Caucasoids. And people would say that there's something rotten in the structure of the play. That, after more than a hundred years of whipping up the most endearing collection of improbable phantoms, all we can whip up is an old man's squirts. Two, in the hush moments of early tomorrow morning...
    (short circuits the protests)
again for the sake of argument, to someone of some seen or unseen matter, even one with a smattering of mattering, he has been left on

the stage as the comment, the residue, the last murmur of our play. Yes...
(indicates SIGGIE)
That there. The sum total. The cadaver left as art. Metaphorically, I trust you get my meaning?

(They 'rise' to him theatrically.)

PARSONS: There. We all feeling better?
(at MISS GLAMORGAN, 'normal')
Page twenty-seven, lovie.
(then)
I tell you, mes enfants, phantoms relate terrible inaccuracies to each other, such that, we, as professional seekers after the underfelt, might never be able to play down.

ALL: Speak, O sage.

PARSONS: (peripatetic) Sit, my pilgrims at the fountain-head of self-preservation.

(While they do so, duly humble, he dons a barrel, holds up a lantern.)

PARSONS: Show me a wise man who is not straining his resources by sitting on them. To that man I would say: leave not the little shit. To put it epigrammatically: show me the man who would leave behind a little shit uncovered and I shall show you a man who stinks.

ALL: Say on, O Wise One!

PARSONS: Consider. He who crashes in a crevasse falls on his gravity. Thus, heresayethwithal, the stage of life being darkened being cold being wet being aching with pain around the tibia region, if not around the anal region while wearing a jock strap, being truly a slimy bin even by a Pythagorean count, better to imprison him in a sunless city drain tormented by little shits until his flesh begins to rot than to leave him holed-up, incarcerated, alone, bound by art's hand-cuffs the whole night through. Who among you would face such a charge?
(general voodoo moaning)

47

Take the hold-on intangible away from its teeth and a rat can be said to be a perfectly beautiful animal. Therefore, I say better draw him out like a perfectly good tooth from a rotten patient than to propagate the species.

SIGGIE: (opens his eyes) Oh, geezy's wept, it's no good.

(They start.)

PARSONS: (at SIGGIE) Are you complaining already?

SIGGIE: Geez, no. I just can't go off. Dummy old me.
  (gets up)
God gave the tiny little birds wings to fly, not me.

PARSONS: No complaint registered.
  (snaps fingers)
Pillow.

> *(MISS GLAMORGAN leaps to oblige, rests SIGGIE's head on one.)*

PARSONS: Cigarette.

> *(JARVIS lights one, puts it in SIGGIE's mouth.)*

SIGGIE: I don't smoke. Didn't like the draw-back.

PARSONS: Siggie old son, we all indulge the fags now and again here. All a question of function.
  (towards BIG JULIE)
 Or primary urges as the case may be. Blanket! Shawl! Slippers!

> *(MISS GLAMORGAN fits him out, stands back maternally.)*

SIGGIE: Geez.

PARSONS: Any complaints?

SIGGIE: Crikey, no.

PARSONS: Registered. Tie, collar. Handle with care.

(MISS GLAMORGAN hastens to loosen his collar.)

SIGGIE: Thank you.
   (up at MISS GLAMORGAN)
Say, haven't I seen you before?

MISS GLAMORGAN: (blushes) I'm Miss Glamorgan, Mr Morrison.

SIGGIE: Siggie.

MISS GLAMORGAN: Siggie.

SIGGIE: You know what Australians are like on first names.

MISS GLAMORGAN: Comfy now?

SIGGIE: My Miss Glamorgan died some years ago... You wouldn't have known her by any chance, wouldyer?

MISS GLAMORGAN: Partially.

SIGGIE: Partly?

MISS GLAMORGAN: (stroking his head) Partially.

SIGGIE: (eyes closed, purring) Did you really know her?

MISS GLAMORGAN: (affirmative) Oh, yes.

SIGGIE: (suddenly alarmed) I don't think you could've.

PARSONS: (avuncularly) That's right. Interrupt as much as you like. Locked, if you like, as we are between your side of the net and the exit.

SIGGIE: (giggles) Gawd, you gypsies. Mouths on you.

PARSONS: Consider us as more. Strange exotic friends, if you like. Close your eyes and sit back to listen to the men strumming cat-gut guitars, the women holding onto pipes and holding back moustaches, all around the campfire. Over the hillock, Toad Hall. Here...
  (sweeps arm)
as you rightly surmise... London airport.

SIGGIE: (suddenly indicates outside) Bloody hell... you see that? It... bounced!

(They look quizzically at each other.)

PARSONS: What bounced?

SIGGIE: That aeroplane that's just landed. It bounced. Do they all bounce like that? Stuff me, I hope mine doesn't have to bounce like that.

PARSONS: Are you objecting already?

SIGGIE: (points out) Look! That bugger of a one bounced too!

PARSONS: (reacting) Is that by way of an objection?

SIGGIE: Me, object?

PARSONS: (angry) Are you objecting to the set?

SIGGIE: Object?

PARSONS: Are you objecting to the sound effects?

SIGGIE: Pardon?

PARSONS: Is he objecting?

BIG JULIE: What if he is? You keep your objectionable shirt on.

PARSONS: It is no registerable objection if he objects about something I myself have already objected to. This buzzing... this orgy of Babel somebody's having with the sound track up there...

(up at control box)
You're fired!...
    (belligerently at SIGGIE)
... that will be corrected.
    (at others)
It is not a registerable objection.

MISS GLAMORGAN: I object to you raising your voice to Mr Morrison.

PARSONS: Over-ruled.

OTHERS: (threat) Sustained.

PARSONS: Sustained.

SIGGIE: (sweetly) I read where twenty thousand. It might have been hundred... Anyway, they all fly out to Australia every year. It makes you think, doesn't it?
    (giggles)
I hope they don't try to fit too many of them onto my plane.

BIG JULIE: Isn't he a sweetie?

SIGGIE: (delighted) When I went down with my dopey old chest, I asked the doctor if I was dangerously ill and he said, no, but...
    (giggles)
I was dangerously old.

    (Only the women laugh. SIGGIE now has the confidence to beckon 'BOY')

SIGGIE: Little boy.

'BOY': Who, me?

SIGGIE: Come and see what Uncle Siggie's got.

    ('BOY' is pushed over to him. From out of a unsavoury-looking pocket, SIGGIE produces a pear)

SIGGIE: Would a smart looking little guy like this nice big juicy pear?

'BOY': Are you kidding? It's got after-birth on it.

SIGGIE: It's only been in Uncle Siggie's pocket. Go on.
    (forces it onto the 'BOY' who holds it gingerly.)
Would you be a dear little boy and go out and see whether Uncle Siggie's friends are waiting for him somewhere?

'BOY': Shit, try the Missing Persons Bureau, mate.

    (And drops pear back in SIGGIE's lap.)

SIGGIE: Your little legs are younger than my little legs.

PARSONS: Keep him sweet.

    (The 'BOY' does a lightning tap dance. Stares back at PARSONS defiantly)

'BOY': That's as far as I'm going.

MISS HOLLAND: It wouldn't hurt you to go out and look.

'BOY': Fucking oath it would.

PARSONS: Go out and have sniff a tin can or something.

'BOY': Gave that up yesterday.

PARSONS: Just as well. It's stunted your growth for the last thirty years.

SIGGIE: I'm sure if you just peeked...

    ('BOY' huffs off left)

SIGGIE: I love little kids. They look up at you with such great big...

    ('BOY' returns from right. Walks past them all, sits.)

'BOY': Looked everywhere.

(Accusing silence.)

PARSONS: To continue. Over the hillock, Toad Hall. Here, London airport. Someone stands. You instinctively recognize him in the pit of your stomach in the light pit of the campfire. Wolves howls turn the frost and the darkness of the night into your soul. Trinkets banging, bracelets tinkling, his voice tremolos up from your fallen arches. He says:

> *(He dons gypsy scarf, ear-rings etc. Gypsy music introduction. But this is quickly overtaken by the MONOLOGUE so that after the first few words he has to shout.)*

PARSONS: ...He says: this is an ancient tale told to me by...

(Stops. Almost immediately the MONOLOGUE subsides.)

PARSONS: ...He says: this is an ancient tale told to me by...

(but MONOLOGUE starts up immediately to swamp him again)

MONOLOGUE: I'd expect better treatment than cats that go around doing disgusting thing anytime during the night and day like cats like you find in any old alley like you'd never find down here because even a cat doing disgusting things day and night like that need a bit of sunshine in its life even if it is night that's why Australian cats have muscles in their doo-doos.

PARSONS: (into air) Stop that!
   (listens, then)
Extrude the outside inclusions.
   (starts again)
As I was saying he says: This is an ancient tale told to me by the seventh son of a seventh son whose great great grandfather foretold the coming of the twentieth century three months before it even occurred. A true tale set in a cruel Northern Land where men eat men for the warming exercise of it all. In this land appears suddenly before

53

all the city folk, dressed in a little pink shirt bought full four score years ago...

SIGGIE: (giggles) Like this old thing. I won it in a pub raffle in Sydney before I left and it's lasted ever since.

PARSONS: (impatiently) Like your pink one.

SIGGIE: Only this white one.

PARSONS: You had a pink one.

SIGGIE: (skeptically) It's gone a bit yellow, I expect.

PARSONS: Pink.

SIGGIE: It used to be so much whiter then.

PARSONS: (now stung) It was pink! I say so!

JARVIS: (at PARSONS) Make it white, for shit's sake.

PARSONS: No.

MISS HOLLAND: Well, it is white.

MRS PRUFROCK: As anybody can see.

MISS HOLLAND: *Now* we can see.
   (waving script)
How do we know what else is wrong in this?

PARSONS: (stubborn) No, you don't. The three most ridiculous concepts in the world are a Jewish igloo manufacturer, a tom cat that had it winking at him and winked back, and the object of a joke in a white shirt. I absolutely refuse.

BIG JULIE: Is it white or isn't it?

PARSONS: (turns on SIGGIE) Look, are you objecting to me calling it a pink shirt.

54

SIGGIE: You've lost your thrilling gypsy accent.

PARSONS: Are you lodging an objection?

SIGGIE: Geez... me?

PARSONS: All right then.
    (resumes).
In a cruel Northern Land where...

> *(MONOLOGUE burst below drowns him. He 'climbs down',*
> *waits for it to subside.)*

MONOLOGUE: And what I've got a right to expect if nothing else is
a bit of help from people. Someone to come up and say Siggie.
Someone to come up and say my name. Just my name. That would
help It's a tremendous bit of help When someone remembers your
name like when they come up and say, Siggie. It's terrible when
someone comes up and opens his mouth to speak but says nothing.
That's terrible. That's terrible. I don't like that.

> *(The burst stops just as suddenly as it started)*

PARSONS: You will notice that despite ringing in my ears meaning
I'm sickening fast, probably with a blood clot coming on, I carry on
regardless.
    (restarts)
... Dressed in a little pink shirt full four score years old, there
suddenly appeared a little doll, a wondrous work of moving parts and
pink little cheeks and authentic body noises as ever wormed its way
around the waistbands of the wives of Man. Of its most magical
movements, none was more magically moving to the wives of Man
than that it talked nothing more than little nothings. Made in the
image of man, it was neither woman nor man, so all the wives of Man
knew it as a doll. Now being a very clever little doll, it knew the
wives of Man did not want it to be anything other than a little doll, so
it spoke to them in its little mechanical voice, saying: 'My, my, aren't
I a clever little doll?' Hearing this, for, remember, this was a truly
clever little doll, the wives of Man said to their menfolk, 'What a
clever little doll!' To which all the menfolk replied, 'Pull this one; it's

got bells on'. But the little doll knew full well that the menfolk of that cold, hard, cruel Northern Land had no cream in the jeans, no loving mother's milk flow for the return of the little doll to its nice sunny little cradle where it was born so to speak. So everywhere the little doll went, it sought out the wives of Man. And thus it was that the little doll survived, disguising itself cleverly as a little doll, for many cold, hard, cruel northern winters in that cold, hard, cruel Northern Land. And the wives of Man marvelled and clapped their hands and said, 'Truly, this is a little living doll, yeah, yeah!'

MISS HOLLAND: (bows in) Well now, one o' the Holy Father's li'l eunuchs himself, he was. A dear li'l ting, if oi may say so m'self. Oi used t'tink o' him as one o' th'li1 people, with that twinkle in t'eye so he had. Every mornin' he'd tippy-toe into t'office, like, and we'd have a wee li'l chat. Oi'll always remember...

ANNOUNCEMENT: 'Attention, please. Qantas announces the departure of Flight QF 625 to Sydney, hoping to call at...'

(The announcement goes dead.

(SIGGIE strains to listen. MISS HOLLAND carries on mindless of it.)

MISS HOLLAND: ...his tiny, li'l voice. Punctuated, t'was, all t'gigglin' an li'l nursery- book sayin's loik 'Glory be', meanin' praise to Himself Himself, loik, an' 'My, my'. 'My, my, what?' oi asked. 'My my oh my' said he. Sweet, loik.

ANNOUNCEMENT: 'Would passengers please disregard that last announcement'.

BIG JULIE: (stepping up to the playacting too) A girl comes across the little pixie in the bush. 'What are you?', she said. 'A pixie, what else?', he said. 'Go on,' she said. 'Let me have my way with you,' he said, 'and I'll grant you any wish you'd like'. 'Fair enough,' she said. Up he climbs, has it away, then goes to walk off. 'Hey, what about my wish, pixie?', she calls. He turns around, looks at her. 'How old are you, girlie?' 'Twenty-eight,' she answered. 'Dontcha think,' the little fellah says, 'that's a bit old to go around believing in pixies, lassie?'

56

Old Siggie, he nearly coughed his tough little breakfast up over that. Good sport, he was.

JARVIS: (steps forward, ditto) From what I could see he had no balls.

MISS HOLLAND: I object! There was no need for that.

PARSONS: (ruling, 'in the frame') Not counted. He extemporized.

BIG JULIE: (at JARVIS) There was no need to say that.

JARVIS: I felt like saying it.

ANNOUNCEMENT: 'Qantas Airways announces the delay, repeat, the delay, of Flight QF 625 to Sydney via Athens due to Athens having gone off the map and Hong Kong. We regret any inconvenience to passengers. Please stand by for further announcements.'

SIGGIE: Oh... *blow*!

JARVIS: You got to have no equipment if all you can say when somebody tells you you've got no equipment is 'blow'. Unless you wouldn't know if a band was up you until it got drunk. Like a few here.

SIGGIE: (conversationally) The doctor told me straight. At my age I ought to be back home under the sun with my brother and sister.

PARSONS: (a martyr resisting temptation) It is not ours to disillusion with reality.

MISS HOLLAND: (knowing him) Don't you dare.

PARSONS: I didn't say a word. I stroll, I strut, I smut, I roll over on my back like a spawning spaniel but I do not... say a...
    (beginning to giggle himself)
...word... about...

(Accusing silence. PARSONS tries to hold himself)

JARVIS: (fanning giggling) Did he say his brother and sister?

(PARSONS is near spluttering trying to hold back outright laughter.)

JARVIS: (quick glance at the script, 'performs'.) 'Ere, Siggie mate, you kept writing those flamin' letters. What dya expect a bloke to say? I'm on me fanny meself. Take a bit of advice. Stay where yer flamin' are. Yer too past it to travel. Stick to yer mad Pommy sheilas. Yer probably a Pom yerself now anyway. Signed, your lovin' brother, Ernie.

SIGGIE: I'm Aussie!

(But PARSONS has broken into outright laughter, so infectiously that the others cannot help themselves either. It breaks the ice.)

PARSONS: (cueing BIG JULIE) The late and loving sister, Mrs Ethel Pot when she hears from him for the first time in forty years.

(BIG JULIE composes herself, steps forward, chews gum, takes gum out, sticks it behind her ear, bites her nails, hoists up a stocking, puts gum back in mouth, looks at SIGGIE mutely and bovinely, then shrugs and turns away.)

SIGGIE: (after her) I wouldn't take up much room!

PARSONS: But what would her hubby, Mr Frank Pot say? And where would they pot you? What with Frank Pot and Ethel Pot and all the little Pot tots - Peter Pot and Pollyanna Pot and Potenilla Pot and the twins, Celia and Cess Pot. Congestion, Siggie, in the Potting shed. And there's Ethel Pot's potty old pop-in-law popping in and out of the pot-hole and Frank Pot a night potter and Pollyanna working in a nights pot and Peter Pot taking pot and Ethel Pot potting her flower pots and in her pot belly another potted Pot spotted... Siggie, what a hotch-pot. Peace pots under all the beds, the whole Pot's place tottering with pots and pottering with tots, everybody taking pot luck from morning's in to night's out... I tell you, Siggie, within a week, you too would have...

58

(He conducts the whole cast)

ALL: Gone to pot!

(Embarrassed silence ensues, except for occasional residual snigger.
)

SIGGIE: (slowly at first) I knew all along I'd finally get here. Even after somebody stole all my savings. I'm not blaming Miss Glamorgan for that. Only I would have liked to tell her I was sorry for what I used to think before she... I didn't like her... woman's smell. It's not that. But I didn't like her sugary tea with all the milk making it all cold. I didn't like to say. I didn't like the runny butter. But I never let on. She had one gold tooth and it used to shine. I wanted to tell her it didn't matter with that gold tooth she could leave the light off...

(The MONOLOGUE increases as he talks until he and it are saying the same thing, then it gradually taking over until he is just mouthing what it is saying and then gives up while it carries on...)

SIGGIE and MONOLOGUE: But what with the milk and sugar in the tea and the biscuit I didn't like but out of courtesy I ate and trying to watch television at the same time which I don't go on and trying not to breathe in and trying not to look at Miss Glamorgan's bandy legs, it was a bit much, I tell you, to take a mouthful and then have to pull out a long strand of hair from out of my mouth. To be straight up, it used to make me go a bit queasy, all that sugary tea and all... Then one arvo I was walking across the green and there were a lot of policemen standing around her. Miss Glamorgan, like, and they took her straight from there to the undertaker. She looked so tucked up on that bench. I wanted to stop. I... One day I was walking along the back lane and there was half a cat lying by the fence. A little girl was standing over it, looking down. If I was my sister, I would have answered my letters. I'm cold and wet. I pain somewhere.

(MONOLOGUE subsides. SIGGIE starts to cough. MISS GLAMORGAN flies to him, cradles him in her arms.)

PARSONS: (quickly) Excuse me, he is emoting, not objecting.

MISS HOLLAND: Now, you've got all those beaut friends and family back in Australia, Mr Morrison.

PARSONS: (conciliatory) Sure. For forty years, Australia's been keeping its glass bongs crossed. From the moment you went to the counter to buy your ticket, the word went out. Oh, yes. Through the salons and the fin de siècles of Europe like a dose of salts. Galloped down the Marco Polo trail, caused the cultural revolution in China, increased the turnover of Aussie beer in South-East Asia, caught Borneo napping. By Darwin, the news of Siggie's returning made the Domino Theory look like chicken feed. The whole country went to rust-resistant seed. In Melbourne, Chloe blushed. In Sydney, Sydney was one mass of frenzied, jerking bodies. Anderson Department of FAT Telegraphed Requesting Communication Urgently Telephone Melbourne 239291.

JARVIS: (taking it up) Some say the earth was feverous and did shake. The sun set its sovereign circumference on the rim of the world and, like a lover whose eyes maynst repair while others ought asleep, kept watch o'er the sweet globe of its beloved returning.

PARSONS:
Then didst the wind pummel to t'fields,
As though th'earth itself had loosed its mighty axis,
The clouds, like naked Neptune concatenated astride
His once proud trident, floundered i' the sea of Confusion's cauldron.

MISS HOLLAND: (following)
Logic, th'Mistress of Nature, did steal from its bed
And left th'house with Disorder. Some say angels
Beating aloft warriors' embellishments drove beasts
With homed heads along the Birdsville Trail...

MRS PRUFROCK:
All Nature werest o'erpotted.
Th'dogs didst railments and g-nashings at th'Masters:
Th'Masters didst derailments o'er th'Mistresses;
Th'Mistresses didst g-nashingments o'er th'Dogs;
Surf Sanderson deceased uponst 'is Board.

BIG JULIE:
The publicans went mad and lashed out free grog;
Only five dollars nonreturnable with each glog-glog-glog!

SIGGIE: (up at MISS HOLLAND) Have we met too?

MISS HOLLAND: Call me Miss Holland.

SIGGIE: How do you do?

MISS HOLLAND: Fine, thank you.

SIGGIE: I know a Miss Holland too. I think you'll like my Miss Holland. She's Irish.

PARSONS: (disassociating himself) Do your worst.

MISS HOLLAND: I'm sure I would.

SIGGIE: She's about the same age as you.

MISS HOLLAND: Really?

SIGGIE: Same hair, same everything.

MISS HOLLAND: What was her first name?

SIGGIE: Joan, I think.

MISS HOLLAND: Mine's Joan, too.

SIGGIE: (giggles) Ain't fact stranger than fiction?

MISS HOLLAND: (daggers at PARSONS) Much better.

SIGGIE: She gave me this coat for a going-away thingmebob.

MISS HOLLAND: How nice.

SIGGIE: And Miss Julie gave me these shoes because they were too small for her.

61

BIG JULIE: I'm Miss Julie.

SIGGIE: (giggles) I thought you might be.

BIG JULIE: Sweetie.

SIGGIE: Even the old dragon herself, Mrs Prufrock, gave me a change of underps, make a man blush.

MRS PRUFROCK: (booming) I'm Mrs Prufrock.

SIGGIE: (intimately, meaning them and PARSONS) I hope I haven't upset him.

BIG JULIE: He's just here to scare away the sharks.

MRS PRUFROCK: (insulted at SIGGIE ignoring her) I'm Mrs Prufrock.

SIGGIE: (cringes) Hello.

MRS PRUFROCK: Somebody might have underchanged you some undies but I did. Not.

BIG JULIE: Sit down and develop.

MRS PRUFROCK: Somebody might have underpinned his underchanges, but not Mrs Profruck. Prufrock. I object to that infertience. What's more, I have said from the initial that using our own names was an invasion of privation.

PARSONS: I've told you before. Get worked up and your diction goes to the pathetic.

SIGGIE: That's it. 'Dictaphone up your diction'.

PARSONS: Dictionary.

MRS PRUFROCK: (not to be pacified) There is a dowuld of diwwerence between playing Mrs Prufrock when I am Mrs Prufruck and having a little man managing to come in... being rude here about a Mrs Purfrock, which I am not, and then dismissing me as though I was not the real Mrs Ruprock. Changing his urdies, indeed!

(Bored silence, except for SIGGIE trying to hold back coughing. New thought...)

MRS PRUFROCK: Especially...

(They all sigh loudly)

MRS PRUFROCK: Especially since if I was since his Mrs Fropuck, Propuck... oh, *shit*!

BIG JULIE: (helpful) Prufrock.

MRS PRUFROCK: Especially if I was since his Mrs Prufrock... you may not care, but happens so it does that the first Frufrocks sailed fleet first with the First Fleet... Then to call her the old dragon.
    (wagging finger)
All I can say, old little man, is that your appetite displays a great meal of inslatitude.

MISS GLAMORGAN: (has to step in) You're all being rotten to him again!

(and begins to wail.)

BIG JULIE: (at MRS PRUFROCK) Now look what you've done, you powdered pole.

MRS PRUFROCK: Well.

BIG JULIE: You avalanche of dishwater.

MRS PRUFROCK: Sticks and bone may break my stones.

BIG JULIE: Smarty pants. And that's a laugh.

MRS PRUFROCK: You're polluted, you are.

BIG JULIE: You couldn't buy a boyfriend on a stick.

JARVIS: Ladies, yuk-yuk.

BIG JULIE: I ain't no lady!

JARVIS: Right.

BIG JULIE: You want a black eye or something?

JARVIS: (dances around her) Come on, you underbelly of a whale.

(They spar)

PARSONS: (renewed animation) Kick him in the crutch. Bounce off her titty and make the cancer come. More stylization. The old Queensbury's make the best. Try John L. Sullivan. Make use of the bare knuckles.

(They stop because of his attempted choreography)

BIG JULIE: Can't anybody put the boot in without you butting in?

PARSONS: Just stay with the action!
  (grabs SIGGIE)
This hurts me more than you.

(And arranges him in a crucified position.)

MISS GLAMORGAN: Objection!

PARSONS: (ignoring her) He comes to us in supplication. Express It, cap I, for me, he asks. What do we do? We box on. We finish the last chewy. We splinter him on wood. Splinters gouging red rivers down his back. Look, his mouth falls open. Unaided, but caught up in the impetus, he moves for one apt summing up of all he has gone through, all he has ever meant to say. What comes out? An 'err' from one end and an airing from the other, then nothing. For all the freedom the umbilical becomes the mortal cord and we choke and die as purblind and bound as when we started.

64

SIGGIE: (but long-sufferingly) Hey, geez...

PARSONS: Quiet. Life begins and ends with the cry of a rift.
Coming, the mother's when we are torn from her. Departing, our own
when it is torn from us. Only one lesson in all our time. How to utter
the last apt animal guttural for ourselves alone and lone. That and that
alone is what is left to all of us. Listen, the rude gasps rippling the
petrified forest of the material world externally.

    (SIGGIE moans.)

PARSONS: One word, one succinct turn of the old verbal twirl... but
grief holds him firmly by the throat. The flies of inexpressible
memory are beginning to blow him.

SIGGIE: I'm aching...

PARSONS: And nobody breaks off from the championship round to
tell him we've all also clapped, very suddenly and very loudly, in
quite the wrong place at a concert. That we've all peeked through the
open blouse at the breast and will peg out haunted, like him, by the
peek-sighting of it or never knowing all the beautiful faces we have
ever seen. That the celibate who said no man is an island was pulling
our pissers. We're too near ourselves to our own inevitable moan,
thanks vee much, so...
  (SIGGIE begins coughing with the exertion)
... so when he coughs, we aim for each other's genitals. He is already
gone and lost from us, like an ice cream on roast. He pleads silently,
but we're too bored and too tired and only want to move our own
bored and tired bodies in rhythm with the St Vitus Dance. Tell him
what we can do, however, is to offer the tenacious sinew that binds all
communities of men... the privilege of arguing the toss over his
carcass.
  (casts a cloak onto the floor. Quick glance at script, then...)
So roll up, ladies and guts... suggest we read gents for guts there...
the die is cast, the dice are upcast. Page forty-three and roll it.

    (Scripts in hand, they shoot dice.)

JARVIS: (first throw) He got on my tit, but I never told him so.

PARSONS: No comment. Next.

BIG JULIE: (throws) I only tried to make him feel protected.

PARSONS: Suffocating. Next!

JARVIS: He had no balls, but I never mentioned it.

PARSONS: No opportunity. Next!

BIG JULIE: The odd bit of folding stuff thrown his way.

PARSONS: Insufficient. Next!

JARVIS: Bought him a beer when he was leaving.

BIG JULIE: A part-time job at my place washing up the glasses.

PARSONS: Upped! Take round one. Round two...

BIG JULIE: Mothered him.

PARSONS: Child substitution. Next!

MISS HOLLAND: (throwing) Let him sit by the library radiator every day.

PARSONS: Virtue too easy. Next!

SIGGIE: (coughing) I... can't...

PARSONS: (above him) Next!

MRS PRUFROCK: My personal attention using my fingers on him

PARSONS: Terms of employment. Cheap easy gestures. Next!

BIG JULIE: (protest) Obliged him when he wanted mothering.

PARSONS: Titty gratification. Disqualified.
    (at MISS HOLLAND)

Take round two.

MISS HOLLAND: Saved all the books he wanted.

PARSONS: Fertilizer delusions, common librarianitis. Next!

MRS PRUFROCK: Council flat, the wall-to-doors, the Wheels-on-Meals, not pooling with his fension.

PARSONS: Upped! But cancelled by typical attitudinizing.

MISS HOLLAND: Invited him to parties.

PARSONS: As Santa Claus. Self-serving. Next!

MRS PRUFROCK: Tidied up after him without saying a word.

 PARSONS: Compounding brag with drag. But fair 'nough! Round four!

'BOY': Let him play with me down by the swings.

> (SIGGIE, unable to hold position any longer, sinks to floor. As he crawls away to the couch, helped by BIG JULIE and MISS HOLLAND, MISS GLAMORGAN bursts out crying again.)

MISS GLAMORGAN: (over him) I could have looked after you so well!

PARSONS: (jumping up, 'riding her') Double seven! Pity and compassion! Can you beat that?

MISS GLAMORGAN: I could have kept him safe!

PARSONS: Oh, bowel-rending stuff!

MISS GLAMORGAN: Proper cooked meals, regular. Electric fire on all day. Tea and crumpets.

PARSONS: Score, score and score! The winner takes all!

(He holds up her hand.)

MISS GLAMORGAN: (wail) And all I did was lose his money!
PARSONS: (lets arm drop) Over-acting.

BIG JULIE: Oh, leave her alone.

MRS PRUFROCK: Well, it was idiotical in anyone's quadratic.

BIG JULIE: Who said it was, you cloistered cluster?

MRS PRUFROCK: All I was saying, keeping his money in a box
under her bed. Really.

(MISS GLAMORGAN wails even louder.)

BIG JULIE: Don't mind them, love. They wouldn't buy grandma a
walking stick if she was one-legged. Anyway, if you'd lived, you'd
probably be as bald as a coot and smelling like a public dunny by
now. Even old Sig wouldn't have looked at you.

MISS GLAMORGAN: He isn't well! I know he isn't well!

BIG JULIE: Corse he is. He'll live to be Australia's first man on the
Moon.
    (turns on PARSONS)
All this is derivative cock.

PARSONS: Traditional.

BIG JULIE: Traditional derivative cock.

PARSONS: The derivative cock of tradition. Subessence of life.

BIG JULIE: Cock.

PARSONS: Cock subessence of life.

BIG JULIE: God, you *gliss*. My word.

PARSONS: Now you're being derivative.

68

BIG JULIE: And you're being bloody Jarry, Pirandello, Beckett, Stoppard... *Their* words.

PARSONS: (dismissive) Foreigners. I'm being Commedia dell' Arte being quintessential subessential cock of the time when goat-herd man sat around on classical boulders being ponderous about the physical similarities of goats being men and men being goats.

BIG JULIE: (shaking script) Are you going to stick to this rubbish?

PARSONS: (defensive) What's wrong with it?

MISS HOLLAND: Wrong with it? After
   (indicates SIGGIE)
he's been here?

BIG JULIE: It's about as real as your mother's womb.

PARSONS: That's cheap and nasty.

BIG JULIE: Yeah, and so's your damn play.

MISS GLAMORGAN: (goes over to SIGGIE) I'll look after you, Mr Morrison dear.

SIGGIE: I... Kids jumping about up top, see. *I want to go home'.*

MISS GLAMORGAN: There, there.

SIGGIE: I knew someone like you. Nice and kind. A... long time ago.

   (Roar of another plane landing.)

SIGGIE: There goes another one.

PARSONS: Don't tell me. Another planey-waney landing.

SIGGIE: Do they always have to bounce?

PARSONS: I bounce too. Look. Bouncey-wouncey. I'm an Indian rubber ball. What are you, some sort of rubber solution subversive?

SIGGIE: (shrinking back) I think I'll have that little shut-eye now.

(The old man closes his eyes.

Long awkward silence. JARVIS and PARSONS break it purely out of tedium. They 'throw' irrelevancies.)

JARVIS: The aggressive confidence of a drunk staggering into a bar.

PARSONS: The staggering confidence of a woman swaggering aggressively into a bar.

JARVIS: The impertinence of someone letting you lie next to her open armpit.

PARSONS: Talking it puts the thought's nose out of joint.

JARVIS: Talking it in the pub the other night, somebody said, 'Whatcha mean I'm drunk? I'm as judger as a sob'. Then sighed like a beer keg being tapped.

PARSONS: Alternatively, the cello isn't a sexual substitute if the lady cellist is clearly seen to be losing her knee grip.

(Another silence. Nobody stirs, until MISS HOLLAND finally does so out of impatience.)

MISS HOLLAND: Oh, let's get it over with!

PARSONS (encouraged) You think so?

MISS HOLLAND: We all think so.

(and they do. MISS HOLLAND takes the lead, glances at her script, steps forward but, first, is stopped by:)

PARSONS: Just a bit.
   (dashes off, returns almost immediately totally confused)

Where's everybody gone?
  (nobody can help him with that)
Well, let's do it ourselves. Give's a hand.

> *(Between them, they pull on a bed, a few mementos on a sideboard, a door, a small section of rails denoting an outside landing, a few prison bars and a desk.*
>
> *PARSONS, during this time, has pulled on an outfit resembling SIGGIE's, before going over to pull MISS GLAMORGAN away from stroking the real SIGGIE'S brow.)*

PARSONS: You too, Florence Nightingale.

MISS GLAMORGAN: He's not well!

PARSONS: Up.

> *(While MISS HOLLAND delivers, BIG JULIE gets behind bars in 'gaol'; MISS GLAMORGAN, shawled and looking pale and weak, gets into bed; MRS PRUFROCK sits at the desk.)*

MISS HOLLAND: Little did oi know at that stage begorrah that, loik t'laxative said, tings were comin' to a pretty pass. There they all were wit' Fate takin' the oupper hand wit' t'help o' t'black-hearted villain Jarvis b'Jesus...

> *(JARVIS makes a flurried excursion onto the stage. General boos.)*

MISS HOLLAND: (continuing) ...stirrin' it all oup. Big Julie ratted on by th'Devil himself...
  (boos)
picked oup, loik, when she happened t'be partakin' of an innocent stroll along t'high street at tree in t'mornin'. An' her twiggin' what was oup, but helpless, loik, in boob...

BIG JULIE: (shaking bars) Helpless! Woe that the time be arrived when having little chats with the opposite sex in the early hours of the morning on the King's highway can land you in trouble. Dobbed in by the skunk, Jarvis, I'll bet.

(Rapid tapping sounds.)

BIG JULIE: (continuing) What's that? Mice? No. Hark. Morse
Code.
    (reads it)
'Help Siggie. Pension Day'. Help Siggie, pension day! Yarbles and
yarsucks, something is trying to tell me Jarvis got me in here so he
could stick poor Siggie up the World's End again! Well, I've still got a
thingo or two up my sleeve. In particular, this hammer and chisel
imbedded in the only outsize bulge that comes with me every time I
goes out!
    (calls)
Siggie, darlin' boy, Big Jools be a-coming!

MISS HOLLAND: An' t'lilly-livered Mrs Prufrock, poxy Protestant
bog, sittin' on her witherin' assets at her desk wit' complaints, loik, o'
immoral practices in t'boarding house an' o' rent not paid. Complaints
be Unknown Sources. ha!

(JARVIS flourishes himself on stage again to boos.)

MRS PRUFROCK: (waves letter) More complaints from Unknown
Sources. It is time for me to invest a little gation.

(She gets up from desk, just as 'phone rings; picks it up, listens
warily, slams receiver down and laughs awkwardly at audience.
The 'phone rings again. She tries to ignore it, but has to pick it
up at last.)

MRS PRUFROCK: (whisper) Not here, Commodore.
    (turns her back on audience)
You know how jealously jealous Cedric jealouses. Ring me in the
park instead.
    (giggles)
Oh, you naughty nanny Commodore. Here...

(She blows noisome kiss into 'phone)

MISS HOLLAND: An' all t'toime, Miss Glamorgan worried out o'
her dear, sick moind for Mr Morrison, God love him for a saint's

72

send-up, an' he not returned again from drawin' his pension, b'Jesus. Her on her sick bed, an' all...

(poked by a rod from the wings, MISS GLAMORGAN coughs weakly, pathetically, gazes with worried eyes at door.)

MISS HOLLAND: (continuing) The rent not paid again. Wit' Mr Morrison's savin's fast safe under t'bed. An' him not realizin' her puttin' her own money in t'li'l box for him t'be able t'go back home to that Australya place an' not payin' her own rent. Loik, t'is more'n enough t'make t'Holy Fadder Himself pity t'poor.

(MISS GLAMORGAN strains over bed to make sure the box is still there, lies back painfully but satisfied.)

MISS HOLLAND: An' all t'toime, the double-dealin' devil Jarvis...
    (general boos)
is gettin' poor Mr Morrison t'wicked booze his pension away again...

(JARVIS and PARSONS, as 'SIGGIE', Come stumbling drunkenly along the landing. PARSONS is singing Waltzing Matilda in a piping falsetto.)

JARVIS: You're one for the boys, skipper.

(He punches PARSONS-AS-SIGGIE in the stomach, pretending to be playful. PARSONS-AS-SIGGIE retches over the landing.)

JARVIS: Goodness me, don't know my own strength. Pardon oopsy-daisy.
    (general boos; cocks finger at audience)
How awfully clumsy.

PARSONS-AS-SIGGIE: Oh my oh my oh my oh my.

JARVIS: What a guy!

PARSONS-AS-SIGGIE: Oh my oh my, I think I must have spent all my pension again.

JARVIS: (back of hand) Twenty pints of beer and fifteen shorts. Or should I say, coloured water? Tipsy, tipsy. Half tipsy for me and half tipsy for the barmaid. Heh, heh.

PARSONS-AS-SIGGIE: Alack-a-day, how can I return to my sunny homeland...?

JARVIS: But you are home, skipper.
    (back of hand)
Home, that is, if he can pay his rent this week. Some hope. Boo hoo.
    (more boos)
Tell you what, skipper, what about a little loan?

PARSONS-AS-SIGGIE: Would you? Oh, would you, Mr Jarvis?

JARVIS: (crocodile tears) If it was only up to me, I'd let you pay, say, your rent next week, but I'm only a humble rent collector. Perhaps...
    (shakes head)
... no.

PARSONS-AS-SIGGIE: Oh what, Mr Jarvis?

JARVIS: Like, say, if someone found the delectable Miss Glamorgan's key lying out here, say, on the landing at, say, midnight tonight...

PARSONS-AS-SIGGIE: (recoiling) Not the fair and virtuous Miss Glamorgan's key!

JARVIS: (back of hand) Damnation! He was supposed to be shikkered.
    (back to PARSONS-AS-SIGGIE)
You goose, it's the only way.

PARSONS: No, no!

JARVIS: I mean to have the lovely Miss G!

BIG JULIE: Stop, you hyena's horseflesh!

JARVIS: (cups ear) What was that?

PARSONS-AS-SIGGIE: Hooray, it came from the direction of the city gaol.

BIG JULIE: You dog's fouling! You physical wreck!

JARVIS: Curses, it's Big Julie!

BIG JULIE: Flee, Siggie, love! Flee from a stinking pig who's gonna get his right up to the stinking sty when I get stinking hold of him! Fly to your homeland, Sig!

> *(JARVIS grabs PARSONS-AS-SIGGIE by the neck. PARSONS-AS-SIGGIE slips him, dashes to MISS GLAMORGAN'S door, struggles to open it. JARVIS lunges after him, but has his wooden leg caught in a knot hole. They both struggle individually. Touch-and-go 'chase' music. PARSONS-AS-SIGGIE gets the door open, slams it behind him.)*

JARVIS: (still caught) Curses! I'll get you both for this!

MISS GLAMORGAN: (wakes up, puts out a trembling hand for him) My Mr Morrison has come back...

> *(and sinks back. PARSONS-AS-SIGGIE hurries over to her bedside. He coughs. She coughs. They cough together and cling to each other. General 'Aws'.)*

JARVIS: (leg still caught) Don't nobody help me, will you?

> *(general boos)*

MRS PRUFROCK: (cups ear) Hark, do I hear retuberrations on the number twenty-seven bus route?
   (she goes up to JARVIS)
Mr Jarvis, kindly your leg out of that stump take, which is blocking that knot hole and preposterating an imperticular affray all over. Town. To wit.

> *(JARVIS hastily unstraps his wooden leg, stands lopsidedly on*

stump to general delight.)

JARVIS: (ingratiating) Mrs Prufrock, lovely lady.

MRS PRUFROCK: Do you think so?

JARVIS: As I half stand here on the lopside.

MRS PRUFROCK: Enough of that, Mr Jarvis, you maughty man, you.
    (brandishes letter)
Hi 'ave complaints.

JARVIS: (confidentially) And it's about time, Mrs Prufrock, pillar of womanhood. If you see what I mean.

MRS PRUFROCK: Do you mean...?

JARVIS: Hi do.

MRS PRUFROCK: Come then, Mr Jarvis!

JARVIS: (behind her) The gravy thickens. Heh, heh.

(He waddles after her.

MRS PRUFROCK knocks imperiously on the door. MISS GLAMORGAN and PARSONS-AS-SIGGIE start, cling more firmly to each other.)

MISS GLAMORGAN: Never you fear, Mr Morrison dear. Nothing will come between you, me and the box.

MRS PRUFROCK: (unlocks the door, enters shocked) Dare I believe my eyes?

JARVIS: Go on, I dare you.

MRS PRUFROCK: So! It is true!

MISS GLAMORGAN: Oh, woe! Caught red-handed!

PARSONS-AS-SIGGIE: We'll pay all rent, Mrs Prufrock, I promise!

MRS PRUFROCK: Never mind the rent. Unless I get an expansion, I shall be forced into a verifirication that...
    (brandishes letter)
you, both of you, are immoral getters-on!

> *(Music. MISS GLAMORGAN sits up shocked, speechless with outrage.)*

MRS PRUFROCK: Nothing to say, eh? Jarvis come then, Mr!

> *(And turns and leaves.*
>
> *JARVIS twirls his moustache triumphantly at them, then waddles after her to boos.)*

PARSONS-AS-SIGGIE: Mrs Prufrock, wait...!

> *(He chases after them to exit. MISS GLAMORGAN tries to follow, still trying to find words of indignation, but gets only as far as halfway across the room before...)*

MISS GLAMORGAN: (to heaven)
Why should the worm intrude the maiden bud?
Or tyrant folly lurk in gentle breasts?
Unruly blasts wait on the tender spring;
The adder hisses where sweet birds sing...
    (and collapses; last gasp from floor)
Oh, sweet Mr Morrison, who will look after you now?

> *(On hearing her call his name, SIGGIE looks up from couch startled, sees her. Alarmed...)*

SIGGIE: Miss Glamorgan!

'BOY': (emerging from under bed) Miss Julie! Miss Julie!

> *(He dashes off)*

SIGGIE: Miss Glamorgan!
   (struggles off couch, staggers over to her)
My Miss Glamorgan!

> *(He collapses beside her.*
>
> *JARVIS returns furtively, slithers over them, steals money box and escapes.*
>
> *Over the ensuing melodrama's musical accompaniment, sound of an ambulance siren.*
>
> *BIG JULIE bursts out of prison, races to the rescue. She throws open the door, sees the two bodies and stops short. Gingerly, she rolls over SIGGIE's body. When the realization hits her, she screams out for real.)*

BIG JULIE: *SIGGIE!*

> *(including PARSONS, they all run back on stage, gasp when they see SIGGIE.*
>
> *Blackout.*
>
>
> *Pale blue lighting illuminates only front few metres of the stage. Funeral music. PARSONS and JARVIS come out from left bearing a coffin. Others follow in a bedraggled procession across the stage.*
>
> *The last is 'BOY'. He is followed at a distance by a pantomime dog. The dog is stopped mid-stage. 'BOY' stops, goes back for the dog.' He kneels down beside it, buries his face in its neck and weeps... then gets up and leads it after the procession.*
>
> *MONOLOGUE rises. It continues until it fills the auditorium and then its surrounds, carrying on throughout the intermission.)*

MONOLOGUE: And go and tell your daddies. Go and tell your daddies or I'll tan your little bums. Go and tell a copper there's an

Aussie caught down here. Tell him I'm not Pommy. Tell him there's an Aussie down here. The only diff was Hailey's Comet. Tell him the only diff was Hailey's Comet. That's all the diff was. Hailey's... what was that book? You know that book. What did that book say? Yes. Hailey's Comet appeared during the battle in which Attila the Hun was defeated by the Romans and the Goths. It was also the sign in the shape of a sword which hung over Jerusalem before the destruction of the city by Titus. It was Hailey's Comet that was pictured in the Nuremburg Chronicle for the year AD 684. If the comet's tail had been straight in nineteen-o-ten, the earth would have passed through it and this possibility gave rise to a quite remarkable excitement. People who should have known better predicted that we should be asphyxiated by poisonous gases. As it was, one or two persons were still turned in the head coinciding with exposure to the unusually large spots on the sun. Causing severe and, in some cases, permanent sun-stroke. One such case was recorded in Australia concerning an eleven-year-old boy caught outdoors. Many have regarded these people as the chosen few. There is an entirely new set of photographs in both full colour and black and white. Ideal for coffee tables. Price, five-fifty and...

(etcetera through interval)

End Act 1

Act 2

(MONOLOGUE gradually becomes indistinct compared to the roar of water in a storm drain.

General stage lighting takes over.

SIGGIE is laid out on airport couch. MISS GLAMORGAN is dabbing a wet cloth on his forehead. The others are sitting back watching him remorsefully. By him is a bottle of beer. The long silence is punctuated only by MISS GLAMORGAN'S whimpering.

PARSONS is about to stick a pin in SIGGIE's hand.)

PARSONS: If he objects to this, it is a cri de coeur, not a complaint.

(Sticks the pin in. SIGGIE doesn't move. Tries again, still nothing. He sticks a wooden chip up SIGGIE's nose. No reaction. Goes around, takes off one of SIGGIE's shoes, reels back. MISS GLAMORGAN screams. The others crowd around, gasp.)

JARVIS: My God, that's just got to be syphilis of the toes.

MISS HOLLAND: (with difficulty) What is it?

PARSONS: Where the water must have got at him.

BIG JULIE: What water?

PARSONS: (shrugs unconvincingly) How would I know?

BIG JULIE (Indicating PARSONS) I don't trust him.

PARSONS: If I told you, it'd only give him an unfair emotional advantage.

BIG JULIE: Something stinks around here.

JARVIS: Stink? He ought to be buried up to his knees in a cemetery.

80

(PARSONS overcomes repulsion to tickle the sole of SIGGIE's foot. MISS GLAMORGAN giggles. He stops. She stops. Does so again, she giggles again; stops and she stops. SIGGIE has not reacted.)

PARSONS: (at her) If he put his hand in a fire, would you?

(PARSONS walks away, sits apart. The others follow, except JARVIS who goes to take the bottle of beer.)

BIG JULIE: (catching him) Hey!

JARVIS: He won't be needing this more than me.

(But SIGGIE's hand flops over, falls proprietorially onto bottle. JARVIS has a tug of war with him, doesn't succeed and lets bottle go. He looks at SIGGIE closely, waves hand across his face but gets no reaction)

JARVIS: The little bugger's determined to take it with him anyway.

(He returns to sit with others.

Long pause.)

MISS HOLLAND: I still say all that was going too far.

PARSONS: During one night in the Depression... and this was in the back stalls... they got so worked up watching the English-tea's silver service breakfasts that three of them had coronaries before they'd even set alight to the seats.

BIG JULIE: He scared seven bells of hell out of me, keeling over like that.

MISS HOLLAND: What are we going to do?

BIG JULIE: We can't just leave him keeled over like that.

81

PARSONS: Did anyone loosen his tie? The manual says, if anyone keels over on you or...

(weak laugh)

... gets keeled, they say step one is you leap in and disarrange the corpus delicto around the larynx region.

BIG JULIE: That's not funny.

PARSONS: Nervousness.

BIG JULIE: You nervous? I nearly underwent my change in woman's life with him keeling over on me like that.

(Pause)

MISS HOLLAND: Why doesn't somebody go out and call an ambulance? Or something.

JARVIS: At least tell them the little exhibitionist just keeled over on us.

BIG JULIE: (daggers at PARSONS) Keel-hauled, you mean.

PARSONS: What's the orangutan underbrow scowl for?

(BIG JULIE snaps her fingers at him. Stung, he goes to SIGGIE.)

PARSONS: Pulse rate... thirteen in ten seconds, multiplied by six... six thirteens... that's still normal, give or take a compression or rarefaction. Heart. Like a baby's on the breast.

(lifts arm, lets it drop)

You can't deny the limbs aren't supple, if sinewy. On the whole, not much sign of excessive, that is to say recently inflicted, rotting flesh.

(lifts SIGGIE's eyelid)

Eyes unrolled, merely staring mindlessly at the world. That's normal too. Respiration. Who knows how to mouth-to-mouth somebody?

(at MRS PRUFROCK)

You've done nursing.

MRS PRUFROCK: No, thank you.

MISS GLAMORGAN: Please.

MRS PRUFROCK: I'm not lipping my pub near a near dead man.

BIG JULIE: It's just the same as kissing only you blow instead of suck.

MRS PRUFROCK: You do it.

BIG JULIE: I wouldn't want to give him my cold.

(Long pause.)

MISS GLAMORGAN: (wail) What are we all sitting around for?

BIG JULIE: (at her) Shut up or you'll bring on my impending heart attack. By Christ, I haven't had such a scare since last week when my own body rejected my advances.

MISS GLAMORGAN:(burst) Nobody's ever given him a thought.

(She whimpers on.)

PARSONS: Someone stop her. I'm trying to think.

MISS HOLLAND: It's too late for thinking.

PARSONS: If this got around...

MISS HOLLAND: You should have thought of that before you did this.

PARSONS: Me? We're all in together.

BIG JULIE: Who is?

JARVIS: I'm not.

MISS HOLLAND: Neither am I.

83

MRS PRUFROCK: I was not certainly.

PARSONS: Now if he'd had the sense to do it on the night. But this. I can't stand bad timing on stage. There is such a thing as taste.

MISS HOLLAND: Now he's blaming Mr Morrison.

PARSONS: Well, he could've keeled over anywhere in Sydney. Jesus, younger than him... they're doing it all the time. You commiserate with them about their pensions and they're liable to conk out over the counter out of sheer bloody spite. Pander to them like you were doing to him about his London lark, and it's like watching the devastation of an autumn gale on dying leaves.

MISS HOLLAND: At least he'd have died happy.

PARSONS: If he dies, he dies.

    (MISS GLAMORGAN wails above him.)

PARSONS: (above her) Even dead saints only look happy because they've taken their false teeth out first. Listen.
    (shouts) '
Death annihilates.
    (again)
Death... anni-hil-ates.!
    (it reverberates)
The phonetifications... another Parsons' personal that we can and should add... alone make you shudder. Compare it to 'Tiptoe through the twilight with a tweezer just to please her'.
    (indicates SIGGIE)
Ask him. If he was alive right now...
    (MISS GLAMORGAN wails louder)
all right, more alive right now... he'd tell you he'd rather live for a thousand more boring years than go through the act of dying just once.

MISS GLAMORGAN: You're callous. All of you.

PARSONS: (first human reaction) You think he's got problems. I'm fifty next week.

(He turns away)

BIG JULIE: Boo hoo. Why didn't you think of that before you done Siggie down?

PARSONS: I did not do him down. It fell to my lot to administer a certain confluence of circumstances. You say walk to an old man and he steps out in front of a car. Who do you apologise to? Circumstances are two metaphors. As delicately beautiful as a harpsichord; as solidly uncomfortable as a pew on which you're sitting listening to it.

(MISS GLAMORGAN whimpers again. PARSONS reacts angrily by pushing 'BOY' off the seat)

PARSONS: For God's sake, take her to the powder room.

('BOY' stands his ground defiantly. PARSONS wearily takes out a packet of cigarettes, offers it to him.)

PARSONS: Here, pretend it's only tobacco.

'BOY': I don't smoke any lousy murderer's joints. C'mon, Aunt Fanny.

('BOY' exits with bedraggled MISS GLAMORGAN)

PARSONS: Did you hear what that thing of small stature called me?

BIG JULIE: It takes some crumby sort of monster.

PARSONS: He walked in here. I don't know why he did, but he did. All I know is he's been wandering around looking for some place to die from the moment he stepped off the plane in Sydney, went into a little jiggle of ecstasy at finally arriving home after forty years and got it right in the flue by the poker of the first passerby. Even I wanted to tell him that. You should've done so.

BIG JULIE: Who asked you for a speech?

PARSONS: (demurely) Just comes and goes.

BIG JULIE: You nearly did for me too, you assassin.

PARSONS: All this is getting nobody to the morgue.

BIG JULIE: Any more of that… just wait for me, there'll be two going.

PARSONS: If the show hadn't carried on, there would have been chaos.

BIG JULIE: Bankruptcy, you mean. For you.

PARSONS: We're actors. The set pattern; life as formal literature; you there, me here, rotate the crystal of life under the strobe, see the pretty pictures. Anyway, up yours. I'm not worried about money. My fifteen dependents are.
    (then)
It was those damn kids that found him stuck down that storm drain and didn't call for help who made it messy for us all. They should have added the coup de grace properly. But then young kids today haven't developed the grace to polish people off with any sort of *je-ne-sais-pas*. Not kids with full bellies. Bombed-out kids might. Napalmed kids, quite probably. Redfern kids with an ounce of community decency, sure. But U-beaut kids out of Banjo Patterson's land, no.

MISS HOLLAND: What kids?

PARSONS: They want to love them to death these days.

BIG JULIE: She asked you what kids.

PARSONS: Who do you know who could be so piddling as to get himself jammed down a drain on his first night back. I mean, you could drive a train through that damn storm drain and what happens… he gets discovered by some kids you could drive a toy train over.
    (impatiently)

86

None of you read Lost'n'Found?

MISS HOLLAND: (appalled) Siggie...?

(PARSONS nods, lifts SIGGIE's foot with repulsion, waves it quickly, lets it drop.)

PARSONS: Yep. Until the flesh began to rot in the storm water. Up, I believe, if you care to investigate, to at least the genital- perineum-anal straight line. A sea-green tide mark. Storm-water vintage

BIG JULIE: You *scunge*.

PARSONS: That's a repetition. I observed scientifically. I am, therefore, morally protected by diminished responsibility. No scientific observer would dare tamper with inevitability. Smoking-dash-cancer. Him-dash-Australia of forty years ago. Both show undeniables of rot-your-lungs-out.

BIG JULIE: You can damn well say what you like. Let's go, girls.

PARSONS: Fine, fine. Let's all go home. He might not be here in the morning.

JARVIS: It's already morning.

PARSONS: (exasperated) Nobody knows that until we look!

MRS PRUFROCK: (at JARVIS) I told you night not day.

JARVIS: I don't fancy coming back here in a few hours and finding him all fly-blown or something.

PARSONS: There are no flies.

JARVIS: I know a lot of flies that'd wake up just to get at him.

MISS HOLLAND: I don't understand this. You mean to say Siggie was that old man caught down that drain a few weeks ago?

PARSONS: Sad, wasn't it?

MISS HOLLAND: Knowing that didn't matter to you?

PARSONS: I was going to tack on a surprise ending. But that wasn't the point. The point is, the poor bugger, being tied right over the bull's-eye, something someone sometime like that would have got him right...
    (uses pin to demonstrate on SIGGIE)
in the guts anyway.

MISS HOLLAND: I'm not talking about that. And stop assaulting him.!

PARSONS: He'll survive. When his little mind dribbles out of that trauma there... which I considered best to inflict for his own tooty-fruity... he'll be with us in body and soul again. He'll remember he's in Sydney. And when he walks out of here, there'll be a silent 'thank you' gurgling somewhere in his dribble.

BIG JULIE: *If* he snaps out of it.

PARSONS: (smirking) Thinking he was still in London. Seeing the set must have blown his mind into a state of thought.
    (listens)
Here it comes again...

    (A MONOLOGUE burst)

MONOLOGUE: When again. the streets are white in London. When the fog is down in London. When the wind whipped up that funny smell in London. That day when I prised open a door in Soho and that big West Indian man standing there, wasn't he? Soho?, I asked him. Not bad, he said. Soho, not bad. Geez, I thought he was going to...

    (It stops as suddenly as it began)

PARSONS: (up at control room) I don't know what wrong with them up there. Where was I?

    (But is immediately interrupted by:)

88

ANNOUNCEMENT: 'Qantas Airways announce with regret further delay to Flight QF 625 to Sydney via Athens and Hong Kong that has followed Athens off the map. In any case, the captain appears to be drunk although he is a great faker and the air hostess is certainly pregnant. Thank you.'

SIGGIE: (suddenly sits bolt upright) Drat.

(The women squeal with joy, fling themselves on him, tickle him, rough his hair, etc. He writhes in delight.)

PARSONS: (joining in) Hey, you remind me of a man!

SIGGIE: What man?

PARSONS: A man of power.

SIGGIE: What power?

PARSONS: The power of Voodoo.

SIGGIE: Voodoo?

PARSONS: No, you do.

SIGGIE: What?

PARSONS: Remind me of a man.

SIGGIE: What man?

PARSONS: A man of power.

SIGGIE: (now giggling) What power?

PARSONS: The power of Voodoo.

SIGGIE: Voodoo?

PARSONS: No, you do.

SIGGIE: Whodoo?

(SIGGIE freezes as 'BOY' dashes back on, pounces on him in delight and bounces up and down on his stomach.)

'BOY': (chant) Siggie, Siggie, good old Siggie... etc.

(MONOLOGUE swells up synchronously.)

MONOLOGUE: Don't hurt my legs. Not my legs. Don't hurt my legs. Not on my legs. Get off my legs. Don't bounce up and down on my legs. Not my legs. Please not my legs. Don't. Not. Don't. Don't...

(MONOLOGUE and 'BOY' stop when SIGGIE cries out, falls back limp.)

BIG JULIE: Now look what you've done!

'BOY': What'd I do?

PARSONS: What have you been smoking out there?

'BOY': I just thought I'd jump on him a bit.

PARSONS: (simpatico) Of course you did.

MRS PRUFROCK: Well, it wasn't every clevery.

SIGGIE: (moans, opens eyes, weakly mouths at 'BOY') Please go and tell your mummy and daddy I'm here...

(SIGGIE closes eyes. BIG JULIE motions 'BOY' off. 'BOY' obstinately shakes his head. BIG JULIE grabs him, pushes him down behind couch. SIGGIE opens his eyes again. Weakly...)

SIGGIE: (angelically) Where's that boy gone?
BIG JULIE: Gone to tell his mummy and daddy you're here.

SIGGIE: Sure?

MISS HOLLAND: Ssh.

SIGGIE: (closes eyes again) I think I'll...

ANNOUNCEMENT: 'Qantas Airways announces the capture of a captain who is not drunk and the air hostess has the baby standing up anyway. Please stand by for a further announcement.'

SIGGIE: (revitalized) Little bottler!

PARSONS: Panic's over, kiddies.

BIG JULIE: Panic's over, he says. I've had another two heart attacks in the last ten seconds alone.

SIGGIE: Fancy the captain being drunk and the air hostess...
    (giggles)
doing it standing up.

JARVIS: Jesus, he's come back even more demented.

MISS HOLLAND: How do you feel, Mr Morrison?

SIGGIE: It was a real deep sleep. Thank you.

PARSONS: Sleep? That was a peel-off.

SIGGIE: I was that tired and when I saw you all come back, I couldn't keep my eyes open. Dumbo me, I thought the plane would leave without me saying goodbye to you.

MISS HOLLAND: We wouldn't let you go without saying goodbye.
    (heavily)
Would we?

MRS PRUFROCK: Never.

BIG JULIE: You have a rest there before you go, lovie.

SIGGIE: I can sleep on the plane.

(They look quizzically at one another.)

SIGGIE: Don't they let you sleep on the plane?

MISS HOLLAND: Oh, they let you sleep on... planes all right.

SIGGIE: Don't they like you to sleep on the plane though?

BIG JULIE: You can sleep on the plane all you want, love.

SIGGIE: I'd have to have a little sleep on the plane.

MRS PRUFROCK: They love you to pleep, sleep, on the splane.

BIG JULIE: Plane.

SIGGIE: Two days on the plane without sleeping...

BIG JULIE: Don't worry. As soon as you get on the plane you sleep and don't you wake up till you reach where you want to sleep to.

SIGGIE: Sydney. Isn't it beaut?

BIG JULIE: (dully) Sydney.

SIGGIE: My father knew Kingsford-Smith.

PARSONS: (with JARVIS and 'BOY' joining in to 'Onward Christian Soldiers':)
Father knew Kingsford-Smith
Kingsford-Smith knew dad
Daddy knew Kingsfordie
Kingsfordie knew my dad
Father knew Kingsford-Smith-ithie...
Kingsford-Smith knew dad... etc.

SIGGIE: I think he did anyway.
   (then)
You sure they won't mind me having a little kip out on the plane?

MISS HOLLAND: Of course not.

92

PARSONS: Those zoo keepers tried to kid along the Russian Panda with the British Panda and nothing came of that pandering.

BIG JULIE: (retort) If he wants to sleep on the plane to Sydney...

SIGGIE: I hope they don't mind if I snore a little. I see you've met my thrilling friend the gypsy.
   (then stiffens)
Mr Jarvis...

JARVIS: Boo!

BIG JULIE: (at JARVIS) Don't you go giving him another of his turns.

   (She holds SIGGIE's head protectively)

SIGGIE: (crushed) Miss Julie...?

BIG JULIE: What, sweetie?

SIGGIE: Could you sort of move your... I think I'm blacking out.

BIG JULIE: (hurriedly let's go, scratching behind his ear) Better?

SIGGIE: (purring) Hmm?

BIG JULIE: Better?

SIGGIE: Uh. Down a little...

JARVIS: Would you like me to go out and buy him a dog's collar?

BIG JULIE: Nobody's asked you.

JARVIS: It's pathetic.

MRS PRUFROCK: A little humbility...

PARSONS: (interjecting) A little what?

MRS PRUFROCK: Humbility.

PARSONS: Erase. Your word, not mine.

MRS PRUFROCK: Humbility hurts nobody.

PARSONS: Oh no? That monstrosity of a tongue trip 'humbility' is hurting me right in the sensibility.

JARVIS: And her coddling him like a teddy bear is giving me the willies.

SIGGIE: (from BIG JULIE's bosom) Oh dear, I hope Mr Jarvis hasn't come here to make trouble. Not on my last day.

BIG JULIE: (at JARVIS) Step back a little, please.

JARVIS: (shaking head) Uhuh.

SIGGIE: (suddenly) You cheated, Mr Jarvis!

JARVIS: Eh?

SIGGIE: He's stole my money!

JARVIS: I never saw his stinking money.

SIGGIE: (tugs her arm) All my savings.

JARVIS: (assumes villainy) Ah, the savings. Hee, hee. Ho, ho.

SIGGIE: (agitated) Thief!

JARVIS: (mock swoop) Whoo...

BIG JULIE: (protective) Scram.

SIGGIE: Thief, thief!

JARVIS: (another pass) Whoo...

BIG JULIE: So help me...

> *(BIG JULIE levers herself up by putting her hand on SIGGIE's head. There is a loud crack. SIGGIE goes limp, motionless, his head at an awkward angle.)*

MISS HOLLAND: Somebody... help...

PARSONS: Trying to help him is like trying to cross upstream after Moses went down.
    (but walks across, grabs SIGGIE's legs)
A couple of you hold his head. You to the left, me to the right. Hold his head down more. Precipitate it. Now.
    (while they try to straighten him:)
The poor old fool's been delivering himself up like water vapour all his life. You can't blame the kids... Try turning the other way... What were they doing? Nothing kids don't do around a park on a Sunday morning. Kicking, jolting, insinuating, insulting their fleeting youth across near the race... course. Take a breather. Throwing and toeing groin-grey... groin-grey being the predominate posthumous primary... groin-grey twigs that look like dogs' turds and dogs' turds that look like groin-grey twigs and not caring one dust-off which is which... Let's get him on the floor.
    (They do so. Try again, while...)
Uh... Hold it. You come down here, I'll go up there... Australia's little kiddies amongst the basted bark breaking bottles. Sharing their first roll 'un made from dunny paper. Directing their explorations at silk and cotton and elastic while heading for the old storm drain... Stop, it's no good.
    (They stand back panting.)
...The old storm drain. Look in. What do they see?
    (points down at SIGGIE)
Lo and behold, that. As though smashed up, covered with sludge and I-won't-say-what-else, was where he'd landed when he'd fallen out of the sky just for them to play with. Who can blame their little minds for filling up with... look, you try pulling your end, I'll try pulling mine... with wondertelly wonderlandment. My word. Their own little poppet discovery. And when it opened its liquid orbs, what does it ask them, bloody near... no good... bloody near drowning in wave after

wave of gutter spill-over? 'Buy us a little drinkie, kiddies.' Try twisting a bit.

BIG JULIE: Why don't you try?

('BOY' sneaks out from behind the couch, creeps up on bottle.)

PARSONS: The least they would have thought was he was a friendly alien from outer space. They fetch the bottle. They spar at first. Then tease a little. He 'bites' like all good fairytale pets should. They dangle, take back, dangle, take back...

(Just as the 'BOY' goes to whip bottle, SIGGIE comes alive, clutches it possessively.)

SIGGIE: Did you tell your father I was here, little boy?

('BOY' walks away in disgust)

BIG JULIE: You're going to have to cut this out, Sig. My ticker won't stand it much more.

SIGGIE: (angelic) I went off again, didn't I? Cripes, I do go off sometimes. I'm really hopeless.

BIG JULIE: (relenting) Don't worry about it.

SIGGIE: I'll be off soon and then you can all forget about a dopey old bugger, eh?

MISS HOLLAND: You don't have to leave until you're good and ready.

SIGGIE: I'll write though.
 (giggles)
When you're all freezing back here, I'll be sitting back all warm and sunny under my sun down there in Sydney...

(But then he has a violent shivering fit.)

BIG JULIE: Did he make me hurt you, love?

SIGGIE: I ache... somewhere. My legs...
  (then)
I don't want to cough!

BIG JULIE: (kindly) You cough.

JARVIS: (unkindly) Cough off.

MISS HOLLAND: You go ahead and cough.

SIGGIE: (recovers) I wouldn't like you to see what comes out when I cough. I don't want to cough because it's not nice when I cough. If you put your head against my chest, just about anywhere, you can hear... gurgling.

> (BIG JULIE signs for them to lift him on the couch, but he goes limp when they try. They give up.)

SIGGIE: I'll be all right though when I get home, like. It's being away from your proper home that causes it. That's what the doc said. Not having the proper rations of sunshine what you're used to as a boy. When will the plane be goin'?

> (He closes eyes again.)

MISS HOLLAND: If you really and truly want to go back to Sydney, the plane's sure to be going soon.

SIGGIE: Promise?

BIG JULIE: On my girl guide's black net stockings.
SIGGIE: (sits up suddenly, searches in pocket, finds ticket) As long as I've got my ticket.

> (Closes eyes again.)

MRS PRUFROCK: Wouldn't you be more couchable on the comf?

> (SIGGIE shakes his head, settles down.)

JARVIS: Don't let him go off again, for God's sake.

BIG JULIE: (cuttingly) Are you talking to us?

 JARVIS: I was only...

MISS HOLLAND: (dismissive) Thank you very much.

> *(PARSONS, JARVIS and 'BOY' draw apart. The women sit on the couch and look down protectively at SIGGIE. Long pause.)*

MISS HOLLAND: (touching head) My old mum's going this way too.

BIG JULIE: Anymore of this and I'll end up the same.

MRS PRUFROCK: Anybody could.

MISS HOLLAND: It's the least we can do… humour it.

MRS PRUFROCK: Yes.

BIG JULIE: Me, I only hope a hundred-metre-wide, five-million-tonne rock falls on me, phfut, before I get to this stage.

MISS HOLLAND: Mum's the same.

MRS PRUFROCK: I know what it's like to be treated as a thing.

MISS HOLLAND: Poor old thing.

BIG JULIE: What more can we do?

> *(Long pause.)*

PARSONS: I'm beginning to feel what his Pommy friends must have gone through when they were really seeing him off. The longer they wait, the more improbable it is that the bloody plane will ever leave. When his back's turned they mouth platitudes to each other about every man having the unimpeachable right to die returning home. They don't look into each other's eyes knowing that not one of them

has even bothered to tell the old boy about pipe dreams, tobacco smoke delusions. What they mean, really, is that they're impatient to get him off their hands. If he's going to go, please, Mr Ratatat, let him bloody go. And quick. It's like dandruff. He's demanded too much attendance.
    (at them)
Come on, let's say it for them. For all the people he's bored to diarrhea wherever he's gone. You bore us, Siggie Morrison. Go away. Go home. Degaussitate... I insist on that standing for its sound value... levitate yourself from our wear-and-tear. Let's each of us admit it and have a good old blow-through.

BIG JULIE: (at him) You blow through.

MRS PRUFROCK: (about PARSONS) Was he parlez-vousing us?

BIG JULIE: He'd be lucky.
    (in SIGGIE's ear)
Siggie?

SIGGIE: (luxuriously) Hmmm?

BIG JULIE: (for SIGGIE's benefit, at PARSONS) Look, you fake gypsy, we've come here to see our friend here off. Now beat it.

PARSONS: I challenge that, on the grounds of over-committing your character part.

BIG JULIE: We said no fortune-telling. Go brush up on your Romany accent.

    (They turn away from PARSONS. He whistles at them.)

BIG JULIE: He's hopeful.

MRS PRUFROCK: I've heard all agout bypsies.

MISS HOLLAND: (in his ear) They're shocking places for it, airports, Siggie. Pick-up merchants.

SIGGIE: (eyes still closed) Yeah, are they?

99

PARSONS: (from afar) I warn you. Beneath that pixie exterior lurks a machine tool with a diamond-hard cutting edge.

BIG JULIE: Take no notice of the nasty gypsy, Sig.

PARSONS: (at JARVIS and 'BOY') It's a joy to watch a professional at work. He's been here a... what?... microdot on Big Ben's main flywheel... and already he's polarized us into sexes. Frail, but as deceptive as transparent armoured glass between the handymen and the harem.

JARVIS: Othello without his urge tubes.

PARSONS: ('music hall') Did you just make that up?

JARVIS: (ditto) I did.

PARSONS: I say, I say, I say. I congratulate you.

JARVIS: Thank you, I say, I say.

PARSONS: I take it you have hidden talents?

JARVIS: I have hidden urges.

PARSONS: To be truthful people only laugh at me when I have a hangover.

JARVIS: (drily) Ha. Ha.

PARSONS: Thank you. Heavy night last night.

JARVIS: Don't mention it. To be truthful, women are inclined to laugh at me for my hang-down.

PARSONS: (drily) Ha. Ha.

JARVIS: Thank you. Swinging sac all night last night.

PARSONS: Was it Othello urging his tube or Hamlet urging tube or not tube?

JARVIS: It was Antony piping, 'O! thello urges lend me your Leers! The quality of Percy is not strained!

PARSONS: Of course it was too. Excuse me.

JARVIS: Heartily.

PARSONS: I had forgotten.

JARVIS: I have forgiven.

PARSONS: Say toodleloo to the nice people.

JARVIS: Toodleloo to the nice people.

SIGGIE: (sitting up) Would anyone like to share a bit of me hard-boiled goog?

BIG JULIE: Aw.

SIGGIE: (fumbling in newspaper packet) I brought it for the trip.

PARSONS: (loudly) Ha.

SIGGIE: It was fresh after it was cooked.

MISS HOLLAND: I'd like a titchy bit, Mr Morrison.

PARSONS: (at women) I warned you. You fool around with post-erection delusions, when you're not even, to be grossly frank, very good at creating hard illusions around erections, and you'll do him more harm than good.

(He snatches egg off SIGGIE, witheringly

BIG JULIE tries to grab it back.)

PARSONS: Before you smother me with your admirable mammae...

(smirks)
hard-boiled and fresh. Well, just watch this.

(And, with flourish, cracks egg on SIGGIE's head. It dribbles over his hair. They all reel back with the rotten-egg smell.)

PARSONS: It's so fresh, it needs an ambulance.
   (then)
You really think I'd waste a good egg?

SIGGIE: (miserably) It seems a bit off.

PARSONS: That's reality, Siggie. The stinking band of a rotten egg tightening around your head. I may be quoted.
   (to the disgusted looks of the others)
Cruel to be kind.

BIG JULIE: Ain't you enjoying it though?

PARSONS: (down to SIGGIE) Look, ancient chappie, I'm going to try to appeal to your sane and sanitary prehistory. Man to... well, look, it's two thousand and fifteen, give or take the last time I gave up the drink. It is not what year in the fifteen century you think it is.

(SIGGIE lies back, closes eyes, smiles angelically at the women. This provoke PARSONS further)

PARSONS: Listen, guy… you're smack in the middle of a stage set, smack in a theatre, smack in Castlereagh St, smack in Sydney, smack in the twenty-first century or what stands for it. Which is smogly snug right in Australia. If you were still in London, would you really have your lunchy-wunchy wrapped in the Sydney Morning Herald?

SIGGIE: Oh, yes.

PARSONS: (smiles, turns to others) Just notice this quick intravenous jab of reality applied as delicately as a postcoital kiss.
   (back at SIGGIE, showing him paper)
With the date of
   (looking)
Twenty o seventeen or whatever...?

(looks closer, then throws paper down)
Old man, you can be black-maria'd for swiping things from the newspaper library.

BIG JULIE: (grabs newspaper) Let me see.

(She hands it to MISS HOLLAND and MRS PRUFROCK)

PARSONS: Are you going to believe that date's today?

(They stare back with animosity. PARSONS indicates SIGGIE.)

PARSONS: Are you really going to believe that bundle of complexes?

SIGGIE: (eyes open) I've still got sarneys. Anyone want a sarney?

'BOY': (doll mimic at him) Mama, mama!

BIG JULIE: (defiantly) I would, love.

MISS HOLLAND: (ditto) Thank you, Mr Morrison.

MRS PRUFROCK: (ditto) Thank you, Mr Mossiron.

SIGGIE: I had to make 'em with marg. because marg. doesn't bring on heart attacks like butter, does it?
  (giggles)
Scribbled on a tombstone, 'Butter got him going'.

BIG JULIE: Ain't he a little living doll?

MRS PRUFROCK: (hep) Yeah, yeah!

(They stop short in a realisation, which is seized upon by PARSONS)

PARSONS: (flips script) Page thirty-four. 'And all the wives of Man marvelled and clapped their hands and said, "Truly, this is a little living doll, yeah, yeah!"'

(They drop the sandwiches back into SIGGIE's lap.)

SIGGIE: I thought you mightn't like the marg. Re-member the war?

PARSONS: The Crimean War?

SIGGIE: (giggles) Oh, you gypsies.

PARSONS: Kooshti bok.

SIGGIE: Pardon?

PARSONS: Freely translated from J. K. Cannonworthy's Die Fragmente Von Zigeuner Gesohiohten using Diels and Franz reference system... for example, D.K.3BI... would come out somewhat loosely from the Romany original as, 'Dig out, ding dong!'

SIGGIE: (indicating observation window) There goes another one. Aren't airports all the go?

MISS HOLLAND: (energy gone) Don't, Siggie.

SIGGIE: No, did you see it?

BIG JULIE: All right, see what?

SIGGIE: That plane.

MISS HOLLAND: (sits upright) Now that you mention it...

SIGGIE: Don't they bounce though?

MISS HOLLAND: I thought I did see something bounce.

MRS PRUFROCK: Mai oussi.

PARSONS: Hey, no plane.

MISS HOLLAND: I distinctly heard a plane sort of bounce.

SIGGIE: (pointing) Two.

MISS HOLLAND: (agreeing) Two bouncing.

BIG JULIE: (at PARSONS) Yeah, two.

PARSONS: News helicopter, traffic, outside.

BIG JULIE: What traffic?

PARSONS: (desperately) Commuter traffic!

SIGGIE: (giggling, pointing) Three.

PARSONS: Helicopters, helicopters, some accident!

BIG JULIE: (surlily confused) Leave me alone.

SIGGIE: I know it will be a bit of a buggery of a diffo when I get
home, but I don't care. If you don't change, you die, don't you? Look
at all those butterflies doing it. That's what I think anyway.
    (pause)
The lovely summers, gawd, do they ever make up for it.
    (giggles)
I'm starting to feel all Aussie again. Did you know, when I get the
proper sun on me back, I come up all pink like a crayfish. Dinky-di.
Oh, crayfish is Aussie for lobster. I think. Yes, and sometimes you
sell lobsters to us and sometimes we sell our crays to you with
vinegar on Then you call them lobsters and we call them crays. Crays
is short for crayfish so I call your English lobsters crays because that's
what I'm used to being Aussie.
    (pause, he gets no reaction)
I read in a book... I always forget the names of books I've always got
my nose in... anyway, crays mate when the Aussie sun is in the
zenith.
    (pointing)
That's up there. It's over there for you. There can be a lot of...
    (thickly)
Zenith-thises. Same as the Zenith-thises for crays.
    (giggles)

If you're a bit-of-a-goer cray bloke and there's a little cray sort here and another bit of a cray sort there, you can always have your zenith here, then zip over and have another zenith there.
  (giggles)
Aren't I rude?

'BOY': (doll mimic at him again) Mama, Mama!

PARSONS: (over SIGGIE, coarse whisper) The bodies are piling up. Already the vultures are consuming the corpses, gulping down the slurpy bits.

SIGGIE: (suddenly) Please... what is this place? My legs are... aching.

> *(SIGGIE shivers while trying to fight off a coughing fit. They watch him. The restrained coughing becomes infectious until they are all doing it. BIG JULIE breaks the infection.)*

BIG JULIE: (fighting off cough) It's no good. There's one part I could never maintain and that's being some sort of Maid Marian from Sherwood Forest. Can you imagine me blushing in a thicket at an English twilight? I'm sorry, Siggie love. I'm going home.

MISS HOLLAND: We can't leave him all alone.

BIG JULIE: (stopping) Hey, anybody know where my home is?

PARSONS: Tell him straight.

MISS HOLLAND: We can't.
  (at BIG JULIE)
Can we?

BIG JULIE: What am I, all of a sudden? I'm trying to go home, here...

> *(BIG JULIE steps back and steps on SIGGIE. He lies there, under her foot, looking up with eyes long-suffering.)*

MISS HOLLAND: Please be careful.

106

BIG JULIE: (jumps off him, growls) Shit! Why doesn't he get up off the floor!

MRS PRUFROCK: I'll go future further and ask...

BIG JULIE: Don't. Just... don't.
   (moves away)
I need a drink. Who's got a drink?

MISS HOLLAND: (anxiously) Siggie? Mr Morrison?

SIGGIE: (pathetically) It didn't hurt.

MISS HOLLAND: (sotto voce) We ought to straighten him out.

BIG JULIE: If you can work it out, you straighten him out.

MISS HOLLAND: We could humour him a little. At least.

BIG JULIE: Humouring him anymore is definitely out, orright?

MISS HOLLAND: You'll feel better up on the couch out of harm's way, Mr Morrison. Let's get him on the couch.

   (The women try again to lift him, but again he goes limp. They
   give up, resume seats.)

SIGGIE: (rolling eyes at them) This is my face here.
   (feels it)
I know I need a bit of a scrub-up, but... excuse me for asking... don't I shine through it anymore?

BIG JULIE: Don't start that again, Siggie. Please.

PARSONS: (fed up, inserts himself again) I object. I insert one formal objection into these whole proceedings. You can add it as an erratum if you wish. Either way, I maintain that it stands and in consequence allows the movement of an adjournment.
   (snapping fingers at SIGGIE)
Go away, go away, go away.

107

SIGGIE: (above him) *Don't I shine through it anymore?*

MONOLOGUE: (sudden burst) You don't shine down on me anymore. You ought to shine down on me some more. It's me. Look, it's me. You ought to shine down just a little bit more...

PARSONS: (up at control room) You're fired up there! And switch off before you go!

BIG JULIE: Don't you get them in a knot too.

PARSONS: I can reposition them. Even laterally. I can hoist them. I can bam them, wham them, slam them on the floor. With a bit of specialized exercise I might even be able to throw them over my shoulder like a continental soldier. But I cannot, repeat cannot, knot them.

BIG JULIE: Just don't knot them.

PARSONS: I cannot knot them.

BIG JULIE: All right, don't get them in a twist.

PARSONS: You cannot get them in a twist. They are either in a permanent state of twist or a permanent state of untwist. If you try to get them to reverse left to right or any other way they will zong back.

BIG JULIE: You've got nothing to zong.

(*Strained silence.*)

BIG JULIE: Sig love, we're all feeling a bit bombed out.

SIGGIE: You go on home. Don't wait for me.

MISS HOLLAND: You do understand, don't you, Mr Morrison?

SIGGIE: Now don't you go waiting for an old cripple like me. If I get lost... oh geez... where can I ask if I get lost again?

(MISS HOLLAND sighs pointedly.)

SIGGIE: No, you go. I'll just stay down here and try to think about being all warm and dry again. And...
   (calculated bathos)
all free again.
   (but this time no one bites)
You go home to your beauty families.
   (pause)
It's just that I'm a bit worried about whether I catch a plane going the wrong way. How do you know if they're coming or going? If I go the wrong way I could end up in Alaska.

(At this JARVIS jumps up.)

JARVIS: Look, cocklehead, this is a villain's cloak. Right? I now put on this cloak. I now take it off. I now strap on this wooden leg. Notice my real leg, all of it, is now bent up behind me. I now put the villain's cloak back on. Dressed as I am now, I now provoke theatrical hissing,
   (waits. Nothing. To wings:)
Hissing.
   (still nothing)
Okay, forget the hissing. Now ineluctably, I am the transmogrified Jarvis, the villain, the dastard. I've been drinking out of mugs like you all my life. All this goes without saying now because by now everybody... and I include the five billion nine hundred million and whatnot people in the world except you... instantly recognize me. I am now about to speak. I say, 'Oops, how awfully-awfully clumsy of me. I've just peed poor old Siggie's savings up against a wall. What a shame!' Note the chuckle, the twirl of the moustache, the... toss of the villainous cloak, the belying symbol of evil's temporality in the wooden leg. I now remove the false wooden leg...
   (doing so)
... the cloak... the false moustache...
   (tries to pull moustache off, but it won't come)
I... am... removing... the... false...
   (hiss to off)
Who's been fooling around? Forget the moustache, cocklehead, for the time being. Except for the stinking moustache, I am me again. Look, Jarvis, once a feeder of mother's milk.
   (then)

So, now, knucklehead, worm your way out of that.

SIGGIE: (sweetly) Geez, I've forgiven you a long time ago, Mr Jarvis.

JARVIS: Would you believe she's...
    (indicates BIG JULIE)
been approached by the Sydney City Council to clear drunks off the streets after midnight?
    (SIGGIE giggles.)
And she's...
    (indicates MISS HOLLAND)
got as much Irish blood in her as the Opera House?
    (SIGGIE giggles more)
Would you believe I was such a darling little boy I was a trustee for the South Curl Curl Cubs?

SIGGIE: (giggles to MISS HOLLAND) I never knew that man had a sense of humour.

JARVIS: Forget I spoke.
    (turns away, then remembering something else)
Miss Glamorgan.
    (prompting others)
Miss Glamorgan. Right?

SIGGIE: (agitated) Miss Glamorgan...?

BIG JULIE: Don't you go making him peg out again.

JARVIS: (shrugs) Suggestion.

MISS HOLLAND: It might work.

BIG JULIE: It'd be risky...

JARVIS: Well, you brace him up with a couple of iron leggings or something, because I'm going to get...
    (nastily to SIGGIE)
Miss Glamorgan.

110

(And goes off.)

SIGGIE: (outburst) He's not fit to speak the name of the dead!

MISS HOLLAND: (soothing) He's gone now.

SIGGIE: (calming) I didn't ask him to come.

PARSONS: Pardon-poke, old son, you say you saw Miss Glamorgan pegged out on a bench or whatever... love of your life, right?... but what if Jarvis just happens to trot back in here with her in tow?

(SIGGIE goes obstinately silent.)

PARSONS: Just say hypothetically.

SIGGIE: Hypothetaltically.

BIG JULIE: His word.

PARSONS: (at SIGGIE) Just answer the hypostalsificating... so top that one... question. Say Jarvis trots back in here with a Miss Glamorgan alive and, I assure you, bleating. But what's more, Australian. What then, little dude?
    (SIGGIE remains obstinately mute)
Nothing? It wouldn't matter? Another black out? Clunk, crash, slam, click, and the old cerebral door thunders down to complete your rhino-hide fortress again?
    (still no reaction; in SIGGIE's ear)
Jupiter.

SIGGIE: (keyed) The ubeaut little radio given to me by Miss...

(He stops)

PARSONS: (nods) ...Miss Glamorgan.
    (command)
Right, up on your feet, old man.

(He gets SIGGIE to his feet but with surprising gentleness.)

111

PARSONS: Just relax old guy. Alternatively, you may shiver whenever, wherever and however you like.
   (and proceeds, not without a show of repugnance, to strip SIGGIE to the waist, looking at the labels of each item of clothing as he goes, while:)
And I bet your father knew Samuel J. Hucker too.

SIGGIE: Who?

PARSONS: Samuel J. Hucker.

SIGGIE: Who was he?

PARSONS: Only Samuel J. Hucker of the original International Dictaphone Company of Australia.

SIGGIE: Never heard of him.

PARSONS: Didn't your father know Samuel J. Hucker?

SIGGIE: Do you mean *the* Samuel J. Hucker?

PARSONS: Who?

SIGGIE: The man who told my father a joke about dictaphones.

PARSONS: Who was he?

SIGGIE: (now giggling) He was the President of the International Dictaphone Company of Australia.

PARSONS: Not Samuel J. Hucker?

SIGGIE: Yes.

PARSONS: Not the Samuel J. Hucker who told your father the joke about dictaphones?

SIGGIE: Yes.

PARSONS: Sorry, never heard of him.

SIGGIE: My old Dad knew him.

(Etcetera, until PARSONS has him stripped to his underpants, tosses his singlet down.)

PARSONS: (triumphantly) Not one item of Pommyland clothing.

(Still giggling, SIGGIE shows the women the label on his underpants. PARSONS cuts them short.)

PARSONS: English underps are common in muck. Note the right hand half turn of the phrase. 'In muck', not 'as common as'.
     (then)
Not even anything in the wallet either, except a lot of holes.

SIGGIE: (grabs it up) I had a fiver.

BIG JULIE: (at PARSONS) Give it back.

PARSONS: How could you, a fellow unionist, think such a thing?

SIGGIE: I had a fiver. I know I did.

PARSONS: (hopefully) Are you objecting?

SIGGIE: I... don't know.

PARSONS: If you think I lifted your fiver, then feel free to object.

SIGGIE: I don't want to be rude.

PARSONS: I demand satisfaction by you objecting. You're objecting about my abuse of your person.
     (SIGGIE shakes his head)
Of your wallet.

BIG JULIE: Don't you object, Siggie.

PARSONS: I invoke an objection out of at least one of your goose pimples.

113

BIG JULIE: He's not objecting just to give you an excuse to make off with his fiver.

SIGGIE: I know I had it just now. You feel the weight, you know.

PARSONS: I'll lend him a damn fiver.

>   *(and shoves it into SIGGIE's pocket.)*

BIG JULIE: You lousy louse.

MRS PRUFROCK: How could you sloop so low?

PARSONS: It would be useless to proclaim the innocence of my rich English uncle who *(a)* still thinks I'm a minor...

BIG JULIE: Very minor.

PARSONS: Who still thinks I'm a minor and *(b)* who likes to think he is helping the 'done-under' colonial branch of the family. Useless. Poor Unc, went head first.

SIGGIE: Can I get dressed now?

PARSONS: Oh, stop complaining!

SIGGIE: (at BIG JULIE) Would you like to hear my chest going, now I'm undressed...?

JARVIS: (panic, off) *Hee-ey*!

>   *(They all stop, watch a frantic struggle with one of the side curtains. PARSONS goes over and rescues a panic-stricken JARVIS. JARVIS grabs hold of him with relief.)*

JARVIS: *Creepy... out... there.*

PARSONS: Calm down.

JARVIS: (feebly) The wind up... funny... ha, ha...

(and trips over SIGGIE's suitcase.)

SIGGIE: (jumps forward) That's my fault.

(And struggles with the weight of the case. JARVIS brutishly elbows him aside, grabs hold of case and, expecting it to be heavy, heaves. Its unexpected lightness causes him to stumble backwards and fall again. SIGGIE is appalled.)

SIGGIE: Mr Jarvis!

JARVIS: God dammit!

(And flings the suitcase off himself across the stage.)

BIG JULIE: How would you like it if I slung around all you've got in the world?

JARVIS: Bloody pretending it's got something in it.

(SIGGIE is struggling to retrieve it)

JARVIS: Look at the old fool now! Falling for the oldest trick in the book.

MISS HOLLAND: You did.

BIG JULIE: Siggie love, don't try our patience anymore.

SIGGIE: (chastised) I'm sorry, Miss Julie. Uh...

BIG JULIE: Put the damn thing away. Somebody'll do themselves a damage to something none of them around here has anyway.

SIGGIE: (struggles to take it off to one side) Uh... if it's a bit heavy for an old codger like me, how's the plane going to go?

MISS HOLLAND: Mr Morrison, it's really empty, isn't it?

SIGGIE: I had to sit on it to get it closed.

(looks from one to another, then desperately)
Miss Julie, what would a man have an empty suitcase for?

BIG JULIE: Sig, don't call me Miss Julie anymore. It ain't my real
name, orrightee? Just take it from me your suitcase's empty. Come
around to my place tomorrow and I'll fill it up with all the male
leftovers I've got hanging around.

*(SIGGIE recoils by backing away from them, dragging his
suitcase after him. JARVIS gets angry again, snatches it off
him.)*

JARVIS: Look, cocklehead!

(Roughly opens the case. It is empty.)

SIGGIE: No, look.

*(He opens case. A few contents spill out as though it was
overflowing. He has to get down on his hands and knees to
retrieve them.)*

SIGGIE: Please look. Somebody look. Look, Mrs Prufrock! Look,
these nice warm socks you got me!

JARVIS: (exploding) Look, beans-for-brains!

*(And grabs suitcase, hoists it high with one finger. Throws it
down.)*

SIGGIE: No, look.

(And just manages to lift it.)

JARVIS: You look.

(And lifts it, twirls it overhead, throws it down.)

SIGGIE: But look. Uh...

(He only just lifts it)

116

SIGGIE: Please, look. Look, I'm going home! Look, they said, don't worry... there's porters to do the heavy lifting, like...

JARVIS: Look, look, look!

(And does an aeroplane spin with suitcase. He loses control and it flies off to knock SIGGIE out. It finishes up on top of him. They gather around, look down at him)

MISS HOLLAND: Not again.

BIG JULIE: Yep.

(Nobody moves to help him. Eventually PARSONS lifts one of his eyelids and holds it open for MISS HOLLAND.)

PARSONS: Tell me if you can see a flicker.
    (then into SIGGIE's ear)
One, two, three, four, five... anything?

MISS HOLLAND: (shrugs) Red rivers... bit nasty.

PARSONS: Only signs of healthy decay... six, seven, eight, nine, ten, eleven, twelve, thirteen...

MISS HOLLAND: Yes.

PARSONS: (leaning back) He can hear then.
    (loudly in his ear)
You can hear, can't you?
    (back at them)
Everybody has to shut down on the world at thirteen. Please hold his eyelids open.
    (JARVIS does so)
Mr Mortified, you are looking upwards. You may genuinely be thinking you are genuinely looking up at the genuine ceiling of a genuine airport lounge. But, when that incontrovertible sense of loss squats finally on your shoulder, comes home, as it were, alate for all the wind on Doomsday of your over-excited synapses, alights and sinks in its talons never again to let go until the flesh finally disgorges

the skull, then one needs, dear old troglodyte, help to see through the
blank blanking-off coming.
    (and)
Now, Mr Morrison, if you look with your mind you'll see how a tiny
transcriptase... nice word, but I shall not brood nor satisfaction show...
of a tiny little pinprick called grief can confuse you about the time
and the place and the whatever other dramatic unity is... Watch from
the mortuary mat.
    (up at flies)
Lower the New Guinea rain forest, Charlie!
    (waits, but nothing
I said, the New Guinea rain forest, Chas!
    (back at SIGGIE)
Replete, you'll notice, with Jap snipers.

> *(Still nothing. PARSONS strides off angrily. The others wait,
> eyes upwards to the flies. PARSONS returns from the other side
> of the stage.)*

PARSONS: (appalled) Deserted. Everybody.

BIG JULIE: Well, what are you? Crippled?

PARSONS: To be frank, I couldn't find the ropes.

BIG JULIE: Everybody's helpless around here.

> *(And strides off herself. Returns almost immediately and sits
> down refusing to say a word.)*

MISS HOLLAND: Well?

BIG JULIE: (shrugs) Who knows?

> *(An unattached scene cloth falls suddenly out of the air. Lands
> near, rolls, and totally buries SIGGIE)*

PARSONS: It's like beating a beach ball on the head with a mallet.

> *(They heave it off him. SIGGIE is still pinned by the suitcase.)*

SIGGIE: (but unmoving) Cripes. About this 'ere suitcase. I was never that strong. Good hearing, but.
    (then)
You've all been very kind.

> (Long embarrassed pause; still, nobody moves to remove the suitcase from on top of him.)

PARSONS: (angrily) Everybody told you not to come back.

> (JARVIS clips on a clerical collar, grabs MRS PRUFROCK. They act.)

JARVIS: I did, Mrs Prufrock. I said do not definitely go.

MRS PRUFROCK: More tea, vicar?

JARVIS: Mannered lady. A little more cream-of-the-squeeze, please.
    (she titters. Lewdly:)
A lot more cream-at-the-two-digit-pinch, Mrs Prufrock.

MRS PRUFROCK: O, you nawgy vicar.

JARVIS: Oodles and oodles and oodles of cream on the push-through, Mrs Prufrock. Hot oodles of oozing cream from the two big fiery furnaces, Mrs Prufrock!

MRS PRUFROCK: Oh, Vicked Wicar!

> (And goes fainting away.)

JARVIS: Mrs P, Mrs P!

MRS PRUFROCK: (one eye open) Call me Ida.

JARVIS: Ida doreya, Ida! Lower 'em lewdly!

> (She leaps upon him. They kiss pantomimely. She breaks away, indicates PARSONS)

MRS PRUFROCK: By Gob, there's Cedric!

JARVIS: Let him take his turn.

MRS PRUFROCK: Alack, I cannot. Not. I've been his prouse these twenty days. My vows got stuck.

JARVIS: (resumes being proper) Two lumps, Mrs P, please.

MRS PRUFROCK: Rock cake?

JARVIS: No, just a little congested; it's just the weather. But to return to the subject, Mrs P.

MRS PRUFROCK: By all salivable means, Vicar.

> *(She leaps upon him again.)*

BIG JULIE: (joining in) Your wife and my vicar swapping spit! Cedric, come here and console me.
    (proffers neck)
Suckle me here.

PARSONS: Alas, Matilda, I cannot... I don't think there's enough suckle.

BIG JULIE: Is it...?

PARSONS: Yes...

BIG JULIE: Not...?

PARSONS: Sadly, alas…

BIG JULIE: You didn't...?

PARSONS: In the heat of the waltz, Matilda. Impetuosity and genetics undid me!

> *(SIGGIE suddenly sits up, claps.)*

'BOY': Goody, goody, goody, Siggie's awake.

(SIGGIE does his best to hide under the suitcase. 'BOY' chants...)

'BOY': We know Siggie's there; we know where Siggie-Wiggie is!

('BOY' begins dancing around SIGGIE. The MONOLOGUE rises. PARSONS endeavours to speak over it. 'BOY' keeps revolving, chanting. Abrupt charivari.)

MONOLOGUE: I can't stay down here. I can't stay down here anymore. I must get out of here. I don't think I can move to get out of here. If I could move I would get out of here. But I don't know whether I can move to get out of here. I think something in my legs must have gone. I think something's cracked. Something smells. I'm cold and I smell. I'm freezing. I won't take any notice of them. I'll make out I don't hear them. I'll make out I don't care whether they're here or not. I'll make out I'm dead. If I make out I'm dead, they'll get scared. If I make out I'm dead, they'll get scared and go and tell. If I make out I'm dead, they'll get scared and go and tell their mums and dads and…

'BOY': Siggie's got a dirty bottle, Siggie's got a dirty pie, Siggie's got a dirty bottle, Siggie got a dirty pie...

PARSONS: (fighting MONOLOGUE) They all said don't go. They were dead right, mate. You get off the plane, flushed, nervy. This is it, your big moment. The only trouble is the sun's in and it's pissing down raining. It's colder than in London and nobody knows you from Adam.
    (looking)
Or Eve. No brother. No Pots. Nobody. You get bowled over by street goons for your money. They get your only fiver. You are turned away from five room-and-boards; you have lost your sister's address; your sole has come off your shoe; your brother has moved. You are tired. This, Siggie, is only your first day. After two days in the YMCA, you find lodgings. Three days after that, you trip over the lino on the stairs and twist your ankle. Back from hospital, you find your suitcase in the hall. Your pension hasn't come through. There's the hospital bill. And there's always the park bench.

MONOLOGUE: …and or someone. If I was their age I would have gone and told someone. I want to be warm. I want to be comfy. If I could get my sun to shine through... if I could get out of here. If I could feel my legs. If they'd stop jumping on these tin sheets. If they were old enough to lift them… boy, would I fly! Would I ever! Boy, would I fly! Would I ever! Boy, would I fly! Would I ever! Listen, if I don't get out of here listen if I don't get out of here... Oh God, if I don't get out of here... Listen, if I don't get out of here...

SIGGIE: (above it all) HELP... ME!

(Cut-off to silence. SIGGIE starts to cough, tries to struggle to his knees.)

PARSONS: (almost kindly) After only three months you're seventy-two years of age according to writ and just another down-and-out Aussie. Try to remember, old son. Don't you remember that day in the park when you stopped up short. The grass was brown. No little dickey birds singing anymore. All the flowers were just burnt out husks... You weren't saying shine on me, but please don't shine on me. Okay? You stalled, stopping the through traffic. You swayed like a Catholic harridan in grief. Somebody... me, I admit it... somebody heard you cry out:

(and orchestrates for:)

SIGGIE: (outcry) What is this place?

(and doubles up in another coughing fit.)

PARSONS: (finishing off) Right. But don't overdo it.

MISS HOLLAND: (kneels by SIGGIE) Mr Morrison, we're only acting. Try to understand.

PARSONS: What she means is you're colliding with what we're colliding with. The elision collision of illusion.

MISS HOLLAND: What he means is our illusion is more powerful than your illusion, Mr Morrison, I guess. Looks like.

PARSONS: She means ours is very well rehearsed, thank you.

MISS HOLLAND: What I mean is it's in the nature of things. We've gone on over it and arrived at a something or other.

PARSONS: She is groping pathetically for the word symmetry.

MISS HOLLAND: What he's trying to so rudely say, Mr Morrison, is that we can't be what you want us to be and act and be ourselves all at the same time.

PARSONS: What she is trying to say is, our real faces are behind our masks. You can't put the faces you want onto those masks. If you could, then there would be no real faces and no real masks because there would be a real face behind the mask and a real face in front of the mask and the mask would then be just one of the real faces in between. If every mask was a real face and every face was a real mask, then there would be only one real face and only one real mask which were the same over and over again. For all of us. And only one illusion which could not be an illusion because then it would be real. And if we had no possible illusions left, old sausage old chum, we'd all go mad.

JARVIS: (jumps up) Who called me mad? When the popinjay sang 'sweet dilly dingle' to the live turkey-turtle, the dead turkey-turtle took off and registered mach three. Causing Herr Vogel to discover Herr Algol discovering the new star Mira Ceti, which he named Mata Hari. Now the repercussions were not, as Lord Lick thought, that stellar was the proper name for a star such as her, but that the naming of a new star stellar should not be a Mata Hari-type plot to immortalize the singing of 'sweet dilly dingle' by the popinjay to the live turkey-turtle.

MISS HOLLAND: (appeal) How do you tell him to go home?

(SIGGIE recovers enough to get to his feet.

He backs away from them, struggles to drag his suitcase with him towards the exit backstage. MISS HOLLAND pleads with him.)

MISS HOLLAND: We only want to tell you you'd be better off home.

BIG JULIE: Watchit...!

(But SIGGIE falls down through open trapdoor. A crash, then silence. They walk over and stand looking down.)

BIG JULIE: I guess he's just accident-prone.

(Pause)

JARVIS: Stopped his cough, anyway.

(Pause)

PARSONS: Australia's vital statistic for the Government's future plan for the twenty-first century, folks. He must be the first man in history whose shadow deserted him for being too dangerous to go around with. I mean, observe it, the final eucharist to the running, jumping, standing-still life. A bony residue of the overheated crucible. All of you were right. I admit it grandiloquently. One extended gaze at him should have told me he needed no literary bromide in his tea. I will renounce my masterpiece...

BIG JULIE: Great loss.

PARSONS: (theatrical) No. No recriminations. No pleas. I renounce it. I cast it into the flames, master flash drive 'n'all. It has been fouled upon by the Real Thing. Bloody impertinence. No. I renounce it.

BIG JULIE: Coming, Sig.

(And goes to climb down into the trap.)

PARSONS: ...except
   (she stops.)
... except to indulge just once more, before burning the Bitch Muse as a propitiation at the stake, pages eighty-eight and eighty-nine, my ducks and drakes...
   (recites)

The supercilious silliness
Of this poor wingless bird
Is cosmically comic
And stellarly absurd

BIG JULIE: (resisting his 'temptation') No!

PARSONS: Please. Just once. For James McKellar who in nineteen ninety-two martyred himself when he dashed up on the stage just as I was on my toes to thrust down with delicate precision the banderillo of my final line.

BIG JULIE: Definitely no.

MISS HOLLAND: Let's just carry him outside and… leave him somewhere.

PARSONS: Please. An artist begs you.

BIG JULIE: Ha.

PARSONS: An ordinary man begs you.

BIG JULIE: (stopping) How ordinary?

PARSONS: Oh, fairly ordinary.

BIG JULIE: How ordinary?

PARSONS: Quite ordinary.

BIG JULIE: How?

PARSONS: Dead ordinary.

BIG JULIE: (satisfied) Let's get the damn ordinary thing over with then.

(They somewhat reluctantly don Hellenic robes. The women in strophe, while JARVIS in antistrophe.)

THE WOMEN:
He has returned
He has returned from the tempestuous journey.
O Lord Zeus, son of Cronus and Rhea,
O Arch-cynic of sisterly intercourse,
See the hero's scars, his wounds,
The weeping carbuncle of life's journey!
Set him, O Zeus, immortal amongst the firmaments!
Paste him into the vault of Heaven
As a navigational aid to the ship of life!

JARVIS: (antistrophe)
Whom do you mean by all that's indecent
In a decent Dionysian orgy?

THE WOMEN:
Oedipus Siggeus, contumelious, vessel of arrogant pride,
But beloved by a majority rule of one -- himself.

JARVIS:
Speak then of Siggie-eus, goat-herd boy; Speak, O speak of Siggie-
eus!

THE WOMEN:
Who he? Who he? Who he? Who he?

JARVIS:
Pitiable wretch of human kind,
Grew up with the herd,
Stayed by the herd until he died.
Surely such tenacity deserveth rewards?

THE WOMEN:
Yesterday he was on the Gods' menu,
Today he is all bone and burp!

TOGETHER:
Oh, wretched little men
Make retching immortals!

SIGGIE: (manages to hoist himself up to see out) Excuse I...

PARSONS: (kneeling) Can this be a germ of an applause? The lute plucked once in singular recognition?

SIGGIE: (outcry) I don't want to die!

(And he grabs out at PARSONS.

PARSONS has to prise SIGGIE's fingers open to stop them both from falling back into the trapdoor. SIGGIE falls back.)

PARSONS: Now what makes you think you're going to die, old fruit?

BIG JULIE: You have.

PARSONS: (down at SIGGIE) I want you to know I deny that, Mr Morrison.

(Mumbles come up from trap. PARSONS motions for silence, strains to listen. Has to kneel down, head in trapdoor.)

MISS HOLLAND: What's the poor love saying?

(PARSONS motions with arm behind him for silence. Finally, he gets up.)

PARSONS: (denigratingly) Well, the official read-out of that little lot was; once upon a time Siggie dreamt he entered upon a small, hillside chapel. This was no ordinary hillside chapel. Oh, no. Because when little Siggie entered this little hillside chapel he found no image upon the altar, but a wondrous flower arrangement. And there upon the altar sat a fabulous Yogi in deep meditation. Now this was no ordinary fabulous Yogi. His flesh was rotting and he coughed yellow and all over his lovely legs and lips were running sores, green with a nice sea-green gangrene. And Siggie saw that the Yogi was wearing Siggie's own face and, because his eyes were closed, Siggie knew he was not only dreaming but more especially dreaming about Siggie. And he knew that if that Yogi ever woke up and stopped dreaming about Siggie, then Siggie himself would no longer be. Now isn't that a nice nursery rhyme?

ANNOUNCEMENT: 'Qantas Airways announce the departure of Flight QF 625 to Sydney via Athens and Hong Kong which have found their ways back on at least the Qantas map. Would passengers make their way to Gate number six and have their boarding passes ready. Qantas Airways announce...'

(and fades.)

BIG JULIE: (incredulous) Did you hear what I heard?

MRS PRUFROCK: I did.

PARSONS: Don't be stupid.

SIGGIE: (struggling up) That's my plane?

ANNOUNCEMENT: 'Qantas Airways announce the departure of Flight QF 625 to Sydney...'

BIG JULIE: (accusing PARSONS) Deny that.

(They stand dumbfounded. SIGGIE starts coughing with the exertion of climbing out.)

SIGGIE: Please...

(But manages himself. He grabs his suitcase, drags it.)

SIGGIE: Which way, geez?

(And struggles frantically off.

Silence, before:)

BIG JULIE: I don't feel real.

PARSONS: Keep our sense of humour...

BIG JULIE: Come to think of it, I feel bloody unreal.

MISS HOLLAND: (indicating after SIGGIE) You don't think he really is... you know. Come to think of it, where are *we* anyway?

PARSONS: That's Siggie's line, not yours.

BIG JULIE: (at PARSONS) I thought you had a stinking gypsy's shifty stinking eyes but I never said anything.

PARSONS: We're all mates, aren't we? We trust each other, don't we?

MISS HOLLAND: My God.

PARSONS: (pointing) See?

> *(SIGGIE reappears from other side of the stage, still dragging suitcase. He comes in near exhaustion, casts about wildly, fighting back a coughing fit.)*

PARSONS: He's just trying to express finding his way out, that's all.
BIG JULIE: Never mind, poor Sig. I want to know what she said, where we are.

, SIGGIE: Geez... which... way, eh?

MISS HOLLAND: Somebody help him.

PARSONS: (at 'BOY') Go and help him.

> *(As 'BOY' approaches, SIGGIE screams, tugs suitcase away, and cringing away from 'BOY', exits again in greater panic.*
>
> *PARSONS resumes equilibrium, takes command, heightened voice after SIGGIE.)*

PARSONS: If you won't listen to us, you're dead, Siggie, old lad. You're back in Australia. All right, they left you to rot. Face up to it. They left you to rot down in that stinking hole, Siggie, and they didn't care a beanpole whether you pegged or not. Let's face it.

> *(SIGGIE returns from opposite side of his exit. He collapses*

over suitcase, goes into another coughing fit. PARSONS holds MISS HOLLAND back.)

PARSONS: You survived, Siggie. That's more than most, old tit. Show a bit of gratitude. Look, if you've got to the stage where you can't tell this...
  (indicates 'BOY')
forty-year-old delinquent from those silly bloody kids...

ANNOUNCEMENT: 'Would Mr Morrison, passenger on Qantas Flight QF 625, please report to Gate number six immediately while it is still on the map. Would Mr Morrison... etc.

PARSONS: (up at it) PIPE THAT DOWN!

(SIGGIE staggers off again.)

PARSONS: (after him) If it wasn't the kids, it would've been someone else, Siggie. Doll butchers have been on your lifeline ever since you dribbled milk down your mother's hard-boiled Australian breast. Prancing around like a pansy in a flower show. Dainty as a little pixie-wixie. That might have been all right in England, but here, Jesus, if you don't face it now, they'll strip the only layer of skin you've got left right off you, you poor bloody romantic sod!

(SIGGIE re-enters. He is in distress. He collapses with coughing. A spotlight suddenly shines down on him. PARSONS at 'BOY'...)

PARSONS: Sit on him quick before he busts something.

('BOY' does so, joggles mischievously up and down)

PARSONS: Forget it, Sig. It's been and gone. Look forward to the day when you slip your pajamas over your little pink shirt and with your dressing gown pulled over your shoulder, shuffle out into the midday sun to sit on the old garden seat and there, Siggie, to commit your last living gesture... fading away while kneading a greasy snot rag between ten digits of bone. So lie back and let the facts enjoy you. Give it up, Siggie!

130

(MISS HOLLAND screams.)

MISS HOLLAND: Blood!

('BOY' jumps away. She turns on PARSONS.)

MISS HOLLAND: Blood! That's what he's giving up!

PARSONS: Coloured syrup!

MISS HOLLAND: You bastard!

PARSONS: Biting his own tongue!

ANNOUNCEMENT: 'Attention, please. This is the final call for Mr Morrison, passenger on Qantas Flight QF 625 to Sydney who has dropped off the end of the world. Would Mr Morrison report...' etc.

SIGGIE: (manages) Wanna go back home!

BIG JULIE: (into air) I want to know where the hell I am!

(SIGGIE leaves suitcase, having just enough energy to stumble off again.)

MISS HOLLAND: Stop him!

('BOY' grabs at him, only manages to tear off his underpants. SIGGIE escapes, his last vestige torn away.)

MISS HOLLAND: *You're all killing him!*

(The spotlight agitates round and round with increasing frequency rising to climax.)

PARSONS: (dancing around it) I'll tell you why, Siggie. Because behind that doll-face and those reveal-nothing eyes, Siggie, anybody can see you've got a scrounging cast-iron lining. Anybody can see you'd outlive us all by fifty years. We don't like that. Not a meat sandwich like you, Siggie. Already they've put an X-marks-the-spot on your head. Do you imagine, with life as it is, a life in which every

131

lurking suspicion would be proved right if one was paranoid enough to check out how paranoid it is... do you think that life will let it rest there? Eh, Siggie? All you can do is forget for a time how tenaciously you have to rely on the inhuman circumstances to stay human. You add up the sum of all the numbers and it always comes to the Number of the Beast. Siggie? Listen, you poor sap, lie down now with the bitter-sweet melancholy of the animal inevitability of it all. It's useless. Your own father was mowed down by a life insurance van. No escape from that unnamed guilt... Ah!

(Spotlight stops stationary suddenly. He triumphantly 'catches ' it with one foot, flourishes.)

PARSONS: Ladies and gents, we have trapped for you... no, we bring you, in the latest putrous... my word, but no thanks needed... putrous-gangrenous-hue never been seen before by the naked eye, the shrewdest, the cunningest, the toughest, the outlivingest, the sweet grindingest, the leatheriest of hide, the real, the one and only indestructible but long-dead gone... Mr Siggie Morrison with his comb and paper!

('Effect' dies down. Silence. PARSONS finally turns to others after 'milking' the effect.)

PARSONS: There, how was that?

(They stare back mutely. PARSONS is hurt.)

PARSONS: Jesus, you're all as sour as an ulcer- bearer's belly. Anyway, even if it is beyond your appreciative faculties, that'll give you some idea of the effect we've got to get. So boost it up a bit next time. Energy. We've got to get them to really feel that...
(indicates stationary spotlight)
this is Siggie. Cornsummate the con.

MRS PRUFROCK: (triumphant) He means consummate the corn.

PARSONS: I mean what I said. We've got to get them to think Siggie's really here. When it moves, they've got to think it's Siggie moving. When Siggie, if we had somebody playing Siggie, cried or coughed his dreadful little ring out, this poor luminosity must evoke more pity because it is the absent image of Siggie. Just remember we're competing with the con of television.

(MISS GLAMORGAN enters)

PARSONS: And where might you have been?

MISS GLAMORGAN: Somewhere.

PARSONS: Don't be ridiculous. Where do you think you are?

(The sounds and shadows of technicians, stage hands etc. appear, continuing about their jobs as though everything was normal. BIG JULIE grabs one, half off.)

BIG JULIE: (desperately) Speak to me!

(Obviously get shrugged off without answer)

PARSONS: (back to normal) Right, shoes.
   (gets SIGGIE's shoes and jacket etc, holds nose)
Phew. Remind me to get some pine forest into these.
   (places clothing in spotlight; down at them:)
There you are, Sig. Say hellosies to the nice kind inept actors.
   (back to them)
Okay, now let's go back to fundamentals. Movement first. Sway. Resonate your bums with the bathos. Psychosomatatize... my word and eminently insertable... psychosomatatize with the pathos. Plug in...

(Voices fade out, although they continue to mime speaking and rehearsals.

Over them and the stage construction noises, the MONOLOGUE resumes.)

MONOLOGUE: And all the stars that were stars but aren't now. All the stars near and far. On the beach. Just before I left, I think. I think it was just before I left. It mightn't have been just before I left. Anyhow, on the beach just before I left, I wrote my name in the sand twenty-four times. Three rows of eight lots of my name. Three rows, each measuring two yards high and thirty great yard long with a dirty old piece of a real gum that must have been washed up on the beach where I wrote my name in the sand with a stick. I thought: if I'm going, I'm going to leave my name behind. Yes, sir. On the beach, I wrote my name in small writing and capital letters and shadow letters and script... I think they call it script... all sorts of different ways of writing my name in three rows all over the place thinking I'd leave my mark. Then a dirty great wave came in. A rotten great dirty great thumping great wave comes pounding in. The dirty greatest ever seen on an Aussie beach and me there with my head out, with my head up, and me there watching the stars come out standing with my feet on my name. And that wave came and whoosh! That's all the thanks you get. Whoosh! Washed it all away. Whoosh! Washed it all away. Whoosh! Washed it all away. Whoosh! Washed it all away. Whoosh! Washed it all away. Whoosh! Washed it all away. Whoosh! Washed it all...

(continuous until auditorium and foyer empty)

(End)

BURKE'S COMPANY

Preface

by Professor Dennis Carroll
('Contemporary Australian Theatre', Currency Press, 1995)

In the mid-1960s, the influence of the Theatre of the Absurd and the writings of Artaud began to make themselves felt in Australia. Of course some of the influence is discernible in the work of White and Hewett, especially in the parody of certain kinds of bureaucratic language and in the creation of mocking or sinister verbal liturgies. But the Theatre of the Absurd and the Theatre of Cruelty are even more pervasively embodied in the plays of Alexander Buzo, Thomas Keneally and Bill Reed. In Buzo's case it is Absurdism which is especially apparent; in Keneally and Reed, Artaudian 'myth' and language-in-space.

Basically, the Theatre of the Absurd playwrights used mild Surrealistic techniques to create existential allegories. Martin Esslin, who coined the term 'Theatre of the Absurd', finds its philosophical foundation in Camus' 1942 essay 'The Myth of Sisyphos', in which Camus characterizes as absurd the condition of man adrift in a meaningless universe, cut off from the roots in the past and the promise of life to come. Artaud's published theory, of course, precedes the Theatre of the Absurd movement, but his influence coincides with and follows it and he takes the philosophical and theatrical implications of the movement further into the heart of darkness. If the Absurdists tended to concur with the existential belief that there is no God and that man's actions are alone what give his life a 'meaning', Artaud believed that the spirits which rule the universe are dark and malignant and the Theatre of Cruelty was a means to make the audience aware of it – not through their intellect and rational perceptions but by means of 'their organisms', like 'the snake charmer's subjects'. By 'cruelty' he meant extreme rigour of action on stage, which would be effected through myth, allegory and his devices of language-in-space. The Theatre of Cruelty would be a 'theatre in which violent physical images crush and hypnotise the sensibility of the spectator seized by the theatre as by 'a whirlwind of higher forces'...

... For Artaud allegory became a ritualized action through a language-in-space which largely dispensed with rational verbal communication and there was an effort through the means to create modern myths. Language-in-space involved an alteration of normal representational delivery. Words were altered to make their sound conform more closely to their semantic meaning, or sometimes used as sounds quite separated from it...

... Bill Reed's Burke's Company has been called 'the first Australian historical play to 'assimilate the Brechtian technical lessons without any obvious sense of embarrassment' but it is more interesting for its Artaudian 'ritualised' action and language-in-space. History is not used here for its factual or documentary illuminations; unimportant details have been pared away and Reed has created a powerful allegory of men locked in battle with natural forces – a myth embedded in the 'collective unconscious' of Australianist traditions. The play was Reed's first to be staged and he was abroad when George Ogilvie directed it for the Melbourne Theatre Company in 1968.

The play is based on the tragic 1860 expedition of Burke and Wills. The first explorers to cross the continent from South to North, on the way back they suffered flukes of misfortune which led to their attenuated deaths in the desert through malnutrition. The play begins with the discoveries of their bodies by a search party. King, the third member of the advance party, is found barely alive, and the play then evolves from the delirium of his memories and the guilt-ridden imagination of Brahe, the man who was supposed to wait for the advance party to return to base at Cooper's Creek and failed to do so. The playwright makes careful use of a pedal point of the confrontation of these two men at the rescue camp sick-bed after the tragedy. The Brechtian epic structure of the play undergoes an Artaudian sea change not only because of the shifting time-space locations of the desert trek but because of the obsessive time shifts through guilt and delirium. The scenes mesh together to form a frightening ceremonial of exhaustive indecision, fateful irony, forced endurance and final agony.

To invest the action with a ceremonial character and give it maximum impact, Reed strips both set and characterisation to allegorical essentials. He suggests two playing areas; a comparatively realistic rescue camp on one side and the rest of the stage much more abstract, a space which 'evokes the Outback heat and stillness, an inimical

whispering quality, infinity of distance yet inanimate nearness...
Behind the rescue camp... a divisive sun shimmers in a darkly
cerulean sky'.

In the production, this was made even more austere. There was a
bare stage and a black sky with a metallic emblem representing the
sun in the centre and no props at all. The play calls for many
blackouts and lighting effects of considerable dexterity. This would
give the necessary illusion of shifting time and space, hallucination
and shimmering heat. Difference in lighting intensity could also
convey the blinding hardness of the sun during the day, the mystery
of dusk, the coldness and terror of night.

In characterization, individuation is carefully restricted except for
Brahe. Burke is shown as a deliberately larger than life hero and his
dialogue has a florid panache which reflects this stature. His refusal
to compromise his self-worth under pressure, his monolithic idealism,
his incipient paranoia are all vividly conveyed. Will and King, the
other main explorers, fall into his shadow: Wills the standard brave
man of reticence, King the standard 'juvenile'. Brahe on the other
hand is no hero. He is guilt-ridden coward desperate for societal
approval and exoneration, an outback Hamlet place in a leadership
position for which he is ill-fitted. Accordingly, his characterization is
more naturalistic and he is full of self-rationalizations and bursts of
hysteria to fend off his terror of the land.

It is this terror of the land which forms the foundation for the play.
For once again the theme is the old Australianist one of man's
relationship to the land, and alienated feeling that if he triumphs over
it, it may strike back in vengeance. As in The Fire of the Snow, a
play that bears more than a passing semblance to this one, disaster
only comes to the party after they have achieved a physical goal.
This marks the attainment of Burke's romantic dream:

'This land can swallow us up right here, I'm telling you. But we've
put the will of man upon it, by God. Once and for all...'

Burke and Wills' final triumph is one of endurance and a
determination to continue the struggle as long as they can, knowing
that this depends on their ability to keep trudging. This theme of
endurance provides the material for those language-in-space

enactments which form the most compelling sequences of the play. A second theme centres around Brahe's double betrayal; his guilt over leaving the Cooper's Creek base a few hours before the explorers' delayed return and his later perjury in stating at an inquiry that there was no evidence of human visitation at the base when he went back later, hence no need to follow the party in search. Brahe's actions suggest consequences of fear of the land, a yearning for safety and anonymity and offer opportunities in one scene for a suitable kind of language-in-space.

This occurs in a scene near the end in which Brahe allows himself to be influenced by his companion into agreeing that there is really no justification for a search party and that to send one out would be dangerous. It is set in motion by a device which superficially suggests the Brechtian theatre: the other man, Wright, breaks out of realistic conversation with Brahe to face front and quote his later evidence at the Royal Commission of Inquiry that there had been no sign of recent European occupation at the base stockade. In a very late point in the scene, Brahe does not acquiesce in Wright's evidence. He fights against it, but with a steadily failing strength. But the inexorable quotations of evidence are a firm indication that Brahe will lose, because they are clearly a 'flash forward' to what will happen later. The device thus indicates the inevitability of Brahe's corruption by Wright, of his acquiescence in the stronger man duplicity. The rest of the scene becomes an atavistic ceremony of domination and submission. Throughout, the sensuous delivery of the words are more important than the meaning of the words themselves and movement and gesture interlock with it to create language-in-space that exemplifies Brahe's mesmerisation by the stronger man. Wright whispers persuasively into Brahe's ears and Brahe reacts as if hypnotised, the two men swaying persistently in a rocking motion. Brahe finally capitulates and speaks evidence with Wright in counterpoint. The dominant man stands above him and croons his last hypnotic assurances like a lullaby. The two men settle down for the night on a symbolically darkening stage.

The more extensive language-in-space of the major action embodies the agonized odyssey of Burke, Wills and King. If imaginatively realised in performance, it can create in the audience a sense of the explorers' experience lived through their perceptions: disorientation under the molten sun, a trance-like sensation of trudging over space and time, an ordeal of repetitive fruitlessness imagined thus by Brahe: 'Heat shimmers, heat shimmers, Burke is slowly moving. The three of them moving, moving. they might be starving with the sun beating down. They might be gasping with the sun beating down. Lead in their legs, their chests gone tight. My head feels light. Dizzy, dizzy, with the sun beating down and heat shimmering, heat shimmering. Burke is slowly moving…'

The ritualize rhythms of suspended animation are created through the repetition of key words and phrases. In performance, these words can dissolve into abstract or musical sounds more closely approximating the emotional states the words suggest. It is with the second trudging sequence which depicts the trek towards Mt Hopeless after the stockade has been found abandoned that this technique becomes very important. King's imagination weaves a stream-of-consciousness monologue, with many repetitions and telegraphic sentences showing confusion and exhaustion"

'How many times, how many… two, three, four, five, six, seven, eight… how many times… how many times… what, what. Blasted hot, blasted flies blasted, blasted….'

The final death trek after the abandonment of Wills is accompanied by the guilt-ridden cries of Brahe tossing in a nightmare and by echoes of earlier verbal motifs.

Of course in production the words function simultaneously with movement and music. The motif of trudging – of marching, moving, crawling on the spot – must be devised by actors and director and must distil an essence of exhaustion, suffering and final agony. It must be stylized movement that can be acted at different rhythms and tempos, and it must be choreographed so that patterns of recurrence, including augmentation and diminution, can register on the audience. It is the repetition of a movement motif that will establish a feeling of 'ritual' just as repeated sound motifs will.

The script invites the stylized choreographing of other incidents, especially those in which extreme hardship or effort is involved. These include the digging of stores from the 'dig tree', the attempts of Burke to get an exhausted camel on its feet, the repeated action of pounding nardoo seed and the incident of Burke driving off some Aborigines. Essentially, the stylisation of these moments involves a slow-motion pattern of movement and gesture which makes an emblem of the action in language-in-space.

The designated music is Peter Sculthorpe's Sixth String Quartet and it is of cardinal importance in establishing all of the body movement in the play. The music was a major inspiration for the play's first director, George Ogilvie. It contains slow passages which he thought ideal for the desert treks and faster sections which suited bursts of excitement and euphoria, such as the passage where Burke imagines the party's triumphant return to Melbourne.

It was Reed in Burke's Company who pioneered Artaudian techniques in a play of stature. If the play is given imaginative production, it powerfully exemplifies one of Artaud's most famous metaphors. The figures on stage will suggest universal human victims burning at the stake, signaling through the flames.

Historical Notes

1860. Robert O'Hara Burke and William John Wills, with a well-equipped party of fifteen men and Aboriginal support, left Melbourne to attempt -- successfully -- to cross the Australian continent from south to north.

The expedition had two springboards along the way:
Menindee: (on the Darling River) where Burke left half his party (eight men) with most of the stores. Under Wright, these were to follow Burke with the main supplies to establish a permanent depot on the next station at...
... Cooper's Creek: (some 700 kilometres from Menindee) where Burke again divided his half of the party and, taking three men with him -- Gray was to die on the way back -- succeeded in the crossing.

Meantime he left Brahe in charge until Wright arrived up from Menindee with the main stores and the other men. But Wright did not arrive. And, after waiting four months with no sign of either Burke or Wright, Brahe left... nine hours before Burke, Wills and King arrived back in advanced stages of exhaustion.

Burke and Wills died of malnutrition two months later. King survived, and was picked up five months later.

Brahe was in the rescue party.

First Staging

Burke's Company was first performed by Melbourne Theatre Company at the Russell Street Theatre, on 7 May 1968 with the following cast:

BURKE: George Whaley
WILLS: Helmut Bakaitis
KING: Sean Scully
BRAHE: Dennis Olsen
MCDONOUGH: Martin Vaughan
PATTON: Graeme Blundell
DOST MAHOMET: John Paton
WRIGHT: Simon Chilvers
WHEELER: Gary Wastell

Director: George Ogilvie
Setting and Costumes: Kristian Fredrikson
Music: Peter Sculthorpe's 'Sixth String Quartet'

The Characters

Advance party:
BURKE
WILLS
KING

Coopers Creek party:
BRAHE
MCDONOUGH
PATTON
DOST MAHOMET: in charge of main party at Menindee:
WRIGHT: doctor in rescue party:
WHEELER

Act
1.

(BRAHE has been left with the packs, while other members of the rescue party are out looking for traces of BURKE, WILLS and KING. A shot is heard in the distance. BRAHE starts, looks up.)

BRAHE: The signal!
   (he listens.)
That signal. Somebody's found something... There's something going on.
   (he listens carefully)
I don't want to know. Whatever they've found, I don't want to see it. Why should I? It's got nothing to do with...
   (turns his back.)
It's spring elsewhere.
   (pause.)
Not here. Here you wouldn't know it.
   (blinking into the sun)
This sun. It brings water to your eyes. Bloody tears.
   (bitterly)
Tears?

   (He looks around, alienated. Drops to his haunches, and takes a handful of sand)

BRAHE: Strange. Nearly a year, almost a year, the first time I camped here. With Burke and co. Then him. Wills. King. Gray. Them, moving off.
   (with a sweep of the arm)
I wonder what they found... out there. Wait, Burke said. Wait.
   (pause)
I didn't have to come back with this lot. If they find anyone... I can say I joined the rescue party on my own free will. I did. Nobody can deny it. I'm doing my best.
   (suddenly thumping the ground, crying out)

But you know what happened to them, don't you, Brahe? They can look, but you-know-don't-you? Eh? EH? Oh, God.
(pause)
I could've waited that extra day for Burke. I could've been here when they got back, with just a bit of luck. A few lousy hours...
(pause. Suddenly)
Damn your damned hide, Brahe! Your rotten luck is what you deserve.

(There comes three more shots. He spins around as though shot. Steadies himself with self-pity)

BRAHE: This place, was I really here? I mean, four months of my life. Here. Around here. It's not possible. In its lap for four months. A day then a day. Waiting, waiting. You built a stockade. Caught rats. And ate. Drank, bloating yourself. And nothing else.
(pause.)
God how you waited. For four, four, four... so long.
(pause.)
Only you up and left the morning of the night they came back.
(pause.)
The animal-land turned round and bit you, boyo. It had the last say.
(pause.)
God, I didn't want to come back here. I'm doing my best.

(WHEELER, the doctor of the rescue party, hurries in from back right)

WHEELER: A tent, get one out, Mr Brahe! My supplies. Where are they?
(rushing over to a smallish pack)
Where the hell are my supplies?
(noticing BRAHE's inactivity)
Quickly, man, the tent, and food, and... they'll do more good up there than here!

BRAHE: Where?

WHEELER: We'll need what you can bring! Half a mile up, other side of the creek, sloping sand...
(leaving)

A tent first, though, to cover him up!

BRAHE: For God's sake, who?

WHEELER: They've found a charred figure...

BRAHE: Who?

WHEELER: They think it's King!

BRAHE: Alive, Wheeler?

WHEELER: Yes, alive, alive!

(BRAHE stops him from running off)

BRAHE: Burke, Wills...?

WHEELER: Dead, both dead. King's the last, but only just...
    (hesitating)
Remember Burke when he left Melbourne, Brahe? The crowds, the
confidence, his confidence...? You should know. Can you imagine
Burke coming to this? Remember how he used to do that boasting
away?
    (brief pause.)
It must've taken a lot to wear down a man like Burke. He rode on his
own dream, didn't he? He's rotting around here, somewhere, now.
We've seen his passing.
    (remembers KING.)
Quickly, man! A tent to cover King up!

    (He exits)

BRAHE: (moving in circles, with remorse) A tent... a tent... to cover
him...
    (suddenly)
to cover up the sight of him!

2.

(Lighting still emphasises the rescue camp. It is a few days later. KING is lying on a bed roll in the shade of the tent. He lies motionless, but his eyes are open. BRAHE enters from front left. He does so, not so much on the defensive, but horrified at what he might see or hear. He whispers KING's name, then, getting no response, approaches)

BRAHE: King?
   (no answer)
My God, King... forgive me, man.
   (pause)
It all got out of hand, that's all. I... I had no idea it was going to turn out like this. I waited four months, King.
   (pause)
I'd give an arm not to have caused this.

   (KING does not stir)

BRAHE: Look, don't die, man. Burke, Wills... you, I can't take it all.
   (No movement. BRAHE waits, longing to vindicate himself, but KING only stares up at him. BRAHE backs away from the eyes, turns to leave)

KING: Brahe.

BRAHE: (turning quickly) King, I...

KING: You're here as well.

BRAHE: I had to come.

KING: I never thought... you're back.

BRAHE: (plunging in) I swear I thought I'd find you all in Menindee waiting when I got back. I swear that.

KING: ... Brahe?

BRAHE: Yes?

KING: You deserted.

BRAHE: No, King, no.

KING: You left us... to die, Brahe.

>*(Pause. BRAHE mutely protests)*

KING: Deserter...

BRAHE: (pitifully) It wasn't how it seems, man. Listen, King, I did what I had to.

>*(But KING starts mumbling, shuts him out)*

KING: (deliriously) Mr Burke... Mr Burke...?

BRAHE: (over him, desperately) There was more to it than any of you thought, King!

KING: Mr Burke...?

BRAHE: (alarmed) Ssh, take it easy, man. You're all right. You're all right now.

KING: (sudden outcry) Mr Burke?

>*(BURKE and WILLS, battered and trudging wearily, are silhouetted, back right)*

BURKE: (remotely) Yes, boy?

BRAHE: (sinking down to his knees, covering his own face) King, it's all right now...

KING: (head straining towards BURKE) Mr Burke. What about me?

149

BURKE: What... boy?

(KING endeavours to rise to join them, but cannot make it. He stays in this position throughout the scene, head straining upwards and backwards towards them)

KING: I've... I've just fallen. How much further?

BURKE: (jubilantly) To Melbourne, one thousand miles, King. To the depot and Brahe, to safety, to civilization, only a few more paces.

KING: (continued struggle) Thank God for that.

WILLS: We will in time. In time, we will.

BURKE: A little way more. A little way more. I promise you, boys, when we pick up Brahe, neither of you will walk another step to Melbourne. Unless on a red carpet, eh? A red carpet you'll be treading.

KING: I'll settle for eggs and a bit of cheese, sir. On my plate or in my belly.

BURKE: Well you may, King. Well you may...
    (urging)
But let's get on boys! You're dragging your heels and that won't do, not for my heroes, it won't! So let's get home -- and Brahe's our darling!

WILLS: (rising to him) Ho, Brahe's our darling!

BURKE: Sure and sing him a song, King! And let's get on, boys.

KING: (stammering in march time)
There was a man who died sans care
All he ever did was to kneel in prayer
There was another who died quite soothed
For he was cunning -- he never moved.
But here is one other who's to trudge his way
And march to exist, not stop to pray
With more than prayers must a man compete

When all his hope is bound in feet.

(BURKE stops suddenly, excitedly)

BURKE: (pointing) Look!
  (peers into the distance.)
I thought I saw...
  (calling)
Cooee! Cooee!
  (he listens.)
Ssh, ssh!

(They all listen)

BURKE: Hear anything?

(But they have heard nothing)

WILLS: No I don't think so...

(Pause)

BURKE: Did you, King?

KING: (earnestly) I'm trying, sir.

BURKE: How far today, Mr Wills?

WILLS: About twenty-five miles, roughly.

KING: (laughing deliriously) A... a long way, sir! Too far to go on an autumn day.

BURKE: All the less to go home, my boy. All the more for not lingering! But let's get these beasts on boys! Hipyah, hipyah, you brutes!

(They move on, with renewed vigour)

BURKE: (trudge lyrics) We'll kiss his cheek, our darling Brahe!
We'll kiss the cheek of our darling boy. On, on, boys, if you're young
at heart!

WILLS: (in time) We'll kiss his cheek, our darling Brahe. We'll kiss
the cheek of our darling boy.

KING: (ditto) On, on, if you're young at heart!

> *(They all chant, giving courage to each other. BURKE stops
> WILLS again)*

BURKE: Wait!
   (calling again)
Cooee! Cooee!
   (pause)
Well?

WILLS: No...

KING: (miserably, sinking back onto bed roll) No, no. The air's so
still. It'd wear you down.

BURKE: Well then, let's get on...
   (chanting, urging)
...on, on, boys. We'll kiss the cheek of that darling boy. Not much
further. There's not much further. You've earned your rest and he'll
be surprised so... On, on, you've a cheek to kiss of a darling boy... our
darling Brahe. A song, John King!

KING: (with little energy)
But here is one other who's to trudge his way
And march to exist, not stop to pray
With more than prayers must a man compete
When all his hope is bound in feet.
   (then)
Can you see anything, Mr Burke? Is there anything to be seen, sir?

BURKE: I... (pointing triumphantly) By God, what's that?

WILLS and KING: *Where?*

BURKE: {not all together but over time} There, you blockheads! I
think it is... By heaven, it is! The stockade, boys! We've made it.
We've made it! Come on, boys, come on! Get -- these -- brutes --
moving! And let's get back! Now let's get back! Start yelling! Yell
those lungs out to high heaven and back! You can do no more than
kiss the cheek of our darling boy... you can do no more!
   (yelling)
Brahe! Brahe!

WILLS: Brahe, Brahe, the boy that's bonny!

KING: (passively) Brahe, Brahe, the boy that's bonny!

BURKE: (moving off) That's it! Brahe, Brahe, the boy that's bonny!
Up with that song, Johnny lad. Let's hear that song as loud as you
can...

   (He exits front left with WILLS)

KING: (laughing weakly, hopelessly)
There was a man who died sans care,
All he ever did was to kneel in prayer.
There was another who died quite soothed,
For he was cunning -- he never moved.
But here is one other who's to trudge his way
And march to exist, not stop to pray.
With more than prayers must a man compete
When all his hope is bound in feet.
Godless there died a parson's brother,
Whose brother's cloak did finally smother,
For, with eyes uplifted, all he could see
Was not his God, but a parson's knee.
But here is one other who's to trudge his way...

   (Re-enter BURKE and WILLS back left near the 'DIG' tree.

   They stop. Silence)

BURKE: (stunned, in a whisper) Brahe?

WILLS: It looks... empty.

KING: (outcry, straight at BRAHE) Brahe?

(He continues to stare at the man's bowed head)

WILLS: They've gone... Brahe's gone, Mr Burke.

BURKE: No...
   (shouting)
Brahe?

(Nothing. And so in disbelief)

BURKE: But where...? How?

KING: (still at BRAHE) Sir... sir... There's no one here, sir! There's nothing in this to meet the eye!

BURKE: No, no.
   (frantically looking about)
 They must've moved up the creek. That's it, they've had to move to another site. They... they must've left word somewhere. Look around, boys, look around! Don't stand there!

(He and WILLS desperately search the stockade)

KING: (back to BURKE) All these things... they've been careless with what they've left behind, sir. Not speaking of us, I'm not.

BURKE: Yes, yes, blast them.

WILLS: (kneeling) These ashes. They're fresh. Very fresh, Mr Burke. Today's or yesterday's.

BURKE: Yes, Mr Wills, I've noticed.

KING: (distraught) Would they have had to move after so long here, sir? I must ask! I can't hold back.

BURKE: They've moved somewhere else, boy, that's all.

154

KING: But they've left the stockade intact. Why haven't they used the wood to build another one? They wouldn't start from scratch again, sir. Would they...? And these boots, left lying here... the feet've gone but the boots are here.

BURKE: (annoyed) King, they've just shifted camp! Look around, man.

KING: (hysterics rising) They've marked that tree with today's date. A tree's been damaged because of today.

BURKE: Blast you, King. I'm telling you they've just pitched camp somewhere else...

WILLS: (from beside the tree) Then, Mr Burke, why did they blaze this tree?

BURKE: What...?

(He runs to the tree. On it, the words -- 'DIG 3ft N.W.' -- are blazed. He runs his finger over them as though reading Braille)

BURKE: The sap has not even dried... Dig! For the love of God, dig!

(All three scramble at the earth with their bare hands, KING doing so where he lies)

WILLS: That... uh... that rake, King...

BURKE: The rake, King.

KING: (deliriously) Yes, yes, the rake. I'll get the rake, Mr Wills, sir. I'll... I'll get the rake! I'll get the rake! You'll find it here within my hands.

WILLS: Uh... Uhh... there's something hard here.

BURKE: Quickly, Wills...

WILLS: It's a box...

155

(He fumbles with it)

BURKE: What's in it, man?

WILLS: ... there's stores and...

KING: And a bottle, sir! It's got a note in it... in the bottle around the note!

BURKE: Give it to me!

> *(BURKE reads the letter in silence. When finished, he looks around confused while the realisation strikes home, then drops to the ground, all energy gone. WILLS snatches up the note)*

WILLS: April? 21st April... it's...
  (in disbelief) ...
it's dated today! My God, my God... they must have left this morning!

> *(From his roll, KING begins to laugh hysterically and then recites the note from memory as though it were his own joke)*

KING: 'Depot, Cooper's Creek, 21st April, 1861. The depot party of the Victorian Exploring Expedition leaves this camp today to return to the Darling River. I intend to go southeast from Camp 60 to get into our old track near Bulloo. Two of my companions and myself are quite well; the third -- Patton -- has been unable to walk for the last eighteen days, as his leg has been severely hurt when thrown by one of the horses. No person has been up here from the Darling. We have six camels and twelve horses in good working condition. William Brahe.'
  (sobbing)
William Brahe! Oh, our sweet darling boy without the cheek to kiss our thanks.

> *(He falls back, his voice conveying heavy bitterness at the motionless BRAHE. Long silence)*

BURKE: They must have camped. They couldn't be sitting more than thirty miles away right now.
(pause, then with obvious effort:)
If we got on straight away... there's a chance that we could overtake them.
(pause.)
Not too many miles, I think. What do you think?

(Neither WILLS nor KING speaks up)

BURKE: Well, Mr Wills?

WILLS: I... I hope that -- I'll never feel so leg-tired again.

BURKE: King?

KING: I'd have to crawl doubled up tight, sir.

BURKE: (nodding wearily) It was my duty to ask.

(Pause. They slump)

BURKE: Would you be so kind as to organise something to eat when you're quite ready, King?

KING: (some determination) I will. I swear that to God. You'll have something inside you if I can help it.

(With a last effort, KING manages to get off the bed roll, but almost immediately collapses alongside it)

BURKE: (general direction of KING) The camels... leave them packed.

(Exhaustion overcomes them. The three of them sleep.

Lights dim to highlight BRAHE who looks up, sees KING out of his bed roll. He tries to speak, but cannot at first. He moves to KING to pick him up, but baulks at touching him as though to do so would awaken phantoms.

For a long time, he looks down at the collapsed man. Then, when he speaks, he does so with pained confusion rising to defiance and self-justification)

BRAHE: (vindictively, aloud to KING) I know what you're thinking! Four months and five days I watched myself rot out here for you... five days over four months -- one hundred and twenty-six days. The land got bigger while I got smaller. Rats, blacks, animals, scouting parties. Nothing moves out here for days on end. You're on your own. It was hard even trying to think, King. Did you ever have to go down to a creek and throw rocks into it to make ripples so that you could watch something move? You find yourself speaking in whispers. You get that way that you can't bear to hear your voice being lost in the distance where you'd never go until someone came who wouldn't.
    (and)
Burke, he made me stay here. I didn't want to. I'd rather have gone with you, you know that. Three months at the latest you said you'd be gone. Wright never came up from Menindee with the stores and the other men like you said he would. You told me I could expect him in a few days. What about Wright? He was second-in-command, not me. He didn't 't turn up!
    (pause)
Four months and five days I waited and nothing I was told would happen did. You left me stranded as much as I did you... What could I do with only three men... and one of them dying?

(Enter MCDONOUGH and the Pathan, DOST MAHOMET, from back right. They are carrying PATTON who is in agony from the effects of scurvy. They put him down and make him as comfortable as possible. BRAHE does not need to have to look at them)

BRAHE: Look at them. What could I do?
    (then to no one)
Would you have let Patton die? Burke? Wills? King? Blast you, give me a fair answer!

(MCDONOUGH moves up to BRAHE, who starts)

BRAHE: What do you want?

MCDONOUGH: Thought we'd take advantage of this breeze.

BRAHE: What?

MCDONOUGH: Thought we'd get him out for a bit of fresh air. He's boiling up and it's not too bad out here now.

BRAHE: Uh...

MCDONOUGH: (pointing) Patton. Patton over there.

BRAHE: How's he doing?

MCDONOUGH: Listen to him breathing. You don't have to ask with scurvy.

BRAHE: (suddenly, a plea) When's Burke coming back? Where the hell is Wright? One of them.

MCDONOUGH: (pointing to PATTON) He's been calling for you all day.

BRAHE: (simply) Yes.

MCDONOUGH: More than usual.

BRAHE: Yes.

MCDONOUGH: He's pretty bad.

BRAHE: All right!

    (MCDONOUGH shrugs, turns away)

MCDONOUGH: Better knock up some tea.
  (to Dost Mahomet)
Put the billy on, old son.

DOST MAHOMET: (looking solicitously at PATTON and nodding) Ye-es, ye-es... pretty bad.

MCDONOUGH: The billy, the billy. Water. Tea. Blast you.

DOST MAHOMET: (going off with the billy) Okay.

    (MCDONOUGH builds up a fire)

MCDONOUGH: (to BRAHE) Where've you been?

BRAHE: Looking.

MCDONOUGH: Up on the ridge again, eh?

    (BRAHE nods)

MCDONOUGH: See anything?

BRAHE: (helplessly) There's nothing to see. Nothing -- to -- see, man. We're trapped here, waiting for one to come back and another to come up.

MCDONOUGH: No sign of anybody again, eh? I've never envied you that little trip.

BRAHE: Going's not bad. It's the same kind of trip back that hurts.
   (then quickly:)
 McDonough?

MCDONOUGH: Yeah?

BRAHE: I... look, how're you feeling yourself?

MCDONOUGH: Me? Reckon I'll last out.

BRAHE: (heavy insinuation) But how are you feeling?

MCDONOUGH: I get plenty of water and more than enough food...

BRAHE: It's going fast...

MCDONOUGH: I still get enough. It's there when I want it. There's plenty of crows and duck about if one of us really wanted to take a few shots. At a pinch, there's the horses... as long as I don't suddenly peg out, like Patton over there, Don't worry about me.

BRAHE: And if you do?

(MCDONOUGH shrugs)

BRAHE: Or what if Mahomet goes over?

MCDONOUGH: That old rag-head? He's fitter than all of us, including the camels. He'd thrive on sand. That's all he's good for, hanging on.

BRAHE: (pressing) But what if he didn't?

MCDONOUGH: That's your problem.

BRAHE: We're all getting worse. If I suddenly went over... what would you do?
  (wanting to know)
 What would you do?

MCDONOUGH: (annoyed) Look... it's your problem, Brahe. Me, I'm still fit, that's all. I'm all right. Don't worry about me.

PATTON: (calling) Where-are-you?

BRAHE: (nervously) He can't stand it much longer, McDonough. I've got to think of Patton!

MCDONOUGH: I can't help you.

(DOST MAHOMET returns with water and sets about making some tea.

The other two move towards him, but PATTON grabs BRAHE's leg as he passes)

PATTON: Brahe... help me, for God's sake!

BRAHE: All right, boy, all right. You'll be fitter soon. Just hang on.

PATTON: Do -- something.

BRAHE: Stick it out, man. That's all I ask.

PATTON: You're killing me...

(He shudders. BRAHE holds him)

MCDONOUGH: (to MAHOMET) Well, Dosty old son, have a quiet time with your pets, today? Did you tread in plenty dung again?

(DOST MAHOMET nods cheerfully, not understanding)

MCDONOUGH: Any trouble with the blacks today? Black fellow?

DOST MAHOMET: Black fellow... Ye-es, ye-es.

MCDONOUGH: Is that so? What happened?

DOST MAHOMET: Ye-es.

MCDONOUGH: I tell you what, old son, they can't say that you and I haven't had some heart-to-heart talks, can they?
    (pause.)
I suppose you went off with one of their lovely ladies again, eh?

DOST MAHOMET: No, no... dirty.

MCDONOUGH: What, even for us?

(BRAHE joins them. He sits heavily. A long silence. Tedium)

MCDONOUGH: (singing lazily)
I'm goin' to see her when she comes
I'd like to stare her down...
Been waiting here for many a day
For the ghost of Nellie Brown.
She tossed her hair and winked an eye
She bared an ankle to me
If that's no promise a-what it's worth

162

I'll be hanged by the mulga tree.
She came upon me one fine night
When the fire was burnin' low
'Dear Johnny boy, I love thee true,
You'll wait for me I know.'
She tossed her hair and winked an eye
She bared an ankle to me
If that's no promise a-what it's worth
I'll be hanged by a mulga tree.

BRAHE: McDonough, I want you to listen.

MCDONOUGH: (singing)
She said: There's just two men in this world
For whom I'd stop and tarry
It's just that the other's got so rich
He's up and made me marry.
An' she tossed her hair and winked an eye
She bared an ankle to me
But twas no promise a-what it's worth
And I'm to hang by the mulga tree...

BRAHE: McDonough.

MCDONOUGH: (singing) .'...I'm to hang by the mulga tree'.

BRAHE: (resolutely) McDonough, listen to me.

MCDONOUGH: Fine by me.

BRAHE: You tell me if I'm not talking sense.

> (PATTON moans, convulses. BRAHE goes to him, wipes the
> sweat from his brow)

MCDONOUGH: (stiffly) Go on.

BRAHE: (over his shoulder) What did Burke say to you before he
left? Never mind what he said to me.

MCDONOUGH: You heard.

163

BRAHE: Didn't he say that if he hadn't returned here in three months, you could consider him perished? Didn't he say that?

MCDONOUGH: He said it.

BRAHE: Didn't he take only three months' rations with him?

MCDONOUGH: That's what he had to hand, yes.

BRAHE: It's been four months now, McDonough, since he left us waiting here.

MCDONOUGH: Well?

BRAHE: He's four weeks overdue, man, and there's not a sign of him. Another thing. It's five months since Wright was to bring up the remaining party from Menindee. Where the hell is he?

MCDONOUGH: (contemptuously) You afraid *we*'ve been forgotten?

BRAHE: Listen to me. God knows, I've had plenty of time to think about it. How are we to know if Burke was picked up by a ship when he reached the Gulf?

(MCDONOUGH shrugs)

BRAHE: How would we know if he's decided to make for the Queensland coast. That way's already been opened up. It's a stroll compared to coming back down here again.
    (pause, then urgently)
They could be sitting pretty back in civilization for all we know.

MCDONOUGH: We would have heard.

BRAHE: But can you be sure of that, man?

MCDONOUGH: (curtly) Can you, boyo?

BRAHE: Look, if they've got back, what would you do if you were Wright -- down there, he'd soon hear about it. Here we are four hundred miles away across a country that only devils and fools would think about crossing for a sociable visit. Don't you think they'd reckon, 'Well, the three months are up. Surely Brahe would have the sense to come back without us dragging ourselves right up there to get him.'

MCDONOUGH: That's up to you. I don't know what orders Burke gave you. I've told you that.

BRAHE: (emphatically) He gave me three months, or until our provisions run short.

MCDONOUGH: We're doing all right.

BRAHE: How much longer are they going to last out? I'll have to leave some buried for them just in case; how much longer can we spin it out and still have enough over to bury? Supposing they're out there dying or stuck in some place unable to move because of water or the blacks. We've got to go back and get help. McDonough?
    (pause)
Look at Patton, man. Just look at the poor devil. He's dying. Any fool can see that. I'm the one who'll answer for it if he dies. One minute he's begging me to finish him off, the next he's cursing me for trying to murder him. And he's right. I've got his life in my hands... whatever I decide boils down to whether he lives or dies. McDonough, I'm not God, man.

(MCDONOUGH does not react. BRAHE realises the other man is turning a deaf ear)

BRAHE: McDonough!

MCDONOUGH: I've told you, I don't know what he told you to do. Anyway, what're you trying to say?

(Pause. PATTON rolls over and moans)

BRAHE: (mustering himself) We're leaving here on Sunday, that's what. That's the twenty-first. I'm too small to gamble with stakes like this.

(He waits for a reaction but MCDONOUGH remains obtrusive. BRAHE strides angrily off back right. MAHOMET watches him go)

MCDONOUGH: (languidly) Well, it looks like that's your lot, old son.

(MAHOMET is looking into his eyes)

MCDONOUGH: Yes, leaving... leaving, old son. Going away. It'll mean giving up your local lasses here. But think of your wages. Think how sick you can make yourself on them. Think how sick we can all make ourselves. Let's get on.

(MCDONOUGH gets wearily to his feet; MAHOMET follows. They slowly pack up their things then go over to PATTON and pick him up. They move off after BRAHE)

MCDONOUGH: (as he goes)
I'm goin' to see her when she comes
I'd like to stare her down...
Been waiting here for many a day
For the ghost of Nellie Brown.

(The stage is blacked out for a short time, then the illusion of day breaking. Lighting emphasises BURKE and WILLS, sleeping where they fell exhausted in their last scene, and KING, sleeping on the ground near his bed roll. KING begins to wake up)

KING: (deliriously brushing away imaginary flies) Ah. Ah. Bloody, bloody flies. Too filthy for hell so up here... Ugh! Let me sleep... So tired, I...
    (dozes, but is pestered again)
Ah. Ah...
    (swallows a fly, coughs violently, spits)
Uh... Uh... so tired. Tired... They won't let me sleep, will they? Will they?

(He is pestered again)

KING: (calling suddenly) Mr Burke, Mr Wills. Breakfast, sirs... Wake up by the flies; breakfast is up. The flies will get it first.

(Struggling to his feet, he staggers over to the others)

KING: There's oatmeal and rice -- and sugar, sir. Sugar! But also for the flies, sirs. You'd better wake up. You'd better hurry; if I were you, I would!

(BURKE and WILLS stir themselves. They sit up wearily)

BURKE: Another day, King?

KING: Oh yes. Another day of flies, but sugar, sir.
   (gleefully)
They can eat all they want, there's still enough.

BURKE: Only for what we need, King.

KING: (rebuked) That's what I meant, sir.

BURKE: How are you feeling, Mr Wills?

WILLS: (getting out his books) Relieved, thank God...

BURKE: Relieved enough to write again, I see. Mr Wills, you're incorrigible. What can you possibly find to write about? And before breakfast, man. Before the luxury of sugar.

WILLS: (with slow levity) Ah, but then, sir, my hand hasn't got a mouth, tell things as it might. It's got better things to do than eat sugar.

(He writes)

BURKE: (unamused about it) Even in this situation, eh?

WILLS: It's this situation that makes the hand itch more than the stomach.

BURKE: (bitterly) To tell the world how we've been left behind?
Marooned by Brahe yesterday like half-wits.

WILLS: (shrugging) The situation's unique. I feel like writing.

BURKE: God help us if it stays unique!
  (pause)
Could you explain it by writing, lad? Months of slogging to be a half
a day late?

WILLS: (chastened) No. I'm not up to that.

BURKE: Write what else then?

WILLS: (with conviction) Same as usual, Mr Burke. To know at what
time on what day we were left stranded, or that that cloud formation
over there is building up, may be useful to someone.

BURKE: But not to us.

WILLS: Precisely that.

BURKE: (good humouredly) You're an admirable fellow, Mr Wills.
I've always admired your book knowledge and -keeping. Your
mind's so accurate you're almost a busybody, do you know that?

WILLS: I suspect I was selected for that.

BURKE: (getting sentimental) No, I was joking. You're one of the
few who've done their duty properly. Remember that. You've done
all that you could've right from the start. You've deserved the glory
that's due to you. We all have, by God. Whatever else happens, that
can't be taken away from us.
  (impatiently)
It would have been a miracle if that blasted Stuart hasn't beaten us in
the crossing after all this.

WILLS: Stuart? I had forgotten him.

BURKE: (theatrically) And so will the world his name.

WILLS: (shrewdly) From the start you were out to beat him, weren't you, Mr Burke?

BURKE: What else? What else?

WILLS: (skeptically) I don't know...

BURKE: (overbearing) Such as, Mr Wills?

WILLS: Exploring, I suppose. Just exploring in general. Taking our time.

BURKE: (walking away) John, I've come to realise something. I'll tell it to you...
   (pause)
Can you imagine what all this is going to be like in a few years?

KING: (aloud) Hot, dry and dying, sir! With flies multiplied by just that much more.

BURKE: (to WILLS) Listen a while, lad.

   (Pause, even KING stops to listen)

BURKE: Can you feel the stillness waiting? A whole new land is waiting. Back on the coasts, men are waiting as well. And waiting for what, John? I'll tell you. Waiting for our word and your books and our return. Waiting for Burke and Wills and King to come back and tell them that man has been putting his great boot over this land. And come away. That they can come on. This land can swallow us up right here, I'm telling you. But we've put the will of man upon it, by God. Once and for all. We've done what thousands of men only dream about.
   (softly)
Do you know what I'm trying to say, boy?

WILLS: (quietly) Almost too much.

BURKE: Whether the South Australian Stuart has beaten us to be the first across Australia or not, doesn't matter. It's men's dreams we're after. It's men's boots we've been marching in. We've taken all those dandies back there across a new continent. And brought them back. We've been fighting destiny for them. And we won through. I wanted to win a race, but I've won a fight.

WILLS: Yes, in many ways we work for ourselves in spite of ourselves.

BURKE: You understand these thing better than I do, don't you? In spite of our ages, you're older than I.

WILLS: I don't think so.

(A long silence)

BURKE: (shaking off his thoughts) Ha, small consolation though, my lad. Ask King.
    (calling)
King, John King, my trusty boy, how consoled do you feel?

KING: (lamenting)
In normal life a man needs more
Than just his body that he keeps in store
He moves its limbs and its face distorts
But knows, by God, he only needs its thoughts
But here is one other who's to trudge his way
And march to exist, not stop to pray,
With more than prayers must a man compete
When all his hope is bound in feet.

    (Blackout. When spotlit again, WILLS is writing. KING is crawling on all fours near the tree. BURKE enters with a fish)

BURKE: Still writing, Mr Wills?

WILLS: Just jotting down a few notes.

BURKE: What are you saying about Wright in your book?

WILLS: (bitterly) I could only guess, Mr Burke.

BURKE: (anguished) What could have happened to the man? If something had happened to him why didn't someone else bring the stores up? In the letter Brahe says no person has been up here from the Darling. Has the whole world forgotten us?

WILLS: All we can do is wait.

BURKE: (annoyed) Wright knew the country. He had a clear run, man.

WILLS: When you took him on, Mr Burke...
  (pause.)
Did you trust the man?

BURKE: (sharply) Why do you say that?

WILLS: Because you put our lives in his hands.

BURKE: What else could I have done? He showed us his mettle. Four hundred miles of land he brought us over as easily as if it were the King's road we were following. And that was during the time of year when others claimed it was impossible to get up to here. It wasn't a question of trusting the man, Mr Wills. He knew the ground and how to overcome it. He was the obvious man to go back for the stores. I had no choice but to trust the fellow.

WILLS: The blacks weren't very friendly, if you'll remember. They behaved all right with our party. But just one man, travelling alone...

BURKE: But why no rescue party in any case?

KING: (calling out) Why just nothing, sir? Why not a cross from hell? Or just a red rude word. Or a rose from the ground? Why the nothing of a deadly silence, or the nothing of fate? They took our clothes away to cover themselves up in our need. They've shot our clothes to pieces. There are more of our skins uncovered than clothed, sir! That's truer than I've ever said, God's truth, Mr Burke!

BURKE: John King, how long do you think it'll last?

KING: (in anguish) What, sir, what?

BURKE: The sugar and things -- our supplies. How long do you think they'll last?

KING: There's three hungry throats and three mouths, sir. There's many a gulp and many a pain in three stomachs. That's the way I figure it.

BURKE: How long, boy?

KING: (almost crying) A month, sir. A month or a little longer. Four weeks or more of not being hungry.

BURKE: You're quite right. Four to five weeks at the most.
    (pause)
Mr Wills, King, I'm going to sponge myself down in the creek. I earnestly suggest that you both refresh yourselves likewise before we leave.

WILLS: (sharply) What are you planning?

BURKE: How do you see the situation, Mr Wills?

WILLS: I'd say, only two avenues. Either wait here for a rescue party or try to make our own way back down.

BURKE: To where?

WILLS: To Menindee. Of course.

BURKE: (to KING) And how do you see it, laddie?

KING: Much the same, sir, much the same. Follow Brahe's track while he's leaving ours behind.

BURKE: (shrewdly) Menindee's four hundred miles away.

    (WILLS puts down his books)

WILLS: What are you thinking, Mr Burke?

BURKE: It's a two months' journey at the least. A waterless journey most of the way. We'd need guts, strength, and supplies to make it to Menindee. And we haven't got that much left of any of those.

WILLS: Something may have delayed Brahe. We might catch him up. Patton's apparently about done up. And a rescue party would certainly come here first. They'd expect us to stay here or follow our old track down.

BURKE: Perhaps there's another way...

WILLS: Sir?

KING: (far-away echo) Sir, sir?

BURKE: A settlement in South Australia is only one hundred and fifty miles away from here, Mr Wills. Just about as far as our provisions will take us comfortably.

(WILLS stands with apprehension)

BURKE: Remember, a man called Gregory did it in '58 in just a little over a week from about here. Even taking into account our knocked-up condition, that way's more our prospect, I fancy.

(WILLS looks carefully at BURKE, as KING agitates. WILLS speaks his last protest carefully and formally)

WILLS: But we're not sure of the way. And should anything go wrong, nobody would think of looking for us that way.

BURKE: (confidently) I doubt whether it will be necessary. But even so, I've thought of that. We'll rebury the box with instructions about what we intend to do.
    (to WILLS's reluctance)
Don't worry, Mr Wills. We'll rebury it in the same place. It won't be missed. God knows that word 'DIG' stands out for anyone to see... And so it should. It's the devil's own writing. No wonder it had to be blazed with fire. This is my intention, boys. I can only hope you're with me.

WILLS: (slowly) You've led us this far, Mr Burke.

BURKE: Thank you. All we can do is pray that the Almighty will be with us.

WILLS: Amen.

KING: Amen, amen. Amen to that, sir.

BURKE: And when you've a spare moment, King, get the animals ready, will you?

KING: (energetically) I'll get them ready, sir. They'll sprint us there. We'll have to tug at them to make them stop, sir.

   (BURKE nods, moves off)

KING: (after him) What'll we need to take, Mr Burke? Besides what we haven't got, that is. Besides our prayers and our knees we'll cry them from.

BURKE: We'll take what we need and leave what we can. That'll do for a start.

KING: But not for an end, sir.

BURKE: More than for an end, boy.

   (He exits)

KING: Where're we heading for, Mr Wills? What was it called? It's hard hearing in this driving silence; the flies are bad and my hearing's shot.

WILLS: I know it by name only. Mount Hopeless, King -- the hill called Hopeless.

KING: Will it be worth the half a day we were left behind, sir? Hopeless is a funny name, a funny name for the price of our heads. It sounds so little to cost so much, when less of a hope is what we don't want.

(They pack up their things. WILLS writes a note, which he places in the box. He then buries the box under the 'DIG' tree)

WILLS: Then let's be off.

(Blackout.

Then slowly lighting reveals BURKE, WILLS and KING struggling towards Mount Hopeless, downstage centre. They trudge on through will only, locked with each other's movement. They stumble often apparently over sand and sharp stones)

KING: (slow rhythm) One, two, three, four, five, six seven, eight, nine, ten, one, two, three, four, five, six, seven, eight, nine, ten, ten, nine, eight, sev... with more than prayers, must, a man, compete, when, all, his, hope, is, bound, in, feet, when, all, his...
    (he stops, picks up the rhythm)
How many times, how many times... two, three, four, five, six, seven, eight... how many times... how many times... what, what? Blasted hot, blasted flies, blasted, blasted.
    (to the figures beside him)
Mr Burke? Mr Wills?

(He gets no reply)

KING: Keep going, four, five, keep going, five six, keep going, six seven, keep...
    (stopping)
Mr Burke? Can you see anything? Mr Wills? I'm so bloody, bloody, bloody, bloody, bloody parched. How's the water, Mr Burke? Sir? How are we for a...? No answer. Miser. Hogging it likely. About time we had a... what's he thinking? Both of them, wonder what they're thinking? Lucky, lucky. They're going to outlast me. They will. Walk me off my feet. Can't let them. Can't, let, them, do, that, two, three, four, five, six, seven, eight, nine, ten, ten, nine... Thirty more steps I'll look up. Be able to see something. You never know, King, you never know. Thirty more steps will make all the difference. You'll see, you'll see. I'll settle for a tree or a pigeon flying over. It's been done before. They're water-seekers, pigeons. Bless them. Bless those

pigeons if there were any. 'How are you King?' 'I'm all right; I'll get by.' 'Good.' 'How are you King?' 'I'm all right; I'll get by.' 'Good.' 'How are you, King?' 'I'm all right; I'll...' rocks, stones, rocks, sand, rocks, stones. My God, I'll... have... to... tell... him... Mr Burke, I... I can't go on. I'll say it like that. Like that. I'm about worn out. It's too far, wherever we're going. This Mount Hopeless, I'll have to, Mr Burke. I'll never make it. No water...

(listens)

Just thirty paces more... thirty paces... then... then I'll look up. If there's not a tree in sight or a pigeon... or some... sound... or a hill I'll pack it in. Thirty paces... One, two, three, four, five...

(looking madly)

He's going to stop. He's stopping...

(He drops to rest a fraction after BURKE and WILLS)

KING: ...Ah. Ah.

(Long pause. And then in cadence 'with' the trudge and the struggle starting up again)

KING: Forty-five miles, sir? Is that all we've come, sir? Really? You say so... I... we'll have to go back. I know it's our last chance, but I can't go on. Sir, I agree with you and Mr Wills. Go back to the stockade is our only chance. There's water there. It's our desert island, sir. We're marooned on it... he, he... after four weeks; it's silly, isn't it, that we can't get away from it?

(he laughs, then stops suddenly)

I'd like to stay right here and let the sun eat me, sir. But, but I'd rather die back there -- I'd rather drown myself there than be shrivelled up by the sun. I would, true to God, sir. Yes, I am ready... sure, very sure, sir.

(Long pause. They get slowly to their feet, turn about to face the direction from which they have come)

KING: Uh... uh... ready... all right, Mr Burke, sir.

(trudging back)

One, two, three, four, one, two, three, four, with, more, than prayers, must, a, man, com… pete...

(Blackout.

At the opening of the next scene, KING is ostensibly trying to get a camel to its feet. BURKE and WILLS watch him, the hope draining from them as they do so. When he has little success, they help him pull and push)

BURKE: (losing his temper) Shoot him, Mr King! Get rid of the lazing, shamming brute!

KING: He'll be all right, sir He's just sickening a bit, that's all. He'll get over it or around. A camel's lonely that's lost his mate the previous day. He'll soon find out that it's not worth his life to pick and choose his company.

BURKE: (determinedly) Shoot the beast, King! He can no longer stand. He's done up and that's all there is to it.

KING: We'll be lost without him, sir.

BURKE: King, I don't need you to point out something that's so painfully obvious, man.
    (pause)
Now do what I say.

KING: (a plea) Can't our three pairs of legs speak for his life, sir? Speaking from mine, he's worth a hope. Can't we hope upon a beast? Can't we hope, sir? And trust?

BURKE: (booming) Trust? Trust what, King? Trust providence? Trust justice? Trust fortune? Trust men, King?

(Pause)

KING: (meekly) Just the grit of a lonely camel, sir.

BURKE: That's all there'll be of him soon. Grit. If we don't finish him off now, he'll go away, die somewhere and rot; we need his meat while we can get at it.
    (pause)

Now, King, listen to me. We got through to the Gulf and back again by sheer guts. Gray died, but we still got through by going to the limit. Now, by thunder and hell, we're not going to perish by waiting around to nurse a sick camel! We'll take our chance without it. Now shoot the lazy brute. And then do what you must.

> *(He turns away, moves off a few paces. WILLS puts his hand on KING's shoulder solicitously, then joins BURKE. They keep their backs turned)*

KING: (sobbing in frustration) Poor Rajah, poor boy. You're done up, did you hear what the boss said? He passed judgement on you because he's the one who can. It's silly to pretend your meat's your own to do what you will. It'll come in more handy to help us do what we want. So Rajah, my fine animal of mine, the next time you'll get up will be to hang up to dry. But I'll make it swift and as quick as that. I'll leave it to the bullet to make it outright deadly for you. We've come a long way, Rajah, haven't we, you and I? Right from India I brought you. But won't take you back. We'll... we'll be lost without you, old boy.

> *(Blackout. A shot through the dark)*

KING'S VOICE: Can you get leather from a camel's hide, Mr Wills?

> *(When lighting returns, it emphasises KING pounding nardoo seed. He is alone on stage and obviously feels alone. From time to he stops, remains motionless with head bowed, then, with visible effort, resumes pounding. BURKE enters from back right. He is singing, is happy -- but euphorically so)*

BURKE: (singing)
In Dublin's fair city, where the girl are so pretty,
I first set my eyes on sweet Molly Malone
As she wheel'd her wheelbarrow through streets broad and narrow,
Crying cockles and mussels! Alive, alive O!
Alive, alive, O! Alive, alive, O!
Crying cockles and mussels! Alive, alive O!

BURKE: Are you a theatre man, King, my boy? Do you often fly to the theatre with your heart full of song? Light opera's me favourite. I don't know about you. Light opera for me, lad...
How happy could I be with either,
Were t'other dear charmer away!
But while you thus tease me together,
To neither a word would I say,
But,
Tol-de-rol, lol-de-rol lady,
Tol-de-rol, lol-de-rol ray,
Tol, tol-de-rol, tol-de-rol, lady,
Tol, lol-de-rol, lol-de-rol lay.
Know that, boy? Beggar's Opera, Macheath to Polly and Lucy. Know it, boy? I do. I should after all.

KING: No, no sir. There's too much in it for me.

BURKE: A young man needs a dream to follow to go to the opera. An old man too. I'll tell you something, boy. I had a dream; that's what made me go. But it was a live one... a dream to hang your hopes on. One as pretty as an angel too. I saw more performances of that opera than you've got fingers.
   (hums, stops, thinks.)
And when I get back, King, that opera's going to see more of me. I'll watch my sweetheart playing her pretty Polly Peachum. By God, I will!
Tol-de-rol, tol-de-rol lady,
Tol,
Lol-de-rol, lol-de-rol lady.

   (Pause)

BURKE: (grandiosely) When we ride back into Melbourne, you won't be able to keep your horse's head, there'll be so much noise. If the bands don't bolt it, or the crowds don't scare it, then the flutter of your heart will, boy.
   (he gets his hat, jaunts.)
Just picture it, King, Melbourne'll be more awake than it's ever been before -- or since we left. We'll ride down Elizabeth Street to the tune of cheering -- bearing the envy of almost too many people. Your back will be straighter than it's ever been, your head knocked back by the

punch of awed stares. Your name when it's called, you can treat with disdain and buildings will rock with people joining in the cheering. Our horses' hoofs will be cushioned by a carpet of hats. That is, those not in the air, boy. And... and the first night back, we'll all -- the three of us -- we'll go to the opera in nothing but style. They'll put on The Beggar's Opera especially for us, and people will clap us more than the show for choosing so well. Centre seats in the front row, there we'll be led while everyone stands up and claps as we come. Even the players will stand and look until we're settled down right, and...
(decrepitly)
and Polly Peachum won't have to stay poor any more, Mr King. Never poor any more. Please be to God.

KING: (to change the subject) You found the blacks, sir?

BURKE: (confused) What?

KING: You found the blacks?

BURKE: (suddenly bitter) Yes, yes, we found them. They were very friendly, King. As friendly Mr Wills likes. They fed us with food as a white man does a starving bird. They gave us whatever we begged for.
(pause)
I'll give the rogues this; whatever we grovelled for on our knees, they handed over. I'll give us this as well; whatever they throw at us, we'll use, won't we?

KING: They'd help us no end if we'd let them, wouldn't they, sir?

BURKE: (lost in his own thought) But then we had nothing on us that they could steal anyway. Except these strips passing for clothes or the teeth from the gums in our heads. They'd see us dead for those too.

KING: They're kind enough, sir. They know we're desperate.

BURKE: They're primitives, King. They don't know the word for charity unless it's for a measure of something we've got that they plan to steal. Don't worry, boy, they'd take our very fire if they could edge us over enough. They can't be watched with too many eyes. I'd repeat that if I didn't know that I've told it to you a hundred times.

180

Lord knows what they'll do to us once they've got sick of the homage we're paying them. They'll cut our throats.

KING: They've been good to us, sir! For our lives, we need them, sir!

BURKE: (bitterly) Yes, we need them. I know that. We need pagan hides to make ours live. We need them. Blacks with the right for us to live. And why not? Oh, I ask, my boy, I ask. Why not? We need them to give us their food or we'll starve by our own. Neither you nor Mr Wills have to tell me that. But if they steal all we've got, then we're just as done up. And it will be because we've gone begging to them.
   (suddenly)
How far must we go down before calling a halt? Falling on our knees lower than the animals we've had to shoot. I've had enough!

KING: Oh sir, how pitifully we've been left!

BURKE: King, my brother was killed, not wanting for anything, on the shores of the Black Sea in '54. His head left his body having been severed from behind after thirty-three wounds hadn't cut off its flow. He was the ninth to be killed on that spot; the eight others before were none but his enemies. I was a Hungarian Hussar, an officer for the bodyguard of the Hapsburg, Ferdinand. Am I now, King, to die like this -- what's promised to us three? A dried-up beggar at the feet of damn natives. To smile at pagans for my life?

   (He looks about shiftily)

BURKE: Must I now suffer a band of them approach me, belying sly smiles and baiting me with crude fish nets like they do when catching their fish?
   (cannot let the bitterness alone)
Must I patiently nod and cower in front and swallow their taunts before the leftovers they fling at me? Is it an attack of fish nets that I must now repel? Is it? Is it that then?

   (Illusion of tribespeople approaching him. He takes a few wary steps backwards)

181

BURKE: Is it our things you're after, you bandits? Eh?

(Petulantly, he picks up his gun, and whispers to KING)

BURKE: I know their intentions. I'll advance alone. Keep our things close, King, and more than watch their course. If they do anything funny don't hesitate to shoot.

KING: (in fear) Be careful, Mr Burke! Be careful, sir! If we could trust them, I'm sure they'd be our friends!

BURKE: What do you want, eh? We'll come to you if we need your help; so there's no need to trouble your little schemes. Fish, eh?
    (peering warily, and smiling knowingly)
Thank you kindly. We'll have a feast and think of you. Put them down on the ground where you're standing.
    (suddenly shouting)
On the ground, I said! Down!
    (he backs off as his imaginaries advance)
Blast your hides! What do you want? That's close enough for sport...
What? No, you don't get on your way! We'll thank your backs or shoot your fronts! Get on with you... oh no, you don't!

(He swings into violent action, knocking imaginary fish from nets)

BURKE: Uh... uh... shoot, King! Shoot! Shoot some hides!

(He fires his gun into the air. His imaginaries apparently run)

BURKE: (exhausted) Godless...

(WILLS enters running from back left. He stops when he sees BURKE and KING, then looks after the Aborigines)

WILLS: Oh no, Mr Burke, you've driven them off. Again, you've insulted them again.

BURKE: They... they came to molest us, to steal our things, Mr Wills.

182

WILLS: (looking at the ground) With fish?

BURKE: (seriously) Yes... with fish, man.

WILLS: (remonstrant) Mr Burke, we can't eat without their help.

BURKE: (miserably) Nor can I without mine.

WILLS: We've got to be friendly to them.

BURKE: (booming) Who wants to exist by their help, by God Almighty? I'd rather they speared me than taunt me to death!

WILLS: They're human beings! More human than us now! You have your choice.

BURKE: (angrily) I know what choice, Wills.

> *(A gust of wind. They turn their backs as it whips them with dust. They straighten, not noticing that it has blown a spark from the fire onto the lean-to in which they keep their things. They don't see the initial smoking)*

BURKE: (more evenly) You'll have to have patience with me. If I had tried to teach myself what you're trying to teach me now, I would have killed myself long ago. This is not Burke.

WILLS: I'll go and see what I can do to make friends with them again.

> *(The lean-to leaps into flames)*

KING: Mr Burke! Mr Wills! The shelter!

> *(They scramble to it, but are beaten back.*
>
> *They can only watch as it burns itself quickly out and slowly dies.*
>
> *Long despairing pause)*

183

BURKE: (brokenly) The stores... everything. It was my idea to keep them in there. Nothing left. Mr Wills, I...
    (brokenly)
Oh, why this total rejection, man?

> *(BURKE almost convulses with rage mixed with frustration and helplessness.*
>
> *When he stops, he looks at the others, his outstretched hands indicating pleading.*
>
> *WILLS and KING can only stare back at him mutely, but their bodies bend together almost jointly, under the inexorable realization that they must surely perish now.*
>
> *With this tableau, lights dim... and slow curtain)*

(End Act 1)

Act 2

(Lighting emphasis on the rescue camp again. KING is back on his bed roll; BRAHE sits on a stool by his side and is looking down at him. Stillness, almost a tableau.

KING slowly awakens. His eyes open wide and stare upward for a time before he makes a sudden and ineffectual movement to get up. He falls back, then turns his head towards BRAHE)

BRAHE: I never really left you, King.

KING: Uh...

BRAHE: I never really left you, man.

(KING continues to stare at him)

BRAHE: Patton died, King. You don't know that yet. But he did. He died on the way down. After all that, he still died of scurvy, poor beggar. We couldn't feed him; his food went in one end, and ran out of the other.
    (pause)
Patton dead. I didn't even have to go; he died anyway. It all needn't have happened.

KING: Patton... dead?

BRAHE: (passionately) Just understand. Just understand what it was like, that's all.

KING: You left us... no clothes.
    (gathers breath.)
Not a thing. Our own clothes you took away... You're a... you're a blasted fool, Brahe.

BRAHE: (helplessly) Understand.

KING: (with some energy, on his elbow) You don't know... you don't know what they're like, the nights up here. Sand storms tear the skin

185

off you. At nights, at nights, the cold comes and you've got to knot yourself up. No... sleep. Burning. Hands, feet, your... head with cold. You scratch at your own flesh. Brahe? No sleep. Look upwards, that's it. Keep your eyes closed. Grip. Grip Mr Burke. Grip Mr Wills. Gripping a cold body...

(He falls back, seems to doze, but then is startled awake by mental demons)

KING: *Brahe*?!
(seeing him)
You lie there and freeze, Brahe.

BRAHE: (pitifully) I... know.

KING: (struggling to ward off sleep) ... Brahe?

BRAHE: I'm here, man.

KING: A curse on you, Brahe.

(He is overcome by sleep. BRAHE watches him)

BRAHE: You should've died as well, John King.

(He gets up and ascertains that KING is asleep)

BRAHE: (bitterly) What about Wright, King? What about him? I'm not going to take this on my own. I've kept my mouth shut for too long. You'll find out some of it, but not all, boyo.
(degenerates into pathos and irony)
You'll find out that I came across him with his party, stranded, on the way down. Yes, Wright. Burke's great bushman. Stranded, with his party on the waterhole at Bullo with five of his men dying on him, his animals about to drop and the blacks at him. He'd had enough when I met him. He was all for turning around and getting back to Menindee. He was for leaving us all marooned up here.
(pause)
That's our Wright. That's Wright. Even when I turned up, he was all for turning back. He reckoned you and Burke were done for anyway.

186

He wasn't going to get sweaty finding out. So he gave his orders and we all started back. A long, black hospital train.

(The stockade and the 'DIG' tree are spotlit behind him. The stage gradually becomes evenly lit)

BRAHE: Even a man like Wright has curiosity, King. The next day, he camped and said he and I were going to ride back here to the stockade. To take a look. The rest were going to wait for us. And that's what we did. Fifteen days after you'd left the depot -- May the 8th -- we arrived back there to whiff your breeze.

(WRIGHT enters back right behind him. And stands looking at the tree and the stockade. He stands confidently. He is a logical man, with a good deal of self-assurance. BRAHE continues to talk towards KING through WRIGHT's entrance)

BRAHE: May the 8th, King. Until I die, I'll know that whatever else I'll do, I'll be no more to myself than I was that day.
   (longingly)
You've yourself, King. You'll never know your limit. You can sleep. You could even have died easily.

WRIGHT: (suddenly speaking to BRAHE) So this is it, is it? A pretty little stockade to be sure.

(BRAHE turns, walks naturally over to WRIGHT in centre stage. Lighting emphasis, if any, is off the rescue camp)

BRAHE: It had to last a long time.

WRIGHT: It outlasted you.

BRAHE: Nobody can last in this vacuum. You get tired of the company. You get tired of not having company. I got tired. I got tired of building the stockade. I, could, not, finish it. I didn't think of Melbourne. I thought of mud and ants and the shadow of the hawk passing over my foot. Sometimes. But, mainly, I didn't think of finishing the stockade. I built it.

WRIGHT: (sarcastically) Desirable summer residence.

LIVING IN BLACK HOLES

BRAHE: What would you have thought about it after a few nights...
   (pointedly)
if you'd arrived, that is. If you had arrived like Burke told you to,
Wright.

> *(WRIGHT moves quickly away, dismissively. BRAHE stares at
> him uncomprehendingly. WRIGHT speaks 'evidence' formally,
> into the air, as though a witness at the commission of inquiry)*

WRIGHT: I started with Mr Brahe and three horses at Cooper's
Creek.

BRAHE: (into the air) What's happened to you?

> *(He gets no reply)*

BRAHE: Why didn't you come up?

WRIGHT: (evidence) I thought that by going back it would still give
Burke two or three weeks longer.

BRAHE: (nodding) There was still a chance.

WRIGHT: I stayed there and had a look around the place.

> *(BRAHE nods at the suggestion, walks around. He looks at the
> flap of leather that was used as the stockade door and from
> which KING had cut a large square)*

BRAHE: That's funny. Funny.

WRIGHT: (evidence) Everything was just as Brahe left it.

BRAHE: A square's been cut out of our leather flap.

WRIGHT: (evidence) The chances were the blacks, as I supposed
they had been at the depot...

BRAHE: A square? A near perfect square?

WRIGHT: (evidence answer) I was not sure whether the blacks were watching us.

BRAHE: What have they got to cut leather so well?
   (thinks, then startled:)
The box...

   (He hesitates, goes over to the tree, inspects the ground)

BRAHE: (with relief) Not disturbed. (measuring) Three paces. I struck roots digging. Nobody helped. You would have thought that somebody could have come to help...
   (looking)
Hold on, I could have sworn I left the rake against the stockade, not here.

WRIGHT: (evidence) Certain things, but the natives could have been playing.

   (BRAHE considers, then nods)

BRAHE: The blacks might have been playing some game...

WRIGHT: (meaningfully) I thought it advisable to be quick about it.

   (BRAHE nods, as though acknowledging some voice in his ear, and carries on with his examination. He notices some tacks, bends down, comes across more. He walks around, bending down frequently to look at various things. In this way, he comes across the ashes of three fireplaces and, nearby, half-burnt and broken pieces of wooden stools)

BRAHE: There's -- things -- here!

WRIGHT: (dismissing him) Everything was just as Brahe had left it.

   (BRAHE picks up a singularly battered pair of boots, takes down strips of leather hanging on the stockade wall, finds a discarded billy and a heap of nails. He looks up)

189

BRAHE: Some people -- Europeans -- have camped here since I left, Wright. Wright?
   (getting no reply)
Take a look at these camel tracks. Take a look at these footprints. Look at these ashes, ashes, three different places from ours. After four months, I know. I made my own track around this place for four months. Around, around, heel where heel is, toe where toe was...
   (confused)
that's not what I'm trying to tell you.

WRIGHT: (impatiently, directly to him) Blacks, blacks.

BRAHE: Blacks, no, blacks not to have broken up our old stools for firewood.

   (WRIGHT withdraws)

BRAHE: Why don't you speak?

WRIGHT: (giving evidence) There were two or three fires about the place, which I supposed had been made by blacks. I looked at those fires particularly, and there was not a stick of wood as large as one of the pens on the table here just as an aboriginal makes a fire; he just brings what is enough to keep a fire, and no more.

BRAHE: I can't understand you. Why won't he look? These... these nails scattered by someone, these strips of leather made up for something, the square out of our flap... this billy; these, these boots. McDonough left a pair behind, Wright, but these aren't them. These've been walked into the ground. Shredded, Wright. Why won't he look?

WRIGHT: (re-emphasised evidence) Brahe found everything as it was, according to his account.

BRAHE: (pleading) I've told you!

WRIGHT: I thought it better to be getting on.

BRAHE: (suddenly) My God, Wright, let's dig, let's dig!

*(He scrambles over to the tree and claws away the earth.
WRIGHT makes no effort to help him. BRAHE pulls out the
cache, struggles to get it open)*

BRAHE: Uh... uh... it's... (flinging open the lid) ... empty! Wright,
it's empty!

*(WRIGHT does not answer or move. BRAHE pulls out the
bottle, tugs out a note from it, reads:)*

BRAHE: It's a note from... Burke returned, the 21st... that's the...
that's the day I left!

(Stunned pause)

BRAHE: How could he return the same day I left? Where are you?
Wright! Help me out!

WRIGHT: (deadpan) I understand.

BRAHE: How can you?

WRIGHT: I understand. Coincidence or bad timing, amounts to the
same.

BRAHE: How can you understand that?

WRIGHT: (unconcerned) Coincidence.

BRAHE: (shaking his fist) Wright, listen, I want to touch that
coincidence. I want to take it by the throat.

*(WRIGHT turns away, collects a few pieces of the stools, heaps
them together, lights a fire, puts on a billy)*

BRAHE: What are you doing? I don't get you. People don't sit
around making fires.
   (watching, fascinated)
 For mercy's sake, talk to me!

(Long pause. BRAHE turns away, stares into the distance. His

voice is dampened at first, rising to near hysterics of ineptitude;
the vocal cadence to a mental image of BURKE struggling)

BRAHE: They might be starving out there. All you want to do is
squat down to tea. Heat simmers, heat shimmers, Burke is slowly
moving. The three of them moving, moving. I left them enough to eat.
They ought to have enough, they would have enough. They should
have enough. But they might be starving with the sun beating down.
They might be gasping with the sun beating down. Lead in their legs,
their chests gone tight. My head feels light. Dizzy, dizzy, with the sun
beating down and heat simmering, heat shimmering, Burke is slowly
moving. Oh, I left them some tea. I left them that.
    (desperately)
You've got to move, Wright.

WRIGHT: (deadpan) Burke's gone again. Wait till it boils.

BRAHE: We're not going to swill tea, Wright. Can't swill tea. People
can't sit around making fires, swilling tea. The dust around here,
what's holding you down. We've got to go after them!

WRIGHT: Wait till the tea's on the go. Wait until the family's settled
in Adelaide. Wait till the salary's guaranteed. I was waiting as I had
no instruction from the Committee.

BRAHE: (very alone) They might be just up the creek waiting for me.
Might be, kneeling, ears to the ground, knocking for Brahe... Nobody
realises that can happen!

WRIGHT: (factually) Have you cocked your gun?

BRAHE: I can't. What are you talking about? I can't.

WRIGHT: Fire away. Blast a rat.

    (Long pause, while BRAHE stares at him)

BRAHE: (displaying letter) Burke says he's going towards Mount
Hopeless, but is weak. Burke says that they're just about done up. He
says they're on their last legs.
    (pathetically)

Why did he want to go and say that?

WRIGHT: The gun cocked, now pull the trigger.

> *(BRAHE makes no movement, except to handle the gun indecisively)*

WRIGHT: But nothing comes near anybody out here. Does it?

BRAHE: (stopping dead) Has someone said that to me before?

WRIGHT: (as evidence) We remained, I suppose, I could not tell exactly, not more than a quarter of an hour at the depot.
    (then casually to BRAHE)
A night won't make much difference one way or another. Hard riding tomorrow.

BRAHE: (thinking hard) A night? It's getting darkish... What was that?
    (listens)
Nothing there. Burke and the parrots stopping for supper now. I left him food. Five weeks' worth. It's all I had left.

WRIGHT: It's all he had. It's all Brahe had to leave. He said.

BRAHE: (reacting) It's all we had, I tell you! (trying to get comfort from him) You don't know how tired you get up here after a while. It's almost too much to raise a gun. When you get up in the morning you dream for the sunset. It comes to clothe you in for the morning again. And the gum tree there, across the waterline.

WRIGHT: (mocking) Originally nine months' stores for eight men. Four go away to cross a continent with only three months' worth on the backs. So four are left with nine months' worth plus that much more...

BRAHE: We didn't have all that much! It goes down, out. It... went.

WRIGHT: (pressing) Of the six camels brought back by Mr Brahe, three were in good condition. His horses, too, were travelling with much less difficulty than could be hoped for.

BRAHE: Why won't you say something? Nobody instructed me to kill those animals for meat! Nobody said they weren't for carrying us back down.

    (gathers breath, then quieter)

A tough journey going back down by ourselves, without Burke. Patton laid up. We might have taken months. The camels with scabs. All of us with scurvy. I itched. I itched. Can I scratch my back? It's no good. The ground spins at your feet, bending like that to shoe the horses. It was to have been a tough journey back down, but I met... you. I was to survive. I had to have my share, fair share, too.

WRIGHT: Four weeks' worth.

BRAHE: (desperately into the air) Five! Come down, come down, I'll give you a number!

WRIGHT: (shrugging) Burke's condition two weeks ago...

BRAHE: Five, four, what does it matter? (keenly) He mightn't have been as bad as he says here!

WRIGHT: (nodding) Burke resting here for a couple of days. Burke, Wills and King in pretty bad shape. With no clothing left. Burke's boots marching into the ground...

BRAHE: He's got McDonough's old pair!

WRIGHT: (encouragingly, fatherly) Yes. And still two camels left. Still Burke's two camels. All knocked up, but in one day, Burke is travelling at least...

BRAHE: (beginning to understand) Ten. I'd get to ten miles.

WRIGHT: (into the air) I put it at eight.

BRAHE: Ten miles; I'd get to ten.

WRIGHT: I left it at eight.

BRAHE: (excited) Burke is travelling at ten, eight, twelve... twenty, why not, why not? Burke might be a hundred and twenty miles away by now. It's in the note. It says...

(WRIGHT has moved near BRAHE, whispers persuasively into his ear)

WRIGHT: It says that Burke is going to the mountain. Burke bent on the outpost at the mountain. Burke, once stranded, is not waiting for a miracle.

BRAHE: (hypnotically) Funny, Wright, listen, Wright, the miracle was that Brahe, me, I, Brahe left them stranded.

WRIGHT: (not to be put off) Now Burke is a hundred and twenty miles away. Now. At least.

BRAHE: (nodding) Now Burke is a hundred and twenty miles away at least.

WRIGHT: (paternally) And the Mount is only a hundred and fifty miles away from here. There. Now you know.

BRAHE: Now I know Burke is only thirty miles from the Mount now. Now I know...
    (realising and brushing him off)
Nobody has a right to talk to me like that!

WRIGHT: (persistently, finally swaying with BRAHE) Now Burke knows he is only thirty miles away from the Mount. Burke is panting near the outpost. Burke is not holding back in search of miracles. Burke even now perhaps on his way to Adelaide along a red carpet.

(Smiling, WRIGHT eventually withdraws, kneels by the fire behind BRAHE)

BRAHE: (recovering his senses) I'm supposing all this! It must be right.
    (suddenly)
But I don't know what sort of country they have to plough through, Wright! I don't know. How could I know? I had to stay locked up

here. Patton knocked up. One man to feed all the horses, graze them. The Afghan scared of blacks, useless. Food, stores, keeping a look out. For Burke. Or you. For you or Burke. Where are you? (no reply; quieter) I know there's fish in that creek, but how do you catch them?
(fierce whisper)
The blasted natives could catch them. I thought of death while I was locked up here.

WRIGHT: (sudden evidence) I knew that Gregory took only a week to do the same trip to the Mount in '58.

BRAHE: |fascinated) Gregory? Didn't Gregory have... fresh men, horses?
(pause)
Burke has a camel, hasn't he? Two.

WRIGHT: Feet like cushions. Beasts to carry a man right across Australia and back, and then on to the Mount on cushions.

BRAHE: (uncertain again) I'll think quietly, make a decision.

WRIGHT keeps up the pressure by jumping up and speaking fiercely into his ear.

WRIGHT: If a man travelled a quarter as fast as Gregory, he'd be there even before you started out after. If a man was left five weeks' rations, he is not going to starve in a two-week trip. If two men, with only one pack horse between them and only two weeks' supply, even supposing they could stretch it out, tried to catch him, they would rot on a sandy plain. If two men think they can go out into a blank with only two weeks' rations, liable to be speared by some black butcher and with their own party over a hundred miles away in the other direction, then they must think like fools or their horses have wings.

BRAHE: (suddenly) I'll be put on the rack for deserting my post, Wright! Burke will point his finger at me...

(WRIGHT whips away again in annoyance, and from association)

WRIGHT: (evidence) I would have marked the tree as an indication had I had the presence of mind.

BRAHE: (on the attack) Presence of mind? Four months and five days I waited up here for you. You never turned hide nor hair to do what Burke told you. Except. Except your back and that was on me. You left us all to rot up here.

(No reaction from WRIGHT)

BRAHE: Wright? Don't put me off, man. Don't put me off. I've got excuses. I had my reasons too.

WRIGHT: A token. Token.

BRAHE: (taken aback) Patton was dying! He was my responsibility!

WRIGHT: (in a whisper) So was Burke, in a way, a way.

(BRAHE stops short, listens. Silence)

BRAHE: (sotto voce) You heard whisperings of your name if you listened at night. When McDonough gets tired of singing, Patton comes groaning, the Afghan is snoring, strange bush noises slide off the moon and shiver an old-time and whisper whisper Brahe Brahe whispering Brahe... I waited four months and five days. My ears buzzed with it. Whisperings. In your ear. What can you do?
    (pause, then breathlessly)
Listen. Is that someone coming?
    (louder)
Is that someone over there, on the horizon?
    (suddenly holding his head)
I don't want to know.

(WRIGHT looks up at the sky. The lights gradually dim to twilight. He nods slowly)

WRIGHT: (paternally) Time to sleep now. Turn over in your thoughts lying down.

BRAHE: (frantically) They're talking down to me. It's come to that. And the dogs howl of an old-time, whisper, hear it coming, in your ear. I... I had my reasons, Wright!

(He gets no reply; pause)

BRAHE: (without energy) Nowhere. I've got to get up and get something going.

WRIGHT: (evidence) As I was anxious to ascertain before finally leaving the area, whether Mr Burke had visited the depot at Cooper's Creek or whether the stores had been disturbed by natives...

BRAHE: That can't be enough.
   (drops tiredly to his knees.)
Tired. Burke's finger pointing at me. You, Wright. At you, too.

WRIGHT: (evidence) Mr Burke used to alter his mind so very often, it was not possible to understand what he really did mean at times.

BRAHE: I think I'll have to go away from here. Things in my head, whisperings, think I'll stay up.

WRIGHT: Dreams in your mind, that's all.

BRAHE: (wrestling with an anguishing image) I... about Burke and King somewhere around here. Something about... ah, where is Wills? Look, sweating. I'm sweating. What does it mean?

WRIGHT: (drawing near again) Burke asleep on feathers tonight. Burke off the Mount, down to Adelaide. Burke cheered towards civilization.

BRAHE: (fatalistic) No, I know he's not.

(WRIGHT pats him on the shoulder in an avuncular manner, then leaves him to his thoughts. He prepares to sleep)

WRIGHT: (while doing so) I thought of camping there that night, but Dr Beckler of my own party had said to me: 'You see the position you are in and the responsibility in your hands. Here are men who will die. You have buried three already. You will be sacrificing these others too for Burke who, more than likely will never come back this way.' Dr Beckler of my own party said that. I had to take his advice, of course.

BRAHE: (huskily) Smell the rats...

WRIGHT: (above him) This morning I reached Cooper's Creek and found no sign of Mr Burke having visited the creek, nor of the natives having disturbed the stores...

BRAHE: Can you smell the rats, body grease, body grease, the stench of dingo bones?

(WRIGHT gets up again, walks past BRAHE, proceeds to re-bury the box by the tree)

WRIGHT: (straining) Everything was as Mr Brahe had left it, according to his account. And being over-cautious, I would not. Take up the box. To put a note in. It.
   (finishes and wipes his hands)
Still, Burke could have seen my horse tracks, which I left as a signal where the cache was buried. I remarked to Brahe he ought to have buried it two or three days before he left and put the horses in under the shade there to avert the natives.
   (heavy irony)
Everything was as Mr Brahe had left it. According to his account.

(BRAHE slowly brings his head around to look at WRIGHT, who returns the took defiantly. He nods at BRAHE. BRAHE, reluctantly at first, nods back his agreement. They speak in counterpoint)

BRAHE: (likewise evidence) I tied my horse up, and so I believe did Wright, near the cache.

WRIGHT: And I said: 'At all events we will put our horses in here now and the blacks will never think of digging there.'
   (as he kicks dirt over the things left by BURKE)
There was no mark obvious above ground showing that Burke had been there.

BRAHE: Because... because of the place being dusty. And... the number of rats. All those rats.

WRIGHT: Mr Brahe immediately placed himself under my orders.

BRAHE: I immediately placed myself under the orders of Mr Wright. (pause, then barely audible) What did we do with the box?

WRIGHT: It's done.

BRAHE: I saw no impression of human feet?

WRIGHT: Done, done.

BRAHE: (continuing evidence) I know a great many things now that I could not know then. If I had known they would have returned the night they did, I should have remained there certainly. If I had any reasons for expecting them back there at all, I would have certainly perished rather than have left...

WRIGHT: I thought the natives had been there...

BRAHE: A few camel tracks, but I supposed them to be ours...

WRIGHT: Natives, on account of the three different fireplaces...

BRAHE: (suddenly\ I want to get away!

WRIGHT: (above him) I suppose, I could not tell exactly, not more than a quarter of an hour at the depot.

> *(Long pause, then BRAHE sinks to the ground, ostensibly to sleep. WRIGHT kneels beside him, pats his shoulder conspiratorially)*

BRAHE: I said I'd lie here quietly, make a decision.

WRIGHT: (almost as a lullaby) And Burke lies back in civilization. Now Burke is cheered in civilization. Adelaide, Melbourne, the way between, and all the streets ablaze. What's done is done now to the final cheer.

BRAHE: (softly) I'll have to... cheer.

(BRAHE settles down. WRIGHT waits until the man seems reasonably quiet, then lies down himself. Lights dim to semi-darkness. Stillness. Suddenly BRAHE raises himself up on one elbow)

BRAHE: Ssh! (listens.) Nothing. Nothing.

(He looks over to WRIGHT, who is already sleeping)

BRAHE: So you've finally come, eh? A bit late. A bit late, Wright. You don't know how I've been waiting for you!

(Then sleeps himself. Stage is blacked out. Through the darkness, heavy grunting and the irregular thudding of rock upon rock.

Slowly the lighting emphasises downstage centre, where BURKE and KING, obviously in states of extreme weakness, are trying to pound nardoo plant. Near them, WILLS lies spent on a makeshift bed of leaves)

BURKE: (weakening) Uh...
    (drops the stone.)
A little rest for a heavy arm... that's useless for pounding any more.

KING: Much more, sir? Much more of putting in what we can't get out of a native plant?

BURKE: With your last load, we should have enough, boy.

KING: It's small but so heavy, sir.

BURKE: (soothing) All right.

KING: (suddenly) How much will we need? I must ask you that, sir, though I know the answer is not for us.

BURKE: We'll leave Mr Wills four days' worth and take enough for two days. That's fifty per cent well divided.

KING: It's been decided then, sir?

BURKE: We've got no other choice.

KING: (agitated) No, sir, no. It's the clouds that are hardest of it all to bear. I tell you what, sir, I've been watching those clouds. They're as barren as the land between here and the Mount. I'm sure you'd find them all dust if they were laid in your way and you had to go through them.

BURKE: It's more than those that are empty, boy. Look around. The blacks have gone. They've deserted us. God only knows where they've pushed off to.
   (pause)
John, never in my wildest fancies did I think we'd end like this!

KING: An end's an end, sir.

BURKE: (defiantly) No, there's finishes to a man that he can imagine and some that he can't. For me there was no such thing as Burke sitting in a black's deserted camp, eating the scraps they'd left behind and praying to God they'd return for his life. Except...

KING: Excepting what of what, sir?

BURKE: ... except with a gun cocked near his head.

KING: (high-pitched voice) Oh, sir, help's on the way. It still is in my mind and that's a start.

BURKE: Don't waste thoughts on hope, boy; it's a miracle we want. A man's got to do that when he doesn't expect the ship that's marooned him to come back!

KING: Even so, sir, my thoughts are too silly for anything to happen. Sir, I'm laughing inside, on the Lord's own truth. It's just that I can't believe John King's sitting behind this voice or you yourself are where you are. Or Mr Wills is watching us now, helpless to help, unable to walk and just able to crawl. It tickles my side because it's really not me. I mean, even when I'm done up, I only want to sleep.

BURKE: You're only twenty-two, aren't you? That's young to have been led into this. You've still the stamp of life upon you.
    (pause)
I'm sorry, John.

    (Embarrassed silence. KING begins to pound some more)

KING: I'll just finish this lot, sir.

BURKE: Never mind. You've baked the seed I told you?

KING: Yes, sir. Over there. Golden in colour, golden in worth to Mr Wills.

BURKE: For us all. (pause.) Water?

KING: Enough to quench him, sir, if he can swallow it down.

BURKE: Wood?

KING: Enough to keep a cold hand full for a good few days, sir. It's laid down by him; there'll be fire to spare.

BURKE: Books?

KING: All buried in lots by his feet but away from the fire.

BURKE: (with bitter irony) Done, eh? The notes, journals, records of the highly esteemed Victorian Exploring Expedition kept to the last and buried with honours for no one to see.

KING: It seems like a grave, sir. You make them sound like a corpse.

BURKE: They're a corpse all right... that is, of what we were. If we don't find those blacks, we'll perish out here and while nature's not kind to the folds of the skin, she'll preserve for time pieces of paper. In time a man may look at their graves and say to the world: 'Here lies the remains of Burke, Wills, and King; not in that order but any way you like.' How would that be, John?

KING: (outcry) Too hard to our extremes, sir.

   (BURKE manages to control himself)

BURKE: Perhaps.
   (pause)
 The letter to his father?

KING: It's in your pack.

BURKE: It'll be heavy to carry and hard to deliver... Anything else?

KING: Sir, I prayed last night, more than once.

BURKE: (wistfully) Yes, I heard you myself. It was hard to keep up.

KING: The cold's a claw that drags you down.

BURKE: Well, there's no reason to delay much more or longer. The cold won't wait nor will the blacks for us and neither should we.

KING: No, sir, if it's been decided...

BURKE: This decision had only one choice.

KING: (looking at WILLS) God rest his soul. I'm ready, sir.

BURKE: And so are we all, except to say, John... I want you to know I tried my all.

KING: Oh, I know, I know.

BURKE: Well...

   (He gets up, followed by KING. They go towards WILLS)

BURKE: (looking, sotto voce) My God, there's more to death than just dying like that. We'll have to find those blacks in shorter days than most -- or die with the looking.

KING: Or die with the looking, sir...

BURKE: (calling) Mr Wills? John?

(WILLS looks up and with the help o/KING gets to his feet)

WILLS: (able to half smile) Ready?

BURKE: A scanty post we're leaving you with, John... water, nardoo and enough wood for keeping you warm. It's providence's help you'll be comfortable with, but ours... ours is the help that'll get you by.

WILLS: Thank you both.

BURKE: It's... it's our thanks to you, sir, that'll keep you most warm.

WILLS: And mine to give you God's speed...

BURKE: John, tell me again that you'll have it this way...

WILLS: I've had no other thoughts. The... the blacks'll be kind and you'll sprint back to me. I must wait at the finish for when you come home...

BURKE: John...

WILLS: (quickly) You seem ready enough.

BURKE: The trek's been long... but I'll never be ashamed of the way you walked beside me.

WILLS: Oh, slightly behind, sir. None better deserved that full pace ahead. Thank you.

BURKE: (quickly) We're away from you... (to KING) The packs please, John.

WILLS: You have my letter? My watch?

BURKE: Yes.

WILLS: (to KING) My pistol?

KING: It's my company of you, sir.

BURKE: (holding out his hand) If there wasn't a chance... no attraction on earth would pull me away.

(They shake hands)

BURKE: Have you all you need?

WILLS: I have a pencil and a field book to plot. There's many a man who'd be half so content.

BURKE: You're incorrigible, John. But you know all that.

WILLS: (smiling weakly) It's God's good grace.

(BURKE turns away, waits for KING)

KING: (over his shoulder) Goodbye... Mr Wills. Goodbye to you, sir.

(They start their last trek.

WILLS drops on all fours, then sinks to the ground.

Blackout of stage, then two spotlights -- one on BURKE and KING struggling to keep going; the other on BRAHE who tosses and talks in his sleep)

BRAHE: (with energy) On, Wright, on let's get on -- dust and my eyes oh, and let's get home where is my...

ECHOES: (taking over\ darling, dust, dust, Brahe's your darling Brahe, is, your, darling, boy, dust and your ...

BRAHE: heavy... feet heavy with me...

206

(BURKE stumbles. KING helps him up)

BRAHE: (with energy) Earth! Wright Wright let's fly on, let's go back, now let's get back spot on my cheek spot on...

ECHOES: on, on kiss the cheek of your darling boy sand and on and sand and

BRAHE: sleep... heavy dust sleep...

> *(BURKE stumbles and falls again. KING drops down beside him. They doze)*

BRAHE: (softly) ... deep dust and my eyes want to go home

ECHOES: sun sun sun...

BRAHE: ...*where are you?*

> *(BURKE and KING shuffle to their feet, leave their packs, and start out again)*

BRAHE: I want to get on Wright, let's get on Wright, I want to get on please get on, where can the sun...

ECHOES: Kiss the cheek of your darling boy bonny bonny ... kiss the cheek of bonny Brahe-oh...

BRAHE: oh no... no more...

> *(BURKE drops again. KING half pulls him to his feet, gesticulating, urging him on)*

BRAHE: (whimpering) ... want to let go now

ECHOES: go home go on go, kiss, the, cheek, of your, darling, boy, Brahe, sun, sun, oh your bonny boy-o...

> *(BURKE drops for the last time. All KING can do is to sit by him)*

BRAHE: (outcry) *Let me up!*

(And he sits bolt upright to stare wide-eyed at BURKE and KING. BURKE stirs)

BURKE: John, you'll... you'll stay by me?

KING: My life's here, sir. It's where you are.

BURKE: There'll be no grave. Give me my pistol. There'll be no grave.

KING: No, sir. None so deep...

(BRAHE remains immobile,. He cannot take his eyes off BURKE.

KING stays by his leader.

After a while, he crawls away, but drops for the final time near his bed roll in the rescue camp.

Slow daybreak. WRIGHT comes awake, gets up slowly, packs his gear. He looks at BRAHE, then half-heaves him to his feet)

WRIGHT: Let's get going. It's going to take some hard riding to make up for this extra day. Cheer up, man. Think of it this way. When Burke gets back to civilization, his vendetta with fate and you by this tree will add just that little bit more to his glory. And he's not going to damn you for that. Is he?

(He nods 'come on' to BRAHE and leaves by back right.

But BRAHE does not follow, nor take his eyes off BURKE)

BRAHE (in an unreal voice) I dreamt... something about Burke and King. Where was Wills? Where was he...?

(He backs warily around BURKE to move without energy to the rescue camp, which is now emphasised by lighting. He stares

down at KING, then heaves him back onto the bed roll, makes him as comfortable as possible, then sits down on the stool. He continues to stare down at KING.

Tableau through... slow curtain)

(End)

TRUGANINNI

The Plays

Play 1: White Exercises

Play 2: Pantagruel In-between

Play 3: King Billy's Bones

First Production

Truganinni was first performed at The Union Theatre, University of Melbourne, April, 1970, with the following creative team:

Play 1:
White Exercises

TASMANIAN WOMAN   Rose Lynorin
WHITE MAN   Stephen Waters
MANGANA   Tom Healy
WONGGU   Michael Myer
TRUGANINNI   Jan Hamilton
GUDJARA   Des Fitzgerald
MR MELLIN   Robert Lewers
MRS MELLIN   Meredith Rogers
LOWE   Bill Saw
NEWELL   David Johnson

Play 2:
Pantagruel In-between

GEORGE AUGUSTUS ROBINSON   Guthrie Worby
REVEREND DOVE   Ian McFadyen
BOB   Derek James
MRS CLARK   Marg Jacobs
SCOTTISH INSPECTOR   Patrick Farrell
BRITISH INSPECTOR   Howard Parkinson
ACHILLES   Andrew Webb
APHRODITE   Alison French
CONSTITUTION   John Jacobs
PIANIST   Martin Arnold

Play 3:
King Billy's Bones

ALEXANDER McKAY   Ian Robinson
GILET   Derek James
DR DINGBY   Jan Martin
MILLINGTON   Jeff Curtis
MOLLY   Roslyn Horin
COLVIN   Dennis Howard
TIMMS   Michael Myer
ATWELL   John Price

DIRECTOR   George Whaley
SET DESIGNER   Jan Martin
COSTUME DESIGN   Sasha Soldatow
STAGE MANAGER   Alex Craig
LIGHTING   Ric Hunter
SOUND   Martin Arnold
SET CONSTRUCTION   Russell Stafford

Truganinni The Lady

She was the daughter of Mangana, Chief of Bruni Island. Later in life, when she had mastered English, she told her story to Alexander McKay. Her mother was stabbed to death by a European. Her sister was carried off by sealers. In her childhood, accompanied by her intended husband Paraweena and another man, she was once on the mainland of Van Diemans Land. Two sawyers, Lowe and Newell, undertook to row the party to nearby Bruni Island. In mid-channel, the white men threw the natives overboard. As they struggled and grasped the gunwale, Lowe and Newell chopped off their hands with hatchets. The mutilated Aborigines were left to drown and the Europeans were free to do as they pleased with the girl.

Clive Turnbull, 'The Black War'

... For example, the Tasmanian Aborigines died out not just because they were hunted like kangaroos for an afternoon's sport, but also because a world in which this could happen was intolerable to them; so they committed suicide as a race by refusing to breed. Ironically perhaps, and as though to confirm the Aborigines' judgement, the mummified remains of the old lady who was the last to survive have been preserved as a museum curiosity.

A.A. Alvarez, 'The Savage God'

Seven years after King Billy's death, Truganinni stood alone, a living relic of her race. She would walk the streets of Hobart Town, resembling Queen Victoria in her voluminous skirts and headdress. She quite enjoyed the curiosity and finger pointing of the townspeople.

Towards the end, she appeared to bear no malice towards her race's persecutors. Growing stoutish, she smoked a pipe and enjoyed a daily jug of beer. But she began to grow ill and as her death loomed, so did the memories of what happened to King Billy's body.

The fear obsessed her like a disease and repeatedly she begged and pleaded that no such horror should befall her.

On May 8th 1876, at the approximate age of 73, Truganinni died.

Only hours after the news, body-snatchers in the Royal Society of Tasmania started to bark for her body. The government tried to fight them off.

She was buried in a secret grave in a plain wooden casket. But the promises made to her were false ones, yet again. Years after her death her body was exhumed with the full approval of the government. Her skeleton was displayed in the Tasmanian Museum, alongside the skeletons of animals.

In 1953, a deputation to the Tasmanian Premier resulted in her skeleton being removed from public display and placed in a box to be opened only by 'bona fide' scientists.

And thus it was that, for decades, in a black casket in Hobart's Tasmanian Museum lay the broken bones of an aboriginal queen – and in her irreverent tomb are squashed the broken dreams of a race.'

Tess Lawrence, Melbourne Herald, 24 May 1974

Author's note: In 2002, there came an official public burial of sorts. Some of her 'hair and flesh' that had been lodged with the College of Surgeons in London were returned to Tasmania, allowing a formal ceremony before the nation's cameras of scattering her ashes on the waters of her beloved Derwent.

Play 1
White Exercises

The Characters

TASMANIAN WOMAN
WHITE MAN
MANGANA, chief of the Bruni tribe
WONGGU, Tasmanian
TRUGANINNI, daughter of Mangana
GUDJARA, the songman
MELLIN, Superintendent
MRS MELLIN, his wife
LOWE, a white sawyer
NEWELL, a white sawyer
CHORUS, as necessary

Production Note
Play 1 is a play for masks. It is not intended as a play in which the actors try to crop a realism artificially out of the Tasmanian Aborigines' culture or language.

It is a play that should be treated in what resembles workshop production -- that is to say, one that presents the theatrical illusion as nothing more or nothing less than the theatrical illusion that is inherent in the actors' masks.

Some 'rhythm sequences' need only be spoken in rhythm, while others should be accompanied by actors beating rhythm sticks. Rhythms can begin sharply or can build up slowly -- but they should always end abruptly and dramatically.

It is suggested that Play 1 should take place with actors moving centrally from sitting around the periphery of an 'acting area'. No exits or entrances, only rhythmic pauses and changes of pace.

Play 1
1.

(A group of actors are seated about the stage as the audience enters. They chat, move as they like. Finally, they pick up rhythm sticks and begin to use them, experimenting individually or in twos or threes. They join into larger groups as the sound builds up to one solid rhythm.

Silence... actors freeze. One of the actresses puts on a black mask and rises. She moves to central area and mimes digging movement.

Renewed rhythm, and one of the actors in a white mask rises and edges up to her. As his shadow falls over her, she jumps up, screaming silently, and tries to escape. He catches her, beats her into submission, and rapes her. Then gets up, looks down at her, bends down as if in tenderness or sympathy, and then simply stabs her in the back. With shame or guilt he simply returns to the circle.

Renewed silence.

Two actors don black masks as MANGANA and WONGGU. They see the dead woman. MANGANA falls onto the woman's body in grief. Finally, they carry her back to the circle. Rhythm again.

Actor as white man walks to front of stage, with his back to WONGGU, who stalks him and, with slow determination, strikes him with his waddy. The white man falls. Down stage, an actor jumps up and assumes a shooting pose. He shoots; all hit their sticks hard. WONGGU falls.

MANGANA crosses to WONGGU. TRUGANINNI is behind him. He looks down at the body for a long time, then picks up a spear. The white man takes up a shooting pose.

In silence again. Long pause.

MANGANA lets the spear fall, picks up the body and, dignity lost, moves slowly away. He walks backward with slow formal steps. TRUGANINNI, bewildered, picks up the spear and follows her father.

Rhythm very slow rhythm begins as MANGANA and TRUGANINNI ceremoniously return the body to the circle. Defeated, MANGANA walks back to the elevated position in central area, where he remains for the duration of Play 1.

His manner throughout is one of having given up all hope. He freezes in position as rhythm builds up. Rhythm changes and TRUGANINNI stands up. TRUGANINNI runs over to MANGANA. Stops. Pause. Then approaches her father reverently, offering food)

TRUGANINNI: The roots of our earth, father. Our people sent them over. For these roots, they said my father will come back into our camp...
    (pause)
I told them I did not think so.
    (pause)
I worked for these, too. Will you eat them?

MANGANA: (desultory) Yes, Truganinni.

TRUGANINNI: Tomorrow, I shall dig with my mother's stick. Today I wanted to work with my hands for you.

MANGANA: I will eat.

TRUGANINNI: Tomorrow there will be more.

    (Pause)

MANGANA: (looking around) You have come alone. Where is your sister? Where is Gudjara?

TRUGANINNI: Gudjara is coming. He follows me everywhere.

MANGANA: Gudjara is my friend.

(In rhythm now)

TRUGANINNI: Why does he follow? Always follow?

MANGANA: Gudjara is your kin, and I told him to.

TRUGANINNI: He is an old man. It tires him out.

MANGANA: Where is your sister?

TRUGANINNI: (giggles) I think Jalmarida is in love.

MANGANA: Where is she?

TRUGANINNI: Down on the shore, she watches footprints until they come up to her. I think she is in love.

(The rhythm-stick beats stop again)

MANGANA: She will come to see me!

TRUGANINNI: Now you are angry.

MANGANA: Have you seen her?

(Pause)

TRUGANINNI: No.

MANGANA: Where has she gone?

TRUGANINNI: Down by the water. I have told you.

(Rhythm sticks up again)

MANGANA: She doesn't come to see me. Something is wrong. Last night I heard a scream from over there. It was her. It was your sister.

TRUGANINNI: My sister screamed.

MANGANA: Why? You tell me why.

> *(Build up rhythm)*

TRUGANINNI: She held her body and said, 'Something has gone in'. The old women laughed. The men threw dirt on her, and danced around. When she had screamed, she went to the fire and burnt herself.
   (pause)
Father, I am afraid!

MANGANA: No, no. Be careful only.

TRUGANINNI: I am afraid, father! Why does Gudjara follow, follow? No women go out to dig any more. No men with their spears. The men should hunt. I am young, but I am your daughter. I know there is something wrong!

MANGANA: They need not hunt now. They stand by the hut; the food is given.

> *(Sudden stoppage of the rhythm sticks)*

TRUGANINNI: What I remember does not happen anymore. The hunt, the chase, the food from the stick... even the old man Gudjara only follows me, a girl.

MANGANA: You tell my people to come over here.

TRUGANINNI: My mother died here.

MANGANA: Tell them.

TRUGANINNI: They won't

MANGANA: (suddenly tired) Tell them.

> *(Rhythm sticks up again)*

TRUGANINNI: I have told them, father. There is no food over here, only my mother. They say before long you will have to go back there too. They wait there for you.

MANGANA: Say I tell them.

TRUGANINNI: There is no hut over here. The old women say they would have to go back to hunting and the white fellows would shoot them. Like my uncle, my mother. My mother. Why do they say that?

MANGANA: They are right.

TRUGANINNI: NO!

(*Rhythm sticks stop.*

In the silence, MANGANA swirls his spear above his head, slams it down on the rostrum. Pace change. No rhythm sticks but spoken rhythm)

MANGANA: Listen, Truganinni. Around, all around, the land that was once ours is now of no use. The white man numbers go on. Each time we went out, our land had got smaller, and two or three of us would not return. Why should they hunt?

TRUGANINNI: We ought to live!

MANGANA: They are too many. The whisperings are great.

TRUGANINNI: The shadows are long, cold winds from the south.

(*Slow build-up of rhythm once more*)

MANGANA: The whisperings, the whisperings, the cold winds from the south.

(*Pause*)

TRUGANINNI: (outcry) *What I remember does not happen anymore!*

223

(GUDJARA, the songman, moves into the central area)

GUDJARA: (pointing to TRUGANINNI) Ah. You.

TRUGANINNI: You leave me alone.

GUDJARA: You go too fast. I shall bring my son Paraweena, along. You would soon slow down for him.

TRUGANINNI: (crossly) When we are married.

GUDJARA: That's why he does not come with me. He does not care either.

TRUGANINNI: (quickly) Where is he?

GUDJARA: (laughing) Oh yes, you would soon slow down for him.

TRUGANINNI: You leave me alone.

GUDJARA: Mangana...

MANGANA: (shaking head) I am going to stay here. They all should come here to me. Once, they would have run behind.

GUDJARA: It's you who have left our people. Come back. They need your counsel.

(Sudden silence from the rhythm sticks, replaced by a slow buildup of low hissing)

MANGANA: Now other whisperings are great. Greater. They have new counsellors now.

GUDJARA: These are not Mangana's.

MANGANA: My wife was broken where I now sit. They then looked for my counsel, and then I told them nothing. Wonggu is dead doing what I said. There can be no more counsel from me. Other whisperings, I say, are greater.

GUDJARA: They don't know that.

MANGANA: They must learn or they are going to die.

(hissing stops)

GUDJARA: But they are lost like children. There was a fight last night. And a spearing. A woman has not come back. The new white man with the food spoke to them sharply. They are children now.

MANGANA: New man? Another?

GUDJARA: He asked for you.

MANGANA: He will come to me.

(Rhythm stick build-up again)

GUDJARA: Come back, old friend. You only sit here alone.

MANGANA: At night, alone, my wife comes back to me.

(Pause)

GUDJARA: Are we dying?

(Rhythm sticks 'die' slowly)

MANGANA: Our land gets smaller, whispering, whispering. Soon where can we go?

(Pause.

During the following, it is suggested that TRUGANINNI and GUDJARA perform a fantasy hunt, with the old man tracking her and she finally falls pretend-exhausted.

The rhythms following their mime stop)

GUDJARA:

The old pig-rat licks his mouth, his paws.
His mouth, his paws, the old pig-rat licks.
Licking, licking, his old coat shines;
Turning his eyes looking for home
The old pig-rat bends looking for home.
For the old sun shines high in his eyes,
Turning his head, the old sun now shines –
Pig-rat filled with the yearning for home.
Across the grey plains, the pig-rat plains,
He looks for home, licking his old mouth,
But the old sun shines high in his eyes
The old sun shines high in his eyes.
Now the new sun only looks towards home;
The new sun only. The old pig-rat is dead.
The pig-rat is dead, and the new sun shines
The new sun shines on the death in his eyes.

(In the ensuing silence, the actors are still.

Finally:)

MANGANA: Last night, my daughter Jalmarida screamed.

GUDJARA: She will be back.

MANGANA: Where has she gone?

TRUGANINNI: I don't know!

MANGANA: (to her) I have asked Gudjara to follow you. You listen to him.

TRUGANINNI: (runs off, laughing) That old man will have to climb trees!

(GUDJARA chases her. They circle and finally drop back into the actors' circle, laughing.

They stop suddenly.

Freeze)

226

2.

*(MANGANA adopts a new position. The Supervisor of
Aborigines and his wife, MR and MRS MELLIN, stand up
formally. They walk tentatively towards MANGANA.*

*Note: They and MANGANA speak point-counterpoint to each
other by way of indicating the difficulty of communication.
Either party tries much anyway...)*

MRS MELLIN: It's him, James.

MELLIN: His spirit must be broken to sit here like this.

MANGANA: What do you want?

MRS MELLIN: What did he say?

MELLIN: (at him) I have heard of Mangana.

MRS MELLIN: Funny, I expected much more. You know what
people say about him, James.

MELLIN: My name is Mellin. This is my wife. I'm here to help you,
Mangana. You can come to me.

MRS MELLIN: Don't promise too much, James. Be the Supervisor.
Try to think what would this one think of you if he could understand
what you're saying? Let's not show weakness right off.

MANGANA: What do you want? Speak and go.

MRS MELLIN: What was that? I don't like the look of him. I'm sure
he's just insulted us. Say something right back from the start.

MANGANA: (annoyed) What do you want?

MRS MELLIN: We can't have this tone, James. Tell him.

MELLIN: (ignoring her) You won't have heard of me as I have of you. These days your people live quietly. All Hobart Town knows that that is due to Mangana.

MRS MELLIN: Look at the brute's scars.

MELLIN: There have been one or two cases. A shooting, a waddying, but nothing like war. Due to Mangana. I am pleased, so I know what you go through to sit here like this. Too many white men speaking against you.

MRS MELLIN: Get on with it, James.

MELLIN: (stilt ignoring her) For my part here, more than the prayers and the rations, I'm here to keep the scum away. It's common knowledge what they come for. While I'm here, they'll keep away.

> (gets no reply. The wife has gone impertinently close to examine MANGANA's face, but MELLIN doesn't bother to stop her... wouldn't think to)

MANGANA: (eyes turned on him) You ask me a question as young as you are. Ask it of your kinsmen who come here at night. If you look, new man, you will see them creeping, wanting from us. You know what they want. We know what they want. We could kill them, as they have us.

MELLIN: Mangana, understand. I have more to give, and I'll see my methods tried.

MRS MELLIN: He should tell his people not to associate with such riff raff. Don't forget the details, the rations, James.

MELLIN: (simply) What would he care about those?

MRS MELLIN: (vexed) Mister Mangana, the question of your rations. I notice that there hasn't been very much order. The door has been rushed and the meat scrambled over. Even more than that, some of you have been coming up twice. Even given the difficulty in spelling your names, don't think I haven't noticed. Therefore, it would be appreciated if a queue were formed not before nine on Tuesdays, and no earlier than church for the Sabbath hand-out. It would also help if proper Christian names were used, or the savages were somehow distinctively marked. As there are now approximately fifty-two of you, the daily ration will be as follows: 3 lbs of fresh meat, 5 lbs of salted meat, 1 lb of biscuits and 4 lbs of potatoes. I trust that proper arrangements can be made for the betterment of all.

(Pause)

MANGANA: Your wife talks, new man. But I think you are able to talk with me.

MELLIN: My name is Mellin.

MANGANA: Mel1-in. You hand out the food, and my people need not hunt. But I think we can talk.

MELLIN: I'm a law-abider, Mangana.

MANGANA: I will not look towards you, for you are only one man. There will be a time when your people will kill all of mine. My daughter Jalmarida is missing. She went off alone.

(He turns away, shuts off)

MELLIN: One last thing. This morning I met a sealer on this side of the straits. He is well known to me as a ruffian. There was a girl with him. She was from here, the camp. I caught them together on the sand, but when I tried to bring her back, she said no. I have no power to prevent him from taking her away if he wants to. Mangana?

MRS MELLIN: Deaf ears, James. Frankly I doubt whether it would even matter to him. Put it in your report. Only cover yourself, James. I keep telling you. It's enough that you should have volunteered for all this.

MELLIN: I happened to believe in this.

MRS MELLIN: Yes, yes. But only cover yourself, dear. That's what reports are for.

> *(The MELLIN return to the circle. Rhythm builds up to herald TRUGANINNI's entrance to centre)*

MANGANA: Where is your sister?

TRUGANINNI: Looking. They are looking for her.

MANGANA: Then you stay here.

TRUGANINNI: Why must you worry? Gudjara will find her. That old man is crafty.

MANGANA: You stay here.

> *(Pause.*
>
> *There is tension between them, which is highlighted by a burst from the rhythm sticks)*

TRUGANINNI: (angry) Can I sit her like my father does?

MANGANA: You do not understand.

> *(Rhythm slows)*

TRUGANINNI: You said we must live how they want or not live at all. Some are bad, yes, father. My mother died here. But I have been thinking. Why should I stay afraid? I walk and run and speak as before. I can dig where I was taught; the roots are still there. The wombat still peers from the dark hole, wanting to escape. My hand can move quickly if I really want to catch him. Why must I go with Gudjara, always afraid?

> *(Buildup of rhythm)*

MANGANA: You will listen to me.

TRUGANINNI: I cannot be afraid all the time. How will you eat? You won't take the food they give from the hut.

MANGANA: Sit here quiet.

TRUGANINNI: (stamping foot) How will you eat?

MANGANA: Wait for Gudjara.

TRUGANINNI: They are not all bad, these people. Have you not changed yourself, father? When do you hunt now? Why does my father not hunt now?

(Renewed silence; all waiting for answer)

MANGANA: Is that what my people are saying?

TRUGANINNI: (softly) Yes, father.

MANGANA: While they eat the white man's food.

TRUGANINNI: They are not happy. They want my father as he was.

MANGANA: They roll over on full bellies, and feel their fathers looking scornfully down on them. Then they speak like that. Only then. It is talk, Truganinni. Talk. You tell them, Mangana says, one day perhaps the white fellow will go on by as he came. The sea will draw him back to it again. Until then, we must wait. Who will sing of their going if we have all died? It is useless to talk. They must wait. You tell them. When Gudjara comes back.

TRUGANINNI: But why should I stay afraid of all white men? There are two who have spoken to Paraweena. Two who take wood from our land. They told Paraweena they don't want to do it or hurt us, but they have to live as other white men say. They told him they would give him and me things if we helped them carry the wood.

MANGANA: You will stay here!

TRUGANINNI: It is only to help them. We have said yes.

MANGANA: No!

TRUGANINNI: (petulant) How can they be bad? They are young like Paraweena. They look at me and I think they smile.

MANGANA: (strikes at her) No!

(Pause. A rhythm stoppage)

MANGANA: (remorsefully) Truganinni, sing. Sing, Truganinni. Listen. It is your mother. Let us bring her here. Sing, sing your mother, for I get so old...

TRUGANINNI: (threnody)
Why do you sit here every day at my grave?
Why do you sit here? The shadows, the night,
The time comes to dance. The moon bone rises.
Why do you sit here every day at my grave?

MANGANA:
Because your body has been burnt and is ready;
The place of your bones is prepared by me.
I am Mangana; you remember your husband.
Mangana, your husband, prepared your bones.

TRUGANINNI:
Why do you sit here every day at my grave?
The place is prepared and I take my rest.

MANGANA:
Come up with your husband, come with me.
Get up from that place. Your husband speaks.
I saw you dancing there just now
I saw you leap when you spoke to me.
Get up from that grave. Your husband speaks.
Come with me, come with your husband.

TRUGANINNI:
You come down here and keep me warm
For I must dance to keep myself warm.
You should rub my body and slap my loins.

You ought not sit there while your wife is dancing.

MANGANA:
My old legs are cold, I shall warm you soon.

TRUGANINNI:
Your wife dances to keep herself warm,
Until you come, I shall keep myself warm...
Will you slap my loins to keep me warm?
My husband, Mangana, will you keep me warm?

MANGANA:
I sit here at your grave. My legs are old;
How shall I prepare you who has died so soon?
My wife, my wife, I shall keep you warm.

TRUGANINNI:
Where I dance is a dry and waterless place.
I am taking you to a dry and waterless place.

MANGANA:
Mangana comes with you to the waterless place...

(End rhythm; action freeze.

GUDJARA enters slowly, others wait for him to speak)

GUDJARA: I could not find Jalmarida.

MANGANA: She is lost.

GUDJARA: She went down to the water and took some flowers.
They say she would not speak to anyone. Now she is gone.

TRUGANINNI: She will come back. Father? Gudjara? If I go for a
walk and you cannot find me, will you say this about me too?

GUDJARA: She ran, old friend. She was running then away from us.
I could see she was going somewhere.

TRUGANINNI: No. She is young like me. She climbed a tree and watched you go by. Now she sleeps and waits for me. She will come back.

GUDJARA: Her tracks stop at the water.

TRUGANINNI: She is waiting, waiting!

GUDJARA: No, Truganinni, I can see.

TRUGANINNI: (softly) She is waiting for me.

    (Rhythm from the sticks builds up again for:)

CHORUS:
She has gone from us,
Where has she gone?
We sit here and wait but Jalmarida is gone.
Jalmarida is gone;
She is gone from us.

GUDJARA:
Crossing the water, she is running there
Wearing the waistband of her mother's hair.
She stops by the wattle
Yellow flowers spreading in her mother's hair.

CHORUS:
She is gone from us;
Where does she go?
We sit here and wait but Jalmarida is gone...

    (CHORUS and rhythm sticks fade.

    Silence.

    TRUGANINNI and GUDJARA return slowly to circle

    One hit with rhythm sticks is followed by lamenting rhythm and chanting.

LOWE and NEWELL don white masks. MELLIN enters and stops short seeing them do this)

LOWE: Listen to that black-hearted thump-thumping, will you? It's wicked, that is.

NEWELL: It is, but who cares?

LOWE: Nights are for blacks, Paddy. I'll see them in the day, I will.

NEWELL: Come on, will you?

LOWE: I'm for waiting, man. I don't like the sound of it. There'll be a chance, another.

NEWELL: I'm hot, Lowe, I'm telling you.

LOWE: They won't let us come near with that noise on. Nights are for blacks, Paddy.

NEWELL: I'll cut a few throats if they try anything. I'm hot, boyo, I'm telling you that. I've seen some of their women run, boyo.

LOWE: Man, we're friendly with a few. We'd best be waiting. We'll go back on chains if we're caught out on this.

NEWELL: They stole an axe from us. Get it? An axe. We're looking for it, see.

LOWE: We'll be back on dragging chains.

NEWELL: Not us. Come on, will you?

(They start to move off)

MELLIN: Stop, you!

LOWE: Christ!

MELLIN: Don't try running. I've seen your faces.

235

NEWELL: And who would you be, cock?

MELLIN: I'll have your back torn for this.

LOWE: He's the new lad running this place. That's who he is, Paddy.

NEWELL: Now what would he want to be yelling at us for, I'm asking you.

MELLIN: While I'm in charge here, your kind will keep away. Now, get off!

NEWELL: (menacingly) Minding our own bloody business, see, and you raising your voice. Did you hear him, Lowe? He wants to see us whipped, does he?

LOWE: Bloody rude, boyo. It's dark now, see.

MELLIN: (raising whip) Scum!

(They back away, but not fully and are menacing)

NEWELL: There's no good in losing your temper, gov.

LOWE: Come on, Paddy.

NEWELL: He won't be writing a report, will he?

MELLIN: They could hang you all and I'd sleep easy.

NEWELL: We came here for a bit of business. Business, we're telling you. A few trees. What else does he think?

(MRS MELLIN comes in tentatively)

MRS MELLIN: James...?

MELLIN: It's me.

MRS MELLIN: God, James, listen to them. That racket they're making. It's like the howling of wild animals. You left me alone.

236

(then)
What's the matter?

MELLIN: I'm not alone.

LOWE: Don't be alarmed, missus.

MRS MELLIN: Who are these people?

NEWELL: We've got some business with one of the blacks, missus.
We work with our hands during the day, y'see, so we had to come
about it now. We're telling you. But your hubby, he won't listen.

MRS MELLIN: You get out of here!

NEWELL: But we've got business. One of them, we've come to see
him about it.

MRS MELLIN: And who might that be?

LOWE: Paraweena. Isn't it so, Paddy.

NEWELL: That's who it is. We cut wood. That black told us he'd
help to get our wood across the estuary, Missus. We'd be paying him
n' all. We need a hand tomorrow, and that's a fact.

LOWE: We were just holding back, like you, missus. Hair on the
back of our necks. Like you, Missus.

MRS MELLIN: James, there *is* such a creature on our list.
Paraweena. He's a young man, usually with that girl Truganinni or
whatever.

LOWE: He won't believe us, missus.

MELLIN: They'd tear you to pieces if you went in there tonight. Now
get out and come back in the light when I can see you.

MRS MELLIN: Don't be too hard, James.

NEWELL: He's a violent man, your hubby is, missus. Come on, Lowe.

(over shoulder at MELLIN)
You ask that Paraweena, gov. You ask, boyo. You do that...

(They return to the circle.

The rhythm sticks calm down)

MELLIN: I lost my temper. That old man was sitting there so heavily, and I know he wasn't believing me.

MRS MELLIN: Ssh, James, ssh. You're trying too hard. Just remember they're only paying you at the probationary rate.

MELLIN: You go on back in. I'll try to find out why they're so agitated tonight.

MRS MELLIN: If you're set on it, James, I can't stop you. Just be careful. They must be near animals when they howl like this.

(Background noise and rhythm build up as the MELLIN return to the circle.

Then silence.

Actors move to places for next scene)

3.

(Scene played in near-silence, low key. All actors seated and very little movement)

TRUGANINNI: Paraweena is going. Why should I not go too.

GUDJARA: Where is your sister?

MANGANA: (fatally) Gone. Gone.

GUDJARA: Your father has said no, Truganinni. You should see why.

TRUGANINNI: But I am to go with Paraweena. Is that different from being followed by you? He is your son; he will be my husband.

GUDJARA: Questions!

TRUGANINNI: He is your son, and it will not take long. Across the water with the wood, then we are back here again. That white man from the hut, he asked Paraweena about it. He knows. What is wrong. Father!
    (pause)
I have not seen over there. If you look in the morning, it comes out of the mist. If you look in the evening, the ripples come from there. You have seen me looking, Gudjara.

GUDJARA: (irritably) Yes, yes.

TRUGANINNI: You see? Father? The white fellow is there, but Paraweena is strong. I shall look from behind him.

MANGANA: No.

(TRUGANINNI stamps her foot, then threatens GUDJARA)

TRUGANINNI: Tomorrow, I will run across the mountains and you will have to follow.

GUDJARA: I would catch you, then use a stick.

TRUGANINNI: (shrewdly) But if I go with those men and Paraweena, and you come too. It is not as far as the mountains.

(Pause)

GUDJARA: (To MANGANA) I would rather go with my son, old friend.

(Pause. MANGANA looks up slowly and nods.

Clap of rhythm sticks.

Delighted, TRUGANINNI runs hack to the circle. The old man follows her as quickly as he can.

Blackout)

4

(Rhythm builds up, stops suddenly.

Late afternoon light circles MANGANA.

MELLIN rises, moves central hesitatingly)

MRS MELLIN: It's no good interfering.

MELLIN: Look at him.

MRS MELLIN: James, you can't understand their ways. They've not been used to anything else. It's in their nature.

MELLIN: If I can, I'll help him.

MRS MELLIN: You can see he doesn't want to know, James.

MELLIN: (sadly) I don't know what I see.

MRS MELLIN: There's no sense in talking to you. I'm going back, James. It's coming on to rain.

> *(MELLIN advances. MRS MELLIN retires, but does not leave the stage)*

MELLIN: Mangana, though you won't look at me, I've something to say.
   (pause)
I'm... sorry, old man.

MRS MELLIN: (shocked) James!

MELLIN: (snaps at her) I said I was sorry!

(then)
Go on back.
    (turns again to MANGANA)
Last night your people were mourning. It was for your daughter Jalmarida, wasn't it?
    (at the name, MANGANA looks up at him)
It was for Jalmarida, wasn't it?

MANGANA: What do you want?

MELLIN: (with signs) Jalmarida - won't - be - coming - back.

(MANGANA understands the 'sense', turns away)

MELLIN: I told you. I didn't know it was her. You didn't understand.

MRS MELLIN: James, it's all falling on deaf ears. Come away.

MELLIN: BE QUIET!

(Silence. Then rhythm builds up)

MANGANA: Now, all but one, my family is gone. I am left with Truganinni and a life I remember. My foolish Truganinni, will you cry for your sister now? I am your father and I want you here now. Darkness comes; you should be here with your father now. We should weep for your sister together. Now your sister comes back no more. A darkness comes. You should be here...
    (then particularly startled)
Truganinni? Truganinni?
    (controls himself)
You are with Gudjara. Gudjara is with you; you have him bring you back now. We should weep together and your father is old...

MRS MELLIN: James, I need to light the lanterns. Look at the sky.

MANGANA: I look at the sky. Black, black. Soon I will see nothing more.
When the sun dies so too will Mangana.
My daughter has not come back and the sun is dying.
Mangana will not see and Truganinni should be waiting.

241

Truganinni should be waiting...

CHORUS:
Ss! Ss! The wind, the sky,
The dark, the night, the moon
The moon is not rising.
Where is Gudjara?
The girl, the young man are still with him;
Truganinni still wanders.
Where now is the old man?
The light dies to be born
The star lizard swims into night
They should return
They should return
We search with our hearts
We are looking with, our eyes
And Mangana is waiting
Ss! Ss! The wind, the sky,
The dark, the night, the moon gone
And Truganinni still wanders.

(In sudden silence again)

MANGANA: Across the air, I heard a scream! Gudjara, Gudjara,
you do not return! Do not stay any longer there; our people now sing.
The night brings the whisper. Listen from here. Bring back my
daughter!

CHORUS:
Truganinni still wanders.
Where now is the old man?
The light dies to be born
The star lizard swims into dark
The moon has wandered
We are looking with our eyes
And Mangana is waiting.

(Urgent rhythm-stick beating)

MANGANA: Gudjara, bring Truganinni!

MELLIN: (at MANGANA) What is it?

MANGANA: BRING BACK MY DAUGHTER!

(Nothing. He rocks with grief)

MRS MELLIN: Don't try to understand this one, James. You will meddle. Has he appreciated it? Has he tried?

MELLIN: There's something more.

MRS MELLIN: (scared) What more could there be? Leave him, for God's sake. Look how dark it's getting suddenly. If he wants something let him go to the proper authorities.

MELLIN: I am the proper authority, woman! Leave us alone for a while.

MRS MELLIN: I can't go back alone. I'm scared, James.'

(MANGANA looks up suddenly. He has heard something. He gets to his feet, peers into distance)

MELLIN: (to her) Wait!

(The three stay silent, waiting. A long pause)

MANGANA: Truganinni...?
   (then)
Truganinni...?

(TRUGANINNI walks slowly and painfully back into the clearing. She keeps her head turned away from her father. When she finally does break the heavy silence, it is in monotone, degraded, introjected)

TRUGANINNI: Father, Paraweena has not come back with me. My Paraweena, he has not come back. Gudjara has not come back with me, Father.

MANGANA: (outcry) *Tell me!*

(All actors freeze, look straight out at TRUGANINNI; essential, economical reaction only.

With abject shame, she keeps her head turned from MANGANA as she speaks and as she slowly sinks down at his feet)

TRUGANINNI: We were... on the water. Those two men had not spoken to us, but they smiled at me. They had smiled at me and were bringing us home. Gudjara fell asleep, the old man was tired. Paraweena held my arm. He... screamed for me when they pushed him over. Gudjara jumped up but one of them hit him. The other slapped me and pushed me down. I saw Gudjara's head as he tried to get back in. Paraweena was calling but I could not get up. I could see their hands. One of those men shouted and picked up an axe. He chopped off their hands as they clung to the side. He... chopped off their hands as they clung to the side, Father. I saw them drown and their hands float away.
    (cringes from MANGANA's attempt to touch her arm)
One of those men was laughing. Whenever he could, he would reach down and touch me. They pulled me to where they wanted to go. My legs were not strong enough to keep them away, Father. Why should that be? I am Mangana's daughter. They would not let me turn my head away.
    (then terribly simply:)
They... hit me, father, at both my ends.

(MANGANA drops his head in utter hopelessness.

MELLIN goes up to TRUGANINNI)

MELLIN: What is it, girlie?

(He has broken the stillness of their grief with this and MANGANA loses control)

MANGANA: Aah... !

(MANGANA leaps onto MELLIN from behind and begins to strangle him.

244

*MELLIN is helpless. MRS MELLIN screams, fumbles in her
bag. She pulls out an old pistol, aims blindly and fires.
MANGANA falls.*

*MELLIN rolls from out under. MRS MELLIN becomes
hysterical. TRUGANINNI looks at her father and does so
without comprehension of any of this)*

MRS MELLIN: (hysterically) I told you. I told you. He was killing
you. He was going to kill you! Oh, why wouldn't you listen?!

(MELLIN walks slowly over to her, leads her out.

TRUGANINNI crawls over to MANGANA, kneels beside him.

The actors freeze in position)

Blackout)

(End Play 1)

Play 2
Pantagruel In-between

The Setting

George Augustus Robinson was the most successful of the 'conciliators' of the 1830s who went out into the bush to 'round up' the Tasmanians peacefully. (Alexander McKay of Part 3 was also one of them.) Robinson went on to be the guiding light of the 'out of sight, out of mind' policy and of the school which was set up for the Tasmanians' so-called education on Flinders Island in Bass Strait. He administered the establishment with (some say) great cruelty. Or was it stupidity? Or was it misguided pity?

The Tasmanians died one by one, just as much through morbid longing for their homeland as any obvious clinical cause.

Later, Robinson was appointed Chief Protector of Aboriginals (Australian) of the Port Phillip District in what was to become Melbourne and its environs.

He was allowed to take five Tasmanians (one of them Truganinni) with him as servants. But he seemed to care little for them. They wandered as far as South Australia; they argued with, and killed, a white man; and the two men were hanged. They had the dubious honour of being the first Australian tribal people ever to be so. Truganinni, perhaps as a woman, was acquitted. But, even here, she witnessed the horrible and mostly-needless deaths of her fellow Tasmanians… perhaps equally as devastating to her as witnessing the postmortem butchery of King Billy. On the first hanging attempt, the gallows trap wouldn't open. On the second attempt, one of the men tumbled and was killed instantly; the other's noose slipped out of place and he suffered an agonizing death. Jack Ketch the hangman got £10 for his 'expertise' at the job.

The Characters

ROBINSON   Chief Protector of Aboriginals
DOVE   his assistant
TRUGANINNI
BOB   Tasmanian
MRS CLARK   a catechist on the Flinders Island 'camp'
1ST GOVERNMENT INSPECTOR
2ND GOVERNMENT INSPECTOR
BOY   young Tasmanian
ACHILLES   elderly Tasmanian
APHRODITE   elderly Tasmanian

Play 2
1.

(The scene is set as though it is another half of the set from Part 1 which itself has seemingly been slid off half the stage.

The alfresco setting is divided from the living-room setting of Play 3 by a curtain or some other similar prop that makes no pretensions to be anything other than an artificial barrier.

Though the stage thus looks incongruous, no attempt should be made to ameliorate this impression. Indeed, it must be as theatrical as George Augustus Robinson is theatrical; it must 'fit' him feeling quite at home in his self-satisfaction if not downright pomposity.

Note: In the directions of this play, the division (whether it be a curtain, a piece of material, a step dividing different levels, a 'wall and door' etc) will be referred to as the 'curtain' for simplicity.

On the living room side, GEORGE AUGUSTUS ROBINSON is slouched at a desk. He picks his nose and, sure that no one is watching, chews on the pickings. He scratches with relish. Other than these, there is no movement positively until someone in the audience makes a noise. (Somebody will sooner or later.) At this, ROBINSON starts and, by reflex action, adjusts his whole bearing into a more 'proper' pose. Thus collected, thus suited for being 'public', he smiles at nothing in particular. It is an awkward smile, managing to convey more fawning than pleasure. Then he gets to his feet, he rounds on a wall mirror and bows, preens before it)

ROBINSON: George Augustus Robinson.

(DOVE appears. He is put out, still buttoning his coat. He stands formally at the rear of the living room)

251

DOVE: ...Esquire. Pacificator and...

> *(ROBINSON claps his hands. DOVE stops. It shows he is quite mindless of DOVE.)*

ROBINSON: (carrying on introducing himself) And my assistant Dove. In my position here...

DOVE: (piping up) ...Chief Protector of Aborigines, by appointment of HRH Queen Victoria, by recommendation of the Prime Minister, the English Prime Minister, through the Home Secretary for approval and the Governor for endorsement, through trickle-trickle clerks and councils and lesser leagues, the commission thereby and duly signed...

ROBINSON: (demurely, again) In my...

DOVE: ...by Royal Seal.

ROBINSON: (above him) In my position here, I need an assistant. But the thing is: do I need Dove? Oh, and I am here with various... sundry... characters out back. Behind here, that is, not the... er, Outback, meaning Interior.

> *(pause, while he assures himself he is happy with the image put across)*

Good. Passably.

> *(He waves DOVE away with an offhand gesture. When DOVE has gone, he gets on his knees. He does this as not a fit man despite his appearance.*
>
> *He is front stage, as near to the audience as possible, but the mirror is still his focus)*

ROBINSON: Song of praise, spoken, in humble reminder, Your Excellency or whoever you are, that there's only ever been one Chief Protector of Aboriginals. Ever. And I'm it.
   (fanfare, which he acknowledges demurely)

A fine fanfare. A good fanfare. A worthy fanfare. Twas first
delivered by my wards after the first whale-boat mail after last
Christmas...

   ('praying')

Dear, good God Who Cometh Good for some of us, I know... Your
some-of-us attempt things that others would not. This is true.
Nevertheless, and all the same, it is a sobering and wonderful thought
that I, me, whichever, George Augustus Robinson, sometime boot-
maker that I was, has been lifted from the last, metaphorically
speaking ha ha, foisted to the first, winched up by Your Divine
Derrick. That I...

> *(Re-enter DOVE. Stops when he sees ROBINSON, just as
> ROBINSON has stopped by DOVE's interruption.)*

ROBINSON: You get any of that down, Dove?

DOVE: I knocked, sir reverend sir. The door was shut, so I didn't
think you were in, sir. Or out. Or both or either, sir reverend.

ROBINSON: Dove, you are a bumbling fellow. You just saw me
here.

DOVE: I did, I did, sir. But I can never believe my eyes seeing you,
an' that's the truth of it.

ROBINSON: (smug) Well, well.

> *(DOVE goes to retreat)*

ROBINSON: Dove!

DOVE: (ducking, then realizing error) Sir reverend sir?

ROBINSON: There comes a time, Dove, when a man must face
himself. Life is like that, my good fellow, although I can't be too sure
about yours. The thing being, Dove... one day you suddenly stumble.
You look down. You see your boots. And that is the time you must
ask yourself questions, Dove. Do you get my meaning?

DOVE: I assure you I knocked, sir.

ROBINSON: Doubts, Dove.

DOVE: (appalled) Not Dove doubts, sir?

ROBINSON: My doubts have arisen, Dove. Doubts standing before you.

> *(DOVE hesitates uncomprehendingly. ROBINSON waits for the penny to drop impatiently, before:)*

ROBINSON: Remember this, Dove…. It is all in the mirrors.

DOVE: What is, Sir reverend sir?

ROBINSON: The smoke, man, the smoke.

DOVE: Did I light something where I shouldn've, Sir?
   (to the other's annoyed click of the tongue)
I really do assure you I had no idea you were in or out or I wouldn't have gone around lighting fires, Sir reverend sir.

> *(ROBINSON turns away in exasperation. Dove is now totally confused)*

DOVE: (sotto voce to off) Did I fluff a cue?

ROBINSON: (heavily, re-prompting) Doubts, Dove, doubts. Have arisen.

DOVE: (tentative) Doubts about your achievements, Sir reverend sit?

ROBINSON: (on the track again) Ah, yes, questions, questions! Self-doubts run a tortuous course, Dove.
   (pause, then prompts)
Yes, you may respond. Broadly will do.

DOVE: Pacificator and...
   (thinks)
Haven't we just been through all this, Sir reverend sir?

ROBINSON: Broadly, broadly. As slow as you like.

(From here on, verbal heralding of rehearsed lines)

DOVE: Pacificator and Conciliator of the species Tasmanoid, the Van Diemens Land Aboriginals.

ROBINSON: (nodding) And today is...

DOVE: Today is the 8th, at the end of November, 1841, being the tenth anniversary of your most successful campaign. Upon which hung a certain tribe's salvation, Sir reverend sir.

ROBINSON: (coolly) Some have viewed it like that.

DOVE: A *whole* race's salvation.

ROBINSON: More have viewed it like that, yes. On a quiet night, one can't help thinking and savouring. And...?

DOVE: And never before had such a white man reached out such a hand to such wild men. Man to savage.

ROBINSON: (self-depreciating) Not exactly savages.

DOVE: Savages comparative.

ROBINSON: Well, well. Natural divisions.

DOVE: Oh Sir reverend sir, though my collar might not fit, my ears haven't been muffled!

ROBINSON: (demurely) I had some help, let's not forget that.
    (homily to mirror)
You may make the shoes, but not the leather. Were you not a mirror, I can be quoted.

DOVE: (going on) Just a black guide or two, that's all.

ROBINSON: For the sake of absolute necessity, mind.

255

(He turns away, sits as The Thinker, causing DOVE to query again his lines. He hisses at 'off')

DOVE: *Are we still with the mirror?*

ROBINSON: (hearing it) Of course we are.

DOVE: (and so carries on declaring) How you went out to save them when most cried folly, let them die off. All those dark days with those nights coming on. You alone with the stealthy bush and who-knows-what creepy crawlies... the strange howlings at night, knowing the primitives lurked somewhere around probably watching you from the country equivalent of dark comers and blood-red rings around the moon. Alone. With none save thyself, Sir reverend sir. Solitary...

ROBINSON: Incontestably.

DOVE: ...trusting in one God, trustworthy and questionably friendly, and two blacks, friendly and questionably trustworthy...

(TRUGANINNI and BOB enter wearily on the 'bush' side and set up camp.

DOVE watches them as he carries on...)

DOVE: Truganinni and Bob. Your only companions. As such.

ROBINSON: Aye, 'as such'. Still, I considered them as people, nonetheless.
   (sighs world wearily. To audience and to mirror)
Excuse me.

(He manages to raise himself, moves through 'curtain' dividing the sets, gets tangled up. Manages to extricate himself, then immediately feigns the extreme exhaustion of a long trek as he crosses to TRUGANINNI and BOB. He flops down)

ROBINSON: It's no good, my friends. They'll just have to come to me. I can no longer pretend that I'm tired, because I am. And to think this morning we were gaining on them. Now here we are, back where

we started this morning. All in all, six complete circles I'd say. It's making me sweat.
(sniffs)
I need a change.
(accusingly at them)
Or is it one of you? If it is, I rely on you removing yourself.

(They don't answer)

ROBINSON: How many would you say are there out there this time?

BOB: Lot.

ROBINSON: (despondent) I thought we had the remainder of the whole tribe this morning.

TRUGANINNI: They will come.

ROBINSON: (shaking his head) Five days is too much.

TRUGANINNI: Now they will come. They could not while we followed. It is the custom.

ROBINSON: (sulkily) You could have said, Truganinni.

TRUGANINNI: They are too tired keeping ahead of us. One of the women, she told me.

ROBINSON: (reacting) One of the women told you?

TRUGANINNI: They are my friends, but I do not like them.

ROBINSON: But I've been chasing them for days, woman!
(but then enthusiastic)
You've told them about my offer, then?

TRUGANINNI: (shrugging) Forgot.

ROBINSON: You couldn't have!

TRUGANINNI: They are bad fellows, these.

ROBINSON: Truganinni, Truganinni, you speak to them.

TRUGANINNI: You go.

ROBINSON: You don't have to be embarrassed by the way they dress... don't dress... like I have to.
  (pushing her)
You talk to them.

TRUGANINNI: They will come.

> *(She helps BOB with the fire. ROBINSON chuckles.*
> *As he speaks, the shadows of the 'wild' Tasmanians he is trying*
> *to 'conciliate' gradually spread across him)*

ROBINSON: The Oyster Bay tribe. Looking like they just come in for a look-see. Walking casually through Hobart Town with them at my side. Hello, Governor. These? Just a few once-hostile family groups I met on the way to tea on the lawn. Easy to tame. Well, Governor, if you don't mind the fact that you're the one who outlawed them, I'm sure they'd be delighted. Cream and one lump all round can't hurt once. Look how outside the inn they cavort and dance and sing and throw spears. Wonderful, isn't it, nature? They're going to love the school you've built for them. Won't we, lads? ... the pearls of the Oyster Bay tribe.
  (giggles)
The pearls of the Oyster. Put that lot of thirty-five in your ledger next to my name, and pamp it down and smoke it.

> *(TRUGANINNI has now stood up, draws his attention to the*
> *shadows.*
>
> *Seeing them so near, ROBINSON leaps to his feet; dangerous*
> *silence)*

ROBINSON: (to her, accusingly) You said they were tired. You said.

TRUGANINNI: (simply) They are looking at you.

ROBINSON: (shrinking) Do you think they can see me?

> *(Menacing silence until it is relieved when DOVE simply put his head through the curtain divide and ...)*

DOVE: (from 'living-room' side) Your track and the savages, Sir reverend sir...

> *(ROBINSON pats 'excuse me' on TRUGANINNI's shoulder and briskly moves back through the dividing curtain, this time without getting too entangled.*
>
> *TRUGANINNI and BOB freeze.*
>
> *ROBINSON 'stations' himself chez lui as before)*

ROBINSON: As our tracks came together with a lustful joining, so did their lives join destiny with mine.

DOVE: Their first white words. They should have understood them. I would have tried to, Sir.

ROBINSON: (nodding; then evangelically to imaginary Tasmanians) I bring you a message from your brotherly white father you may call Governor or Gov at a pinch. He has told me to tell you he thinks of you more as first cousins than subjects. It is hard, he has told me, to list an official return about you when you make him shoot you with only half the certainty. For that numbers have to be stabilized, he said. He promises you protection, a good place to live, plenty of food, warm coverings for your genitals in particular you will be glad to hear. He wants to protect you and those genitals. He wants to invite you home. He says he would like to have you to tea in his big house, the one with the most interesting topiarized tea-trees south of the Cape of Good Hope. So, come, come. Your sins are forgiven, some even forgotten. Follow in my footsteps and learn to walk with God!
   (pause for afflatus to subside, then nods end-game to DOVE)
So, Dove, there is your mirror and there is your smoke. I recommend it to be remembered.

> *(He returns to TRUGANINNI and BOB, takes up former position of fearful apprehension. And quakes in the direction of*

the shadows of the 'wild' Tasmanian tribespeople)

ROBINSON: I bring you a message from your brotherly white father. He has told me to tell you he thinks of you more as first cousins than subjects. It is...
  (into air)
Etcetera, etcetera.
  (then musters:)
Come! Come!

TRUGANINNI: (pointing out the fact) They have come. And gone.

ROBINSON: Where?

TRUGANINNI: (shrugs) Places around.

ROBINSON: What, then?

TRUGANINNI: Bad fellows, these.

  (Chanting and rhythm sticks begins off)

ROBINSON: (fearful again) What's going on?

TRUGANINNI: They are jumping around.

ROBINSON: (agitated) It's getting dark.

  (They settle. When they have done so, ROBINSON gets up, hurries into 'living-room' side and resumes declarations to mirror, to audience as though continuing public speaking)

ROBINSON: There were nights when I could not be sure of seeing the dawn again. Such a night was that one. Try though I might, I could not get to sleep. Next morning, because of it all, I'm afraid my edge was somewhat dampened. And I overslept. But, even with that, I still could not bring myself to curse the day they were born.

  (He quickly returns to 'bush' set, lies down in sleep again with woollen cap.

Quick and theatrical dawn.

Shadows, obviously with spears, fall across the group.
TRUGANINNI springs up)

TRUGANINNI: (eventually defiantly) What are those spears for?

ROBINSON: What's that one saying?

TRUGANINNI: He says, not right to kill you like this with that thing on your head.

ROBINSON: And?

TRUGANINNI: (laconically) Others say who cares.

 ROBINSON: More, more. He is answering.

TRUGANINNI: He says best you undress first.

ROBINSON: (outraged) What? Take up the cloth?

(The spears are raised. At this, TRUGANINNI and BOB bolt,
leaving ROBINSON to be enveloped by shadows)

ROBINSON: What do you want? Eh? Eh? You want me to meet my Maker as naked as the day I left Him? Look, one day you'll be reasonable people. I wouldn't use force to stop you... being reasonable.
    (stops confused by himself)
That's not my nature, you see. If you really have to leave, please don't feel wildly free. Or...
    (weak laugh)
freely wild. I give you my word as a man of ... OH, GOD!

(He bolts too. As he does so, and thankfully for him, BOB
springs back into the clearing as a decoy)

BOB: Ay! Ay!

(All freeze.

261

As quickly as is possible, ROBINSON dives on stage from the wings on the opposite 'living-room' side. Pauses to gather his breath, before...)

ROBINSON: I could only be thankful to my Maker that, in his panic, Bob had stumbled back into the very clearing he had bolted from. It was a fortuitous diversion. I ran, of course. Any one of you who has had to hop it through the Van Diemens Land bush with wildmen pounding along behind will know what it's like to... to be chased by blacks through the Van Diemens Land bush with wildmen pounding behind. Anyway, all I could do was to break more wind and leave what was left to Providence.

(ROBINSON exits. As immediately as possible, he re-appears -- backwards and crouched -- from wings on the 'bush' side.

At the same time, TRUGANINNI enters in the same manner upstage.

They creep in parabolically until they theatrically back into each other)

ROBINSON: Aagh!
  (recognising her, casting about wildly)
Where, where?

TRUGANINNI: (matter-of-factly) They have killed him, I think.

ROBINSON: Who?

TRUGANINNI: The other. That Bob who saved you.

ROBINSON: I don't want them to have to answer to God on account of me!

(TRUGANINNI shrugs. ROBINSON notices the river)

ROBINSON: The river. Truganinni! Our main camp over there! Our soup's up here!

262

TRUGANINNI: The river, yes.

ROBINSON: It's flowing swiftly. We'll have to be sharp. Keep up, woman, and I'll see you safe yet...!

(Grabs her arm, goes to dash off. But stops when DOVE, from the 'living-room' side, speaks...)

DOVE: And so they did.

ROBINSON: (prompts across 'divide') Yes, yes, and what...?

DOVE: Did follow you to salvation. More than a gross of them.

(ROBINSON lets her arm fall. He walks, puffed, to front of stage)

ROBINSON: Much nearer two, Dove.

DOVE: They did by the hundreds. You saved a whole nation.

ROBINSON: Noble fellows all. I remember a number of them quite distinctly. Matter of fact, I believe there's still quite a number of them left.

(theatrical pause, then he turns back to TRUGANINNI, takes her by the arm again, then resumes position of midflight.')

ROBINSON: Keep up, my good woman, and I'll save you yet...!

(and theatrically dashes off with her, but stops a second time after a few paces. Incredulous, dawning pause)

ROBINSON: I can't swim... You know I can't swim. Truganinni!

(she shrugs what-to-do)

ROBINSON: The raft! Where is it?

TRUGANINNI: (pointing across river) Across there.

ROBINSON: How did it get there?!
   (she shrugs lugubriously)
Then how did we get here?

TRUGANINNI: I and Bob carried you. Anyway, they have seen it.
Some will be waiting for you with smiles on their faces.

ROBINSON: The cunning black bastards!

   *(Realising this mistake he quickly turns back to front stage and,
   either to mirror on other side or to the audience, recants:)*

ROBINSON: You understand I was under considerable strain having
voluntarily put myself in such grave danger.

   *(He waits to see if he hears no objections; hears none; then
   nods got-away-with-that and turns back to TRUGANINNI, but
   DOVE's voice stops him before he can resume flight)*

DOVE: It can't be true about those two, sir!

ROBINSON: (suspiciously) Which two?

DOVE: Those two guides, Truganinni and Bob. You can't owe your
life to them on a number of occasions, Sir reverend sir, the word
going around.

ROBINSON: Don't be a complete duffer, Dove. There's slander
abroad, mind, my lad.

DOVE: Oh infamy, sir...

ROBINSON: And men who make them. Men who make them. What
do you yourself think?

DOVE: Some fool did assure me, Sir reverend sir.

ROBINSON: Pure flights of fancy. Some agnostic fantasy. Can
God's work be done by spear-throwers, lad? I mean, *think.*

DOVE: Heaven forbid, Sir reverend sir.

ROBINSON: Well.

(Satisfied he has countered that, he moves into the living-room side and presents himself)

ROBINSON: Speech to the Parramatta Party for Preserving Preventions, New South Wales, late 30's. Despite minor heckling...
  ('delivering')
That one called Truganinni if I remember... she informed me, under such trepidation that I had to knock it out of her, that they had killed the other native. In the circumstances, this proved untrue, but wholly understandable. She then rather pathetically urged me to hide in the bushes nearby. I explained to her the inadvisability of that course for the moment, whereupon I explored the possibility of broaching the river across which either she or the native Bob had so carelessly left it. Finally, after repeated attempts to manage both the camouflaged tree trunk fashioned out of my own hand and the woman's hysteria, I reached the safety of the other bank whenceupon I then proceeded to my main encampment.
  (pause)
I had brought the native woman along through all this, rather careless if I may say to my own safety. Her name was -- perhaps still is, although they chop-and-change so -- Truganinni. It was interesting to note the woman's subsequent devotion to me, and probably quite justified.

(Pause for a lacklustre applause by DOVE. Then ROBINSON returns to TRUGANINNI and assumes flight position with her)

ROBINSON: Over *there*? My God, Truganinni, that means the raft's out when it should be *in*!

TRUGANINNI: There is a tree down over there. It will float with you if I pull it after me.

ROBINSON: Truganinni, dear, dear woman, long-time companion, for the love of God, try!
  (dashes off to hide)
Call me when you're ready!
  (stops on thought)

265

But not too loud with the calling!

(TRUGANINNI follows him out, walking. Blackout on 'bush' side.

ROBINSON re-enters on 'living-room' side, catches breath by flopping into chair at desk. Then assumes academic pose with letter in hand.)

ROBINSON: Correspondence to a friend in...

(stops for a long 'unrehearsed' pause. Whispering and then prompts from wings and DOVE.

After a while, ROBINSON tries again)

ROBINSON: Correspondence to a friend in...
     (stops, irritated)
It's no good, you know.

DOVE: (psst) Sir!

ROBINSON: (annoyed) It's no good. Something's very wrong. Today...
     (clicking fingers)
today...?

DOVE: (emerging) Today is the 8th, sometime in November, eighteen forty...

ROBINSON: I know that.

DOVE: ... one. The tenth anniversary of your most successful campaign. Upon which hung...
     (stops)
I definitely know we've been through this bit.

ROBINSON: (out of character) Oh, keep it to yourself, will you?

DOVE: (down from his 'role') You packing it in then?

ROBINSON: Listen, Dove or whatever your name is, there's something else today. A man doesn't stand around boot to boggle without something-being-very- wrong deep down. I don't know if it's something I forgot before that bloody bus was late getting me here, or it's something you'n'I have buggered up. It's got to be you when I think of it. I can't think of anybody I'd doubt less than me.

DOVE: Fair go.

ROBINSON: Something ain't right, I tell you.

DOVE: You get a touch of stage fright, like?

ROBINSON: I tell you something's not right. What about the fumbling, bumbling start. You made.

DOVE: Me?

ROBINSON: The lines you fluffed. Me feeling stared at being caught in that curtain thing there. Listen, caught picking my nose! Don't think I don't know that.

DOVE: (patting his shoulder) Don't take it so hard.

ROBINSON: Get your hands off me! There. Even you. Give you an inch and you take a mile.

DOVE: (coy) You didn't say that last night.

ROBINSON: I was trying to forget... something... last night.

DOVE: Go on, it's probably only the trial.

ROBINSON: (reacting) The trial!

DOVE: It's probably that. Your Truganinni-not doing what she was told, and all.

ROBINSON: By God, that's it! Bloody hell, what treachery! No wonder I couldn't sleep.

DOVE: Take it easy.

ROBINSON: It's all right for you. I've got responsibility, a position. Oh, why did they have to go and kill some... some white trash on some trashy open road where everybody could see because that's what they're always looking for, trash.

DOVE: There you go. Can I go back to Sir reverend sir again?

ROBISON: What could I do about it? I didn't even know they'd got out through the bars, let alone been gone a week.

DOVE: It was atrocious behaviour, Sir reverend sit!

ROBINSON: Too right it was. I told 'em, I said, no atrocious behaviour while you're my wards in this house. This is Melbourne now, I said, not your Hobart Town. And you tell me, Dove, what's more atrocious than breaking out and all five of them, walking overland to Adelaide.

DOVE: Atrocious... them walking or Adelaide, sir?

ROBINSON: Adelaide, of course. And nearly getting there. If they hadn't killed that white trash... and I do wish you wouldn't keep calling him that, Dove... if they had made it to Adelaide, Dove, can you imagine Adelaide being more worse for wear?

DOVE: Shudder, sir!

ROBINSON: After all I've done for them. Bringing them to Melbourne, letting them share the glory of my promotion. Allotting my own servants' quarters to them. There's right and there's wrong, man; you yourself have heard me personally getting them to repeat that in English, Dove.

DOVE: I have, indeedee,

ROBINSON: And damn it, murder is wrong!

DOVE: It is, Sir reverend sir.

ROBINSON: They could have asked you that. You would have known that. The years I've spent in trying to get them to speak properly. The Robinson stress on the adverbial and all that, if I may say so m'self. The father I've been.

DOVE: Mustn't upset yourself, sir.

ROBINSON: (hotly) Father, I say! When I could have been fathering elsewhere!

DOVE: Ssh, sir, you'll need the sleep tonight.

ROBINSON: Only last week, that Truganinni stood right there where you are, Dove, and said, pitiably, 'You be Father; I'll pour'. And now this. Some Yankee whaler killed, some ordinary little judge holding a public trial, and my name dragged through the mud. I'll wager that. My sacrifices will mean nothing. Instead, I will have to stand by and watch while the fruits of my labour drop, plop.

DOVE: Not plop?

ROBINSON: Yes. Splat plop. Gallows, you know.

DOVE: Poor unfortunates.

ROBINSON: Murderers, murderers. Let's not mince words. From my voluntarily-given protection, my own house. Truganinni, that one. That Bob. Jack. Yes. Matilda. ...what's the other's name?

DOVE: I don't think you'd quite gotten around to giving him a name, Sir.

ROBINSON: Harried, harried, Dove.
   (then tedious decision)
You'd better go.

DOVE: Beg yours?

ROBINSON: You'd better attend the trial. Call me when I'm expected in court but delay it so I can't possible make it.

DOVE: (indicating stage) But I haven't finished a few scenes here yet...

ROBINSON: I can manage on my own. Underlie any bits you think important.

(DOVE is confused, hesitates)

ROBINSON: Go on, I say.

DOVE: Oh, why is it always me.

(and huffs off in irritation.

Long pause. Finally, ROBINSON goes wearily back to the desk, sits, picks up the letter again)

ROBINSON: (tries again) Correspondence to a friend in...

(DOVE pops his head back in)

DOVE: The letter. Are you sure you can manage?

(ROBINSON waves him roughly away, re-arranges himself)

ROBINSON: Correspondence to a friend via a letter, care of Oswaldtwistle Presbytery, Sussex, England. Authenticated as being my hand writing when Superintendent of the camp on Flinders Island for additional remnants in Bass Strait running with Antipodean undercurrents...

(As he reads, lighting on 'bush' side of set, where MRS CLARK mimes teaching, preaching, beseeching and singing of prayers, and the 1ST and 2ND GOVERNMENT INSPECTORS mime officialdom)

ROBINSON: 'Well. Floriana, History does not furnish another instance where a whole race has been treated to so humane a policy of conciliation and protection.'
  (to mirror)
Let those in court answer that.

(back to letter)
'After I and others...
　　(adds in correction)
a *few* others... had gathered these piteous primitives like wild flowers
to the bosom of God, we had them repatriated to this school. Ah, and
what a singular establishment it is! Nowhere else could Stone Age
bodily functions come to express perfectly Christian prayer. A one
Mrs Clark and I have to carry the burden. Even so, we furl and unfurl
did a-furling go the Union Jack each and furl and unfurl did a-furling
go every sunset and sunrise. Sabbath day observation and no moving
around; nightly prayers at six and eight. No unsupervised dancing
allowed and even then only in neck-to-knee garments. Latin
inscriptions, not just your ordinary catechisms. But I won't go on.
After thousands of years in the dark, you can imagine how they take
it. Even now we are all eagerly preparing for the annual Government
inspection...'

　　(At this stage, MRS CLARK and the INSPECTORS are waiting
　　formally for him. They look mutely in his direction. He puts the
　　letter down)

ROBINSON: (finalises reading) 'I'll carry on with this later, dear
Floriana.'
　　(gets up and moves over to her side)
Right, Mrs Clark, if the Inspectors are ready, let us proceed.

MRS CLARK: (nods, but hesitated) Er...?

ROBINSON: (patiently) Call in the advanced class please, Mrs
Clark.

　　(She titters out. He turns to THE INSPECTORS)

ROBINSON: Gentlemen, this won't take long. When they know we're
ready for them, you can't imagine the excited state they get into.
They'll positively stampede in.
　　(waits. Fills in with:)
They've been waiting six months for this. Some of them get so
wound up they want to know what six months is.
　　(waits, but still nothing)

271

You'll see yourself how proud they are. Indeed, we are all proud! I
and my staff are certainly bulging chests have. I trust that you too will
leave here feeling that there's something worth saving in these sad,
sad creatures.
   (calls)
Mrs Clark?
   (nothing)
Poor Mrs Clark, can't get around like she used to. Not too sprightly.
Hips don't you know.
   (silence now embarrassing and produce verbal burst)
One thing I am certain of, gentlemen. Skin colour, sun-exposed or
not, barbarian or British stock, it's not quite the whole story.

   (He dithers while still having to wait)

2ND INSPECTOR: (not understanding) Quite.

ROBINSON: As you will see. Despite voices raised against us,
gentlemen. Many voices.

   (Still more waiting, dithering)

2ND INSPECTOR: (platitude) A great man proves himself above
such rumours, I should have thought, Mr Robinson.

ROBINSON: Precisely, sir.

1ST INSPECTOR: (dislike) You are aware, then, that there are some
expressions of doubt about your school here?

ROBINSON: (appeals to mirror) What could that possibly mean?
What was meant by that?

   *(He remains with his circumspection, his back to them, until
   finally MRS CLARK returns. She has one boy in tow)*

ROBINSON: (roughly) The whole class, Mrs Clark.

   *(MRS CLARK signs to speak with ROBINSON privately.
   He goes over in annoyance)*

272

MRS CLARK: (near tears) They can't be found.

ROBINSON: They're just excited. Look around, woman.

MRS CLARK: 'Ere, they're gone. Scarpa'd. We found this one in a vat. The sergeant had to shut him in to keep him there.

ROBINSON: Well, leave the boy here and bring in the women. Quickly. Now what are you shaking your head for, woman?

MRS CLARK: The women, sir...

ROBINSON: Well?

MRS CLARK: They took off before the men did. Then they came back and started washing their clothes.

ROBINSON: Don't be preposterous!

MRS CLARK: The sergeant says they refused to come up at first. Then they changed their minds. In a while, they told him.

ROBINSON: Washing their clothes?
  (light dawning)
But they'll be standing there naked!

MRS CLARK: Not will. Are. As the day they were born, Mr Robinson!

ROBINSON: They wouldn't dare.

MRS CLARK: They did. All the Sergeant says he can do is look on.
ROBINSON: I bet he would.

1ST INSPECTOR: (aloud) Are you inconvenienced by our visit, Mr Robinson?

ROBINSON: (hard smile) Nothing, nothing. One or two over-excited extra backsides, that's all.
  (back to MRS CLARK)
 Quickly, woman, the men. Bring back the men.

MRS CLARK: (bursting into tears) Oh, Mr. Robinson...

ROBINSON: Oh, no.

MRS CLARK: Yes. They've run off with the women's clothes!

ROBINSON: Depravity! Depravity all around us!

MRS CLARK: There are one or two stragglers, Mr Robinson.

ROBINSON: Can there possibly be?

MRS CLARK: Taking advantage of the open vat the Sergeant found the boy in.

ROBINSON: Bring them in before they've done with it!

> *(MRS CLARK rushes out.*
>
> *ROBINSON recovers to be the genial host again)*

ROBINSON: My apologies, gentlemen, it seems the excitement... We don't believe in a lot of discipline...
    (darkly)
as yet.
    (then, brighter)
Take this sturdy young specimen. What's your name, lad?

BOY: Constitution.

ROBINSON: (proudly) Almost first thing, I renamed them all. Though not one of our more advanced, the boy can count...

BOY: (too keenly) One... two... three... six.

ROBINSON: ... and slightly add, all at the same time. As I recall, he reads well from the authorized text of 1609, but has been known to stumble on the Revelations. The days of the week and the months are also well within his grasp. What's today, boy?

BOY: Constitution!

ROBINSON: Has slight trouble with oral skills, but attends family worship every evening, arriving in good time. Ah.

(Re-enter MRS CLARK, virtually pushing ACHILLES, the old man; APHRODITE, the old woman; and TRUGANINNI.

The Tasmanians are dressed in the most clownish hand-me-downs as though TRUGANINNI has deliberately outfitted them so from the clothing store.

They form a really burlesque-looking group)

MRS CLARK: (introducing) Achilles. Aphrodite. Truganinni.

2ND INSPECTOR: Who?

MRS CLARK: Truganinni, sir.

2ND INSPECTOR: I say, original aboriginal. Which one?
   (pointing to the old woman)
Her?

(The old woman, graced by this attention, stands in a lewd 'femme fatale' pose of come-on at him)

MRS CLARK: That's Aphrodite. That's the Goddess of Love.

(The 2ND INSPECTOR backs off quickly)

ROBINSON: Truganinni's father was Mangana, chief of the Bruni tribe.
   (intimately)
A princess, locally, but you have to keep a bit of a straight face. Somewhat obstinate. Most of our women were rescued from captivity amongst the sealers. Think of the depravity. Now, to all who know, they exhibit virtues formerly reserved only for vicars' wives and governors' ladies. The leather binding of certain parts help there.

2ND INSPECTOR: They certainly look well fed.

MRS CLARK: (whispering) Mr Robinson, I don't think they're going to stay very long.

ROBINSON: Proceed, Mrs C.

MRS CLARK: (confronting the Tasmanians) Now wait for the questions...
   (begins formal catechisms)
Who is God?

BOY: My father!

MRS CLARK: Who was Jesus? Achilles?

ACHILLES: My father.

MRS CLARK: Who is the Reverend Robinson?

APHRODITE: (senilely, but eager) My father, my father...

   (and continues to chuckle and indicate he and her should get together...)

MRS CLARK: How can you get to heaven?

ACHILLES: (rushing ahead) Keep clothes on!

MRS CLARK: No Ach...

ACHILLES: Make own bread!

   (And interrupts MRS CLARK each time she goes to speak with...)

ACHILLES: Drink tea! No dance, no song! No kill sheep! No bugger-bugger!

BOY: Run away chop-chop!

ROBINSON: Stop interrupting, boy! Go on, Mrs Clark.

MRS CLARK: Have you a soul?

(General puzzlement)

MRS CLARK: Truganinni? Have you a soul?

TRUGANINNI: (irritably) Yes.

MRS CLARK: Will you die?

BOY: (eagerly, hand up) Me!

MRS CLARK: Who crucified Jesus?

(No volunteers)

MRS CLARK: Truganinni?

ROBINSON: (aside) Our brightest pupil...

(But TRUGANINNI still refuses to answer)

MRS CLARK: Who crucified Jesus, Truganinni?

TRUGANINNI: (softly) I hear him scream in the night, longing for home.

2ND INSPECTOR: I say...

1ST INSPECTOR: (to MRS CLARK) Would you repeat that? What did she mean?

(MRS CLARK looks at TRUGANINNI^ but gets no explanation)

MRS CLARK: I don't think she knows herself, sir.

ROBINSON: (quickly) Go on then, Mrs C.

1ST INSPECTOR: Wait a minute. I want to question this...

277

(ROBINSON jumps between him and TRUGANINNI and conducts them like a choir-master. After each concerted answer, there is a fanfare off, which he acknowledges with the rococo gestures of Commedia dell'arte)

ROBINSON: Did you know anything of God before you came to this establishment?

BOY: NO!

ACHILLES: NO!

APHRODITE: NO!

ROBINSON: Did you ever pray to God when you lived like savages?

BOY: NO!

ACHILLES: NO!

APHRODITE: NO!

ROBINSON: Were you happy before I taught you about the Lord?

BOY: NO!

ACHILLES: NO!

APHRODITE: NO!

ROBINSON: Are you lost to God's kingdom?

BOY: NO!

ACHILLES: NO! NO!

APHRODITE: NO NO!

ROBINSON: (final flourish) Hurrah the Good News!

(Final fanfare. ROBINSON sweeps a bow, stands mannered and plumed.

After a while, he snaps his fingers in an over-the-shoulder gesture, obviously expecting the INSPECTORS to disappear from his horizon.

He turns and casually walks toward the curtain divide. The 2ND INSPECTOR has to waylay him)

2ND INSPECTOR: Mr Robinson.

(ROBINSON stops)

2ND INSPECTOR: I am frankly worried. I fear my report will look bad, sir.

ROBINSON: I hope there are no grounds for complaint, Mr Inspector?

2ND INSPECTOR: Absolutely not, you understand. I would not have brought the matter up had it not been for this wretched report to be accurate as possible.

ROBINSON: I understand perfectly.

2ND INSPECTOR: It's these blasted returns.

ROBINSON: Trouble?

1ST INSPECTOR: (sarcastically) Just a little matter of a deficit of thirty or so natives since the last return was lodged a year ago.

2ND INSPECTOR: (puzzlement) I've added and re-added. I'm worried about the comment in the margins the matter might draw, you see. Really messify the ledgers, you know. Perhaps if I could just round them off as escapees ...?

(ROBINSON shakes his head sadly)

ROBINSON: That would indicate a certain dissatisfaction amongst the natives, would it now?

2ND INSPECTOR: No deep well around the establishment they might've fallen into…?

   (ROBINSON shakes his head again)

2ND INSPECTOR: No natural catastrophe last winter?
   (ditto reaction)
Well, what about rounding to the nearest ten whole numbers?

ROBINSON: It is difficult, I agree.

2ND INSPECTOR: It seems so lame to put down 'Inbuilt Obsolescence', that's all.

1ST INSPECTOR: (confrontation) On my arrival, Mr Robinson, I found one quarter of them on the sick list. Since then, less than a week, more than a half have been ill in one way or another. This thing, whatever it is, consumption or mental irritant, could wipe out the whole race before long.

ROBINSON: (self-concerning thought) It's God's good air, sir. I don't know what you think I can do about it.

1ST INSPECTOR: Have you ever considered a connection between this disease and your attempts to civilize the poor devils?

ROBINSON: Impossible. Why, I myself have had more than a slight cough lately, and look at me. And Mrs Clark here was laid up for two days last week with nasal congestion. Sophistication has nothing to do with it.

1ST INSPECTOR: Need I point out that you have only forty left?

ROBINSON: I realize how some people are talking. Just you remember that when I go to Melbourne to take up my post as Chief Protector of Aborigines ...

2ND INSPECTOR: (admiringly) Congratulations, by the way!

ROBINSON: (nodding acknowledgement) ...when I go as the newly-created Protector of Aborigines of the mainland, I am taking five of them with me. Five, sir. Not for my own attendance, either, I may add, but also for their health. Across the Bass Strait, sir! It shows how worried I am.

1ST INSPECTOR: Might you be able to suggest where it will all end?

ROBINSON: Probably not even a thank-you for me.

1ST INSPECTOR: I meant, what do you plan to do about it?

ROBINSON: I shall continue to do all that is humanly possible, adding as I always do 'humane' to that.

2ND INSPECTOR: (exploding) There's only a bare, miserable forty left, Mr Robinson. For-ty. Four 0.

ROBINSON: I know! I know!

(And escapes across the curtain divide.

Immediately, lights off INSPECTORS.

From the other side, ROBINSON jerks a finger at their going. Feels safe to return and to return to declarations)

ROBINSON: Of course I knew that. Honestly, some people...
(pause)
The death rate was one frustration, certainly. But I am firmly convinced that my concept would have borne divine fruit had not the mortality rate been so damn high. I mean there are only so many balls one can keep in the air at one time, no?
(calls)
Dove?
(no reply)
Dove?

(DOVE finally puts his head around the door)

281

DOVE: Be fair, Sir reverend sir. I've only just got back from trying to keep that man's ledger falling out of the boat.

ROBINSON: Did it?

DOVE: Much as I tried, Sir, much as I tried.

ROBINSON: Well, well, let's get on with it.

(And waves him out)

DOVE: All right, all right, I'm going as fast as I can, mate.

(And shuts himself out. ROBINSON thinks of making an issue of DOVE's out-of-character irritability, but thinks better of it, and:)

ROBINSON: ('delivering' again) Of course, I have not been 100 per cent right 100 per cent of the time. But I am content. I have had, by Fate, the Tasmanian Indians... and they in their turn have had it by me. As I have watched over them, I have seen a lot of water pass under the bridge which fell down less than a month after they build it. Let's make it water passing these shores. Oh, yes... currents move while tides ebb and flow. Growth and decay, it's the natural order of things. I may be quoted. Why, even when I...

(Re-enter DOVE without knocking, slams door behind him.)

ROBINSON: Dove! I was meditating.

DOVE: I knocked, didn't I?

ROBINSON: You did not.

DOVE: Knock, knock.

ROBINSON: What's gotten into you, man? You interrupted my train of thought.

DOVE: The door was shut. I didn't think you were in. Or out. Or where you'd gone to.

ROBINSON: Let's not start that again.

DOVE: How do you know I was looking for you, anyway?

ROBINSON: Then who are you looking for?

DOVE: You, of course, 'Sir reverend sir'. That's why I knocked, right?

ROBINSON: I just said you didn't. *You* just said you didn't.

DOVE: Well, the door was shut, so how was I to know someone was behind it in a train of thought?

ROBINSON: It is probably best we are soon parting way, Dove.'

DOVE: Yeah, take five of them but not me.

    (disgruntled pause on either side)

ROBINSON: (exasperation) Can we get on?

DOVE: Ask away, 'Sir reverend sir'.

ROBINSON: (back in role) What do you want, lad?

DOVE: I want to apologize for knocking when I didn't think you were in, sir.
   (surly aside)
What the hell else?
   (then)
Oh, and you're being waited on in court.
   (another aside)
Couldn't happen to a nicer bloke.

ROBINSON: (blow-it bombast) The court, the trial! Why is this world so confoundedly cold?

DOVE: (outcry with him) Issue a few more of those nice new blankets you're got in store, for a start.

ROBINSON: The scandal, the smear of it all!
(and)
Well, Dove, what's the informed opinion?

DOVE: (just to get things right) We've moved on to Melbourne now?

ROBINSON: (with apologetic laugh to mirror or audience of both)
We are, Dove, we are. The pitter-patter of it, lad.

DOVE: (back in character) Bob and Jack to hang's the money's on.

ROBINSON: Strong ropes, Dove, strong ropes. I could never keep them on the dangle.
    (and)
What about the females Truganinni and the other, if it was a female.

DOVE: The women acquitted, sir. For humanity's sake. But I've come to tell you, that court there's waiting on you. There's a crowd outside and it's howling your name. So are the accused.

ROBINSON: (pleased) A crowd, you say?
    (waving him on)
Well, I'll not shirk my duty, Dove. Chief witness for ...
    (vaguely)
whomsoever.

    (DOVE stops in his tracks)

DOVE: What did you say?

ROBINSON: Chief witness for the whomsoever.

DOVE: (incredulous, not acting) For the defense, not whomsoever. It should be whosoever, anyway.

ROBINSON: What possible defense, Dove?

DOVE: Hey, now listen...

ROBINSON: (over him) I'll be letting the judge know I tried my human best. That's as near as I'm going.

DOVE: (now angry) You're supposed to say for the defense!

ROBINSON: And I'm supposed to be in court too, but I'm not, am I, because you're stopping me.

DOVE: I know the score. You're supposed to send me out to tell the defense lawyer you're coming. I go ahead and you wait here to show them you're not above a bit of playing to the crowd. While you're waiting for the right moment to appear, you stay here and, for sure, you're going to read out the speech you intend to deliver in court.

ROBINSON: Why would I do that?

DOVE: I don't know. How's about to hear your own voice?

ROBINSON: (disgusted) That speech.

DOVE: Yes, that speech.
    (rummages around desk)
This... this...
    (finds it)
this speech.
    (looking)
Say, you're not fooling are you?

    (ROBINSON remains obdurate. DOVE gets angrier)

DOVE: I'm telling you, you're supposed to read...
    (reading from paper)
'Your Eminence Benched so, members of the jury, ladies and gentlemen inside and all those outside straining to hear... yes, I am acquainted, one might say, with the prisoners. As you all know, I have endeavoured to civilize them. I can therefore assure you that they know right from wrong and if that right be my right, then so be it. I was discussing this very point today with my assistant Dove. Thus it is quite probable that the poor wretches feel guilty about the

whole affair of letting down the trust I put in them. I would say more in their defense, but what more can I say, Your High Honour? Thank you, and I say that humbly.'
    (then)
That speech.

ROBINSON: Take it away.

DOVE: (not relenting) At least it was *something*! And then... and then...
    (searches speech again)
you were supposed to say...

ROBINSON: (mimicking himself) 'Must do everything I can, dear world, everything I can.' Right?

DOVE: Right!

ROBINSON: With heavy irony. Brutal callousness. Yes?

DOVE: Yes!

ROBINSON: And then leave for the trial dripping with a poisonous sneer over my contemptuous arid face...
    (waving vaguely at mirror and audience)
and they say what a horrible, overblown, nasty little man, before they get up and shake off the peanut shells. Right?

DOVE: No!

ROBINSON: George Augustus Robinson to go out fawning and insufferable. Nothing more than a damn despicable death-dealing dolt as to what appears to public opinion?

DOVE: It's not like that! It's a sense of... I don't know... something!

ROBINSON: Look, Dove or whatever your real name is, you don't seem to realize it, but I've got critics. None of your long-haired sufferers with third degree burns looking like tattoos and wigs, but real live critics. They're not going to be satisfied if I come out with a transparent effort like that speech, then cap it with a rotten little drawback of a line like, 'Everything I can, dear world, everything I can' and a sneer. Leave after that? To boos and catcalls? Why should I be jeered off just so everyone can rub their sense of shame on me? I looked after these people; never mind I got a bank balance for the first time in my life. It's my bank balance. I'm the one who's got to sign for it.

(remembers something around banking)

That reminds me. I have to…

DOVE: (cuts him off) Truganinni and the others are calling out for you, man. Save them!

ROBINSON: I've got the reputation to keep, thank you. One does not keep reputations going into any old court and speaking on behalf of murderers. Or those who thought of doing it. Scriptures, Dove, scriptures.

(DOVE stares at him for a long time, then simply turns about and leaves in disgust)

ROBINSON: (after him) Yes, mate, me. George Augustus Robinson. Antidestinarian! Foul godless Reformation voice!

(then to audience, indicating DOVE)

That's what you get. Stop for a brief human pause on the historical path, and they think they can take liberties. One moment in time… one… a certain day, a couple of blacks do in some white nobody, and my name is hauled over hot coals. Two years in the Flinders Island hell hole and where were those hot coals then? Nowhere! If it wasn't for me, they wouldn't even be alive to be standing trial today. And more especially with that hanging horror up on that bench with his buck teeth. I mean he's more than likely to rope me in too! Hey, hey, look, Judge, you take that Truganinni. Do you see the effort put in just with her alone? My advice… word to the wise… keep her out of your private chambers. Trouble with a capital T.

(turns outright to confront mirror on wall)

You be the judge.

(He stops and seems to listen to a judgment that has to be coming from his own mind)

ROBINSON: And I most definitely concur.

(He straightens his clothes, cocks his hat with a defiant flurry, then leaves the room.

Blackout)

(End Play 2)

Play 3
King Billy's Bones

Introduction

Hobart, 1869, during the funeral of William Lanne, or King Billy, reputed to be (certainly at the time) the last full-blooded male Tasmanian Aboriginal.

'William Lanne (King Billy), the last Tasmanian male, died in 1869 at the age of 34. She (Truganinni) thought of the deaths at Flinders Island, the horrors of the trial and executions of Port Phillip... she thought of King Billy, with his hands and feet cut off, and the skull lying on the blood-soaked earth by the broken coffin. "Don't let them cut me up", she begged as she lay dying. "Bury me behind the mountains". She was buried at Cascades, Hobart, with great precautions against the body-snatchers. Today, her bones are strung together in the Tasmanian Museum -- no longer on public view, but in a 'coffin-like' box in the basement.'

Clive Turnbull, *The Black War*

(Also see earlier Author's Note to Part 1: White Exercises)

The Characters

McKAY   'authority' on Tasmanian Aborigines
GILET   his ticket-of-leave servant
DR DINGBY   general Hobart practitioner
MILLINGTON   undertaker
MOLLY   barmaid
COLVIN   whaling boat captain
TIMMS   whaling boat captain
ATWELL   colonial Under-Secretary
TRUGANINNI

Play 3
1.

(The drawing room of ALEXANDER McKAY, gentleman of Hobart, member of the Royal Society, authority on the Tasmanian Aborigines.

The room reflects McKay's secured position in his society. The furniture has been pushed back against the walls to make space for a table that stands in the centre of the room. On the table, and the floor underneath it, are white lilies and carnations.

McKay is finishing arranging the furniture. GILET, his servant, enters)

GILET: Dr Robert Dingby has arrived, sir.

McKAY: Send him in, send him in.

(GILET goes to leave)

McKAY: And if any other guests arrive, let them find their own way in, Gilet. Today we won't stand on formalities.
  (pause)
And don't refuse entrance to anyone. Understand?

(GILET affirms, waits, McKAY reflects)

McKAY: When the coffin comes, lend a hand, will you? And tell them to be careful. For once in his life, even though it's too late.

GILET: Shall I leave the door open then, sir?

McKAY: Best to. None may come, but then the whole town might turn out.

GILET: Front or back?

McKAY: (sharply) I said we'd stand on no ceremony.

GILET: Yes sir.

McKAY: You've seen to it that the invitation has got about?

GILET: Everybody should know about it by now, sir.

McKAY: Good, good. Send in Dr Dingby.

(Exit GILET; after a time DINGBY enters)

DINGBY: (reflecting good friends) Dr Robert Dingby, slowed by Fate, passed by time, extinguished member of the Royal College of Surgeons, London -- and I think I still remember where that is -- colonial surgeon and turned out very well because of it, has come to present his present state. How are you, my dear boy?

McKAY: Come in, Robert.

DINGBY: Bring the room to me, Alexander. You're obviously taking it somewhere.
    (noticing and touching the flowers)
With your scientific mind, what sort of insects do you expect to catch with these?

McKAY: (not wanting to be frivolous) I asked you here with good reason.

DINGBY: Ah, it's my serious friend. Alexander McKay, you were never so bluff. Nor so decorous. It must be something serious.

McKAY: Serious, interesting. Some might laugh -- certainly not many are going to lament.

DINGBY: Interesting, serious, in a fete-like arrangement. The Governor's coming, is that it?

McKAY: Damn his eyes, man. If he cared, this wouldn't be necessary.

DINGBY: No? Then it's certainly not laughable. His neglect of state is only humorous when he attends to it. What then? A theatrical performance in John Citizen's parlour?
  (pause)
Ah, I see I'm being over-flippant.

McKAY: King Billy has died.

  (DINGBY glances away)

McKAY: You hear? King Billy died last night.

DINGBY: (more soberly) Last night, I know.

McKAY: The last one gone.

DINGBY: The last male surely, Alexander, but let's not forget our Queen Truganinni, though she might be of less academic interest, I'll warrant. She still warrants the mention, though, don't you think?

McKAY: He was to have been buried early this morning, but I had it postponed. Do you know why?

DINGBY: (theatrical again) Why? Alexander McKay, the best living authority on the intellectual endowments and the martial character of the now almost extinct Tasmanian Aboriginals. By right of word and interest, you have the authority. Why not you, after all? Though I'll ask. Why?

McKAY: To my knowledge, nobody knew he died last night. Nobody would have even been at his burial. No hats taken off, no standing still. King Billy, the last male gone, put away at nine and nobody the wiser. A few minutes past nine, then an end to the story?
  (pause)
We shouldn't get off so lightly. I had his burial postponed. I'm taking it on myself. Guests are coming; I've ordered my front door left open.

DINGBY: To all and their sundries?

McKAY: One burial. One decent, endorsed burial, Robert. Don't you think the race deserves that?

DINGBY: Of course. A minor request, the least, etcetera. Full rites to the ground, a spear, a waddy, union jacks, the unfurling of prayer; at last you'll see people bowing their heads over one of them. A Tasmanoid mourned. You've been trying for years.
    (pause, then slyly)
But peace in the ground? That too?

McKAY: (quickly positive) Peace in the soil that we took them from.

DINGBY: But drop the last male in and just let him lay there? Don't you know how valuable the skeleton of that man is?

McKAY: (looking) Be serious, Robert.

DINGBY: I am; you've seen me so before. What is a burial when Science and Anatomy are concerned? No, I'm serious in this case. Should we dig in what shouldn't historically ever be dug in?

    (McKAY is dismissive)

DINGBY: Look, a letter came to me a few months ago. It was from the Royal College, still crumbling around it's edges and I speak not of the letter's paper. I know that. But they asked of the possibility of procuring the bones of the last Tasmanian male. They want it for dangling in some comer to delight their old fools over vintage port back in London. That's all. But they want it, nonetheless.

McKAY: One decent burial, that's what he'll get.

DINGBY: No, no, you're forgetting real Science! It never even let the Industrial Revolution rest in its grave. You don't think it'll let Billy do so? Alexander?
    (meaningfully)
You ask your own Royal Society.

McKAY: If they've been waiting for his death like a pack of jackals, I'll resign.

296

DINGBY: The Royal Society's been digging up old bones and new for years, dear boy.

McKAY: He'll have a burial, a reception of the minimum of respect! And he'll have it this afternoon.

DINGBY: And you are going to give it to him. Well, who else?, as I've said.
   (losing interest)
Why did you invite me especially?

McKAY: I don't know. To help. To help me.
   (looks into the flowers, then, needing assistance...)
For years now people have come to me. 'Let's talk about the Tasmanoid', they say, 'What do you know?' A night's sky is black. Some people are. I am not. That's all I've been able to say.
   (then)
Yet I've dared to clear my throat and try.

DINGBY: You are the authority, Alex old son. It's that curious fame given by the Curious
.

McKAY: Fame? Attachment, rather. A vulture at the end of a hardening artery. I just thought I might need a comment on this afternoon... somebody to assess it, to say how it goes off. I thought you might be interested.

DINGBY: In anatomy, Alexander. Not in absolution of consciences.

McKAY: In humanity, damn it!

DINGBY: (doing so) Well, I'll arrange the flowers. The tip, the do. I was a choir boy once. You and me together. Don't you remember?

McKAY: (morbidly) Other things have been once.

DINGBY: Alexander, dear boy, why do you tie yourself up over them so much? From the outside, it's so... impotent. I mean, why don't you just do as most would in your position? Love the idea of them if you can't warm the flesh. After all, let's not get sordid. The

world needs thinkers. I mean, where would I be without thinkers? Some of my patients I loathe the sight of. Yet I still tickle them.
    (pause)
Even now you look disgusted with yourself. Did you kill him? Did you, in your secret way, aim silver at his heart?
    (gets no answer, holds up a flower)
Why not red? More dramatic.

        (Re-enter GILET)

GILET: It's arrived, sir.

McKAY: (relieved) Is Millington there?

GILET: He brought it with him.

DINGBY: The head tucked under his arm. That's our caretaker.

McKAY: Help him bring it in, Gilet. And go carefully. It will have enough rough treatment before today is over.

        (GILET nods, goes out. McKAY and the doctor wait expectantly.

        GILET and MILLINGTON, both struggling, come in with the coffin)

MILLINGTON: (conversation for the sake of it) He's all ready as you asked, Mr McKay. He's heavy though, heavy. A strapping lad, he was. Had to use all my strength on his biceps, ha ha.

McKAY: Put him on the table there.

DINGBY: (inappropriate and knowing it) A pyre fit for a king. I'll set a match to this table leg. Alexander, you'll have your final ritual. Wilting, curing, smoked and all.

McKAY: (for himself) He'll rest in my house for a while.

DINGBY: Now you're altogether too intense, Alex. You'll have all the ladies of Hobart following you with their tongues out. Our own pale and fiendishly attractive Alexander-Hamlet mooching along the scent trail of a ghost. A thimbleful of gin, spoonfuls of Madeira and all those chasing ladies will be thinking that Alexander McKay is fading on a pine-away. All that mothering instinct; they won't be able to resist you! And all the rest of us feeling so unmercifully human by comparison.

McKAY: (strained) Robert, you are my friend.

DINGBY: Professed and admitted.

McKAY: Will you be quiet, or will I throw you out?

(DINGBY shrugs, then turns away. GILET edges off)

MILLINGTON: (evasively) I did as much as possible, sir.

McKAY: (reacting to the hint) What's wrong?

MILLINGTON: ...Nothing, Mr McKay sir.
   (then quickly)
Nothing, like. The parlour has been busy this morning. Like a weight on my mind. You understand. People die, sir.

McKAY: (quickly bitter) Yes, yes. People die. We stretch out in the final measure. The fattest, the tallest, the heaviest, and so to the shrivel. People die, well said.

DINGBY: (amused, back in game) Don't be too hard on him, Alexander. To our esteemed undertaker, it's merely guild-like observance. Isn't it somewhat similar with our own guilds as well?

McKAY: As well as what? When you go will one human direction become extinct as well? And me who's done all the talking, and Millington here who's done all the laying-out, and Gilet who's done all the running after, will some unique human pathway dry up when we go? What's taken off the sum of things when we gasp our last?

MILLINGTON: (in ignorance) Somebody has to do the arranging, sir.

McKAY: (turning on him) Today, Millington, today, between the tiresome passings that cluttered up your parlour, there has been a death that will be thought on over. And on the imagining of the scene in this room, some man some time will lay down a farthing. A farthing for its worth… next to nothing, okay. But it's still a worth, Millington. And whoever he is, he will think on past us, past the geometry of this room, past that box and he will come to a halt when he comes to the fate of a poor black man who died and cluttered up your parlour for a time there. Yes, people die, Millington, and God bless the light!

(He strides from the room)

MILLINGTON: I say something wrong, Doctor? People do die.

DINGBY: (facetiously) They do indeed, Millington. And you were quite right in saying so, my good man. The world needs thinkers, though I've just said so. Take this room, this coffin. Take the flowers, or me. Take yourself, for instance...

MILLINGTON: What have I done, sir?

DINGBY: A blush in time, all, but we have to stand firm, being victims ourselves.

MILLINGTON: (confused) Pardon?

DINGBY: (leaving) Wait here, Millington. The guests will be along in a moment. I, with God's grace and the twinkle in His eye, will to Mr McKay with verbal balm.

(DINGBY leaves.

Alone, MILLINGTON furtively goes over to ensure that the lid of the coffin is securely screwed down. While he is doing so, enter MOLLY)

MILLINGTON: (mumbling) Sometimes I wish I had some competition. I hate political copses.

MOLLY: (right behind him) What did you say?

300

MILLINGTON: (startled) Who are you?

MOLLY: Molly, dearie, Molly. If you don't know me, you don't listen in the nice'n'naughty places, Gawd luvya. I know who you are. Carrying on with dead bodies like you do. Shame.

MILLINGTON: (scandalized) I beg yours?

MOLLY: I haven't got one. The day's all blue outside. I got talking with a spotted dog. Old Billy would have loved today. A good day to get buried in, if you're not out working. Molly of the Dog and Partridge; you must have heard of me. I mend sailors' legs by taking out the cork.
    (winks)
I can fix them up too, given half the chance.
      (She goes over to the coffin)
Is this Billy here?
    (knocking on the top)
Is this you, Billy?
    (theatrical wait)
It's you all right. No good denying it, eh?
    (remembering something)
Wait. Wait.

> *(She searches in her purse, pulls out a shilling, and ceremoniously places it on top of the coffin)*

MILLINGTON: What a filthy habit.'

MOLLY: Oh, I don't know about that, cock. I owe it to him in a sort of way. What I mean is, he didn't prove up to it, but he was brave, my Billy was. He'd have a go and pay his way. Last week-end, he paid up front, like.
    (can't suppress giggle)
It must have cursed his luck. If you get over-generous, something's sure to happen. I know, I know. I'm Molly, Dog and Partridge.

MILLINGTON: (formally) How do you do?

MOLLY: Passably, they say.

(then looking)
You must be the dirty old man who put him there.

MILLINGTON: I have only business relations with my client.

MOLLY: He was new to it, like most things, Billy was. Spotting
whales. But he never got sea-sick, not Billy. I used to sing him
shanties, so I ought to know. Though he was black, he was a bit of an
abo. I know the type, poor lovie. You can tell by their eyes they can't
leave it alone. He'd get paid, off he'd come, we'd have him at the Dog
and Partridge till... till... you know what?... till some dirty dog
laughed at him. And then he'd go; up and go.
     (pause)
I never come at that. The brats on the streets were the worst. They'
throw rocks. I didn't come at that, neither.
     (pause)
He was not bad, Billy wasn't. He was handsome and good. Honest
with money, he was. You could tell he wasn't used to it. And famous
as well. Lots of things... He met Prince Alfred, f'instance. Tea and
cakes and doilies to match. Billy said it was the first deck he hadn't
had to scrub while he was down there on his knees. It was aboard the
Royal yacht, see. It's a shame he's here.
     (dabs her eyes)
That's why I'm here. That's his shilling, all said n' done.

MILLINGTON: I didn't mean to be inquisitive, miss. Doesn't pay in
my profession.

MOLLY: You're a queer one, you are.
     (pointing at the coffin)
Who's going to do you like that when the time comes?

MILLINGTON: (eagerly) Oh, I know it all off by heart!

> *(Then realizes, when she laughs, he's said something foolish.
> He turns away and sulks. MOLLY walks around the coffin, as
> though there might be a peek-hole in it.*
>
> *Re-enter DINGBY, effects 'love at first sight')*

DINGBY: An apparition. A vision. Venus unthroned. Stop exactly where you are.

MOLLY: Oh, it's you.

DINGBY: Me, my chick-a-dee.

MOLLY: (petulantly) Hoi, I've come to be solemn. My friend is in here.

DINGBY: Millington?

MOLLY: No, just resting.

(and laughs raucously)

DINGBY: ('rising' to her) What a coincidence! Millington, my dear chap, truth and lies here do dovetail and pattern. This sweet, once dear and still costly creature is here because of Billy's mind. I am here for his body. You are here for what you can get out of laying both to rest. What a travelling troupe we three would make! And he, how our King Billy has danced to our tune!
    (to MOLLY)
Ah, angel, the thoughts you inspire.

MOLLY: (sulkily) I've come to be respectable, not talk to gentlemen.

MILLINGTON: Dr Dingby. Miss. Please. Decorum.

DINGBY: Millington is right. Undertakers invariably are in the end.

(Pause)

MOLLY: Come and have a look.
    (to MILLINGTON)
You too. Come on. For him, just a peep. Come on, old Bill won't bite.

(The three gather to look for a solemn moment over the coffin)

DINGBY: Far away. A memory already.

MOLLY: (softly) Kids would throw stones at him.

DINGBY: (but with wider meaning) Foreshadowing the surgeon's cold mind?

MOLLY: All kids are like that, little buggers.

DINGBY: And men with scalpels.

MOLLY: (looking at him sharply) What d'you mean?

DINGBY: (too innocently) Why, the word, that's all, my cluck. 'Scalpels'. Have you ever rolled it around your tongue and noticed the way it rattles... oh, yes, rather, rattles... about one's head? Scalpels is an incisive word, scalpels is. It comes from the word scalp, I imagine and appropriately.

> *(The others don't even pretend to know what he is talking about, even more so that he has become quite serious.*
>
> *DINGBY shrugs, tries to laugh his way out of it)*

DINGBY: Well, what's deemed fashionable must be done or by God the board of governors of the old Society will burp his annoyance very rudely and loudly across the whole of London. Wouldn't want our Billy to cause a gush like that.

> *(Enter the two whaling boat captains COLVIN and TIMMS. DINGBY welcomes them, almost rudely)*

DINGBY: Why, gentlemen, whoever or whatever you are, you're the perfect guests. Come in, come in. Seat yourselves for the showing. If you're good at arranging flowers, you might make yourselves useful in the meantime.

COLVIN: (gruffly) We heard of the invitation.

DINGBY: To be sure.

TIMMS: Is that Billy?

DINGBY: He's the only guest that has not said so.

> (COLVIN and TIMMS don't take kindly to his supercilious attitude. They go over to the coffin. They openly inspect it before:)

COLVIN: (suspiciously) Where is McKay?

DINGBY: The deceased was one of your crew, I gather?

MILLINGTON: (disapprovingly) He was. They engage half-castes as well.

DINGBY: And still bring in whales? That harpoon's extremely well...
   (for phonetic)
...cast.

COLVIN: (brushing that aside) Where is Mr McKay in all this?

DINGBY: The invitation was only for poor Billy. Mr McKay is very much alive. When his day comes you'll hear in good time; I shouldn't worry.

MOLLY: (playfully) I'll be here too if he gives me fair warning.

DINGBY: Alexander McKay won't die without completing arrangements, sweet girl. Invitations will go out, signed by his own hand. Just listen for the bells, and RSVP. as soon as you can.

MOLLY: You are a fool.

DINGBY: A doctor second. In order of merit.

COLVIN: (scornfully) Is this a funeral?

DINGBY: (amused) Not due to begin for another few seconds. I believe the guest of honour is here, but not the toaster. Until he charges us to fill our glasses, I hope you'll forgive a man for working up a little tickle of a thirst.

COLVIN: (booming) I said where's McKay?

McKAY: Here.

> *(They turn. McKAY, with GILET, has entered the room.*

> *He shakes the Captains' hands, which they give grudgingly)*

McKAY: You must be Colvin and Timms. I hear you treated Billy kindly, so thank you for that.
    (to GILET)
Do we expect any more to arrive?
    (GILET shakes his head)
Right, we'll begin then. Who's to carry with me?

COLVIN: (cutting him short) Wait a minute, McKay.

TIMMS: It's a decent thing you're doing for Billy, but there's just one thing we'd like to know...

COLVIN: ... why are you doing this?

TIMMS: Aye, we'll have an answer before you go on.

McKAY: Who else, if not me? Some government clerk?

COLVIN: Us! We'll break our backs carrying the lad alone, if need be. We'll hear the truth and either leave or join you.

McKAY: (impatiently) You may leave or join us, as you wish. That coffin is mine.

COLVIN: (really aggressive) But not what's in it, McKay.

McKAY: Come or go, either way.

TIMMS: We'll stay only if it's not a vain show, McKay.

McKAY: Good. We're going to need all the hands we can get.

COLVIN: Then open that box. We'll have a look inside.

McKAY: (arrested) What? What did you say?

TIMMS: We're sea captains. McKay. Before we join a ship, we'll look inside her.

McKAY: Have you gone quite mad?

COLVIN: (booming) Will you open that box, or will I tear it apart?

McKAY: No! I'll leave that to God. Now get out of my house!

> (TIMMS sees MILLINGTON trying to edge off. He catches the
> undertaker, and twists his ear)

TIMMS: Your rats are deserting McKay.

MILLINGTON: (squirming) Why me?

TIMMS: Tell us, what have you and your friends done with our boy in there. We'll hear it out of your own mouth, then we'll leave you all alone. To talk and be damned.

McKAY: You're speaking nonsense!

MILLINGTON: (hysterically) I do what I'm told to!

TIMMS: (twisting harder) More!

MILLINGTON: Lamp and shades'. Mr McKay...!

> (Enter ATWELL, the Colonial Under-Secretary)

ATWELL: (impeccably) Now, now, Captain Timms, release that creature. You will have to be in his hands too one day.

McKAY: Atwell.

ATWELL: I see I've come at just the right time, Alexander.

DINGBY: (oddly bitter) Ah, the government imprint has arrived. See the tortoise behind its shell. Slow moving but well cased in.

ATWELL: Ever observant, Doctor Dingby.

DINGBY: But, my dear Atwell, you are dressed for important work. The tie, the suit, the brolly, the felt hat; it's all so meaningfully drab.

ATWELL: It's not my best finery, I grant you.

TIMMS: Official or not, Mr Atwell?

ATWELL: Alas, Captain, with service for the public, one is never off duty. I'm always glad to be amongst friends, though. And on rare occasions that gives me the chance to indulge my natural curiosity.
    (meaningfully to DINGBY)
Doctor, you should know.

DINGBY: (strangely uncomfortable) There is a ring of novelty in this situation, I agree.

   (And turns away 'into' himself)

TIMMS: (had enough) Come on, Colvin.

McKAY: Wait!
    (turning to ATWELL)
You are here officially. That's obvious. What isn't is why?

ATWELL: The Governor's discretion and, I confess, his slight bemusement. After all, Alexander, the government was to pay for the burial, but at nine o'clock this morning. Not now and not here. You see our problem?

McKAY: The same cost to bury a pauper, nothing more.

ATWELL: But nothing less.

McKAY: A few formalities fit for a human being that's what I expect from a government that's never done anything for them before.
(then to COLVIN and TIMMS)
You came here because of something you heard. I know nothing of this.

TIMMS: (looking) Perhaps you don't.

McKAY: What was it?

TIMMS: It's got around that Billy has been tampered with, McKay. That more than his clothes were taken off him.

(McKAY turns sharply towards ATWELL who does not commit himself. He then moves towards MILLINGTON)

McKAY: Millington?

MILLINGTON: (backing off) I only do a job, Mr McKay.' I've got no competition, see!

McKAY: Open that coffin.

(MILLINGTON looks towards ATWELL)

McKAY: OPEN THAT COFFIN!

(MILLINGTON is jolted towards the box)

MOLLY: 'Ere, is that allowed? I mean, would you like it?

DINGBY: It's a question of property, not propriety, my dear. The bird may have flown his coop or gone to seed. It's better to be sure.

MOLLY: But that's my Billy in there! That's my shilling on top. How would you like it? How would you like to be caught in a position like that?

McKAY: (to MILLINGTON) Get a move on.

(Finally, MILLINGTON gets the coffin lid loosened.)

McKAY moves forward as do the others. He opens the coffin.

A general recoil. MOLLY turns away, gulps back nausea)

McKAY: (stunned, staring) My God, my God.

COLVIN: (to ATWELL) I should tear your bloody heart out for this.

McKAY: You're in on this, Atwell?

ATWELL: Officially, that's all. I was sent here to prevent just this sort of thing, Alexander. Please calm down, all of you.

(His normally overbearing manner is just right for this occasion. They all stop to gather themselves)

TIMMS: (quietly) He was a fine young man with arms as strong as any's. He would have bred had girls survived for him. I had a photograph taken of him last year. It was 'too' black for him, he said. Too black' for him. We had him thinking that way. That was a crime.

McKAY: (almost deadpan at ATWELL) You've stumped his legs and cut off his hands. Why not his heart? Why not his… personals? And why his skull as well, when so warm, Atwell, when it must have still been warm? Answer me that, Atwell. Why butcher him? You're not going to answer?

ATWELL: (finally) The Governor is sorry for what has been necessary. Let me explain...

DINGBY: (genuinely, to McKAY) No, don't turn away, Alexander. Atwell is right. We run and walk in this world, but one or two of us do so watched. King Billy was one. King Billy and his life; it's been ours right from the start. Think on it. He himself knew he was a public performance.

ATWELL: Millington, go and get a seal. No one else must open this coffin again.

(MILLINGTON leaves gladly)

ATWELL: (to McKAY) Your own Royal Society thought our museum should have Billy's bones. They petitioned the Governor demanding the right of the skeleton. He agreed in principle over other institutions that made applications but not in fact. In other words, your colleagues...

McKAY: No longer my colleagues.

ATWELL: ... your Royal Society colleagues were told that if any one group should have the bones it should be them, yes... but since no one group could, their claim was denied.

McKAY: What about me?

ATWELL: The Governor would bank on Billy being safe in your hands, Alexander.
    (then looking meaningfully at DINGBY)
It seems that our other scientific institutions were after the corpse as well. Is that not so, Dr Dingby?

DINGBY: (not now taken aback) Mr Atwell, sir, you're a crafty rascal. I had to make enquiries for my College of Surgeons, yes. Wonderful great bellies, the bunch of them. An oath of allegiance stretches out into the colony's way, sir. Which shows it up for its own stupidity, I agree.

ATWELL: Well put.

DINGBY: Not well put enough to secure Billy boy.

ATWELL: That is right, too.
    (turns back to McKAY)
Alexander, last night while the body lay in hospital, its head was skinned and the skull removed. We don't know who by but
    (pointing to the coffin)
that one you see in there, ill fitting, was from a dead white man who had his skull similarly removed. You perhaps will grant the Governor had to act quickly. It was obvious that somebody wanted the skull to blackmail us for the rest of the skeleton. Crude but effective. After all,

what good is a skeleton without its head? As worthless as one without
hands or feet. As your Royal Society friends were quick to point out.
They feared body-snatching for the rest of the body in the grave
tonight. So they re-petitioned the Governor and reminded him of his
decree. Under sanction, therefore, they were allowed to remove what
they called 'the extremities'. Hands and feet to us. They've been
stored in a safe place, the Governor is told.
    (pause)
It is now hoped that whoever took the skull will realize it to be as
worthless as a part of a body sans 'extremities', and hence return it.
McKAY: You people, you want to carve up everything we kill?

ATWELL: (kindly) Not that.

McKAY: (to DINGBY) What did you know of this?

DINGBY: Only what was pre-ordained, Alexander.

McKAY: (nodding, quietening) You warned me.

DINGBY: I did, my friend.

    (GILET comes into the room)

GILET: There's one more outside, sir. Shall I let her in.

McKAY: More's the point: will they let us out?
    (then)
No, Gilet, nobody else.

GILET: (intimately) She's the one you wanted me to keep a look-out
for, sir.

McKAY: (reacting) Truganinni! Bring her in! Close that coffin,
quickly!

DINGBY: Why, haven't they met?

McKAY: Fool! Fool!

ATWELL: Do it, Gilet.

(GILET hurries to attend to the coffin, but is fumbling. He stops inexplicably when TRUGANINNI enters.

She is now nearing seventy years old... an old lady. She shuffles over to the coffin, looks down at it, then backs away to a chair. She does not speak, and sits, staring ahead with little involvement.

The others watch, then seem to forget about her.

COLVIN brings their attentions back to the coffin.)

COLVIN: He was our boy, the top-of-the-mast man. They don't come often, not as good as that. Something about being black; he could see a whale when it wasn't there for us. One of the best.

MOLLY: He always paid, if not beforehand.

TIMMS: (at her) Aye. He knew you, too. You're from the Dog and Partridge. He was a bit of a young stallion. He would've known you.

MOLLY: He'd try, try. I'll grant you that.

COLVIN: Though a black first, he was a sailor first, mark.

TIMMS: No, man... I reckoned a black first, a sailor after. Strange that, strange.

COLVIN: It didn't worry me. Nor him. Nor none, well enough. When they got t'know him.

TIMMS: You'd see his old crony women ...
    (indicating TRUGANINNI)
like her, poking and scratching, laughing at him. Him asking could any of them have kids because he's just found out he's the only man left.
    (pause)
Further back too. He'd tell us things. A boy, taking his first steps, his mother laying a lizard across the palm of his hand, and humming to him:

313

Be good
Be kind
Do not touch things that belong to others.
Do not touch any such thing.
Be good.
Be kind.

COLVIN: Aye, there were the songs, one or two. To warm the night. He was scared of the sea. But his eyesight was good, and so were his songs.

McKAY: (painfully) We won't wait any longer.

(Re-enter MILLINGTON with wax and an old brass stamp)

MILLINGTON: I couldn't find a seal, sir.

ATWELL: Then what is that?

MILLINGTON: A brass stamp from out of our dispensary.
    (looking at it oddly)
I think.

ATWELL: (impatiently) Has it got a pattern?

MILLINGTON: (nodding) I can't make out what it is.

ATWELL: It will do. Just get on.

(MILLINGTON applies the wax in several places. He presses on the stamp, looks, and takes an involuntary step backwards. Laughs weakly)

ATWELL: What is it now, man?

MILLINGTON: (apologetically) It was all I could find, Mr Atwell.

(DINGBY pushes the undertaker to one side, and looks at the seal)

314

DINGBY: (with hard humour) Alexander, this is for your sense of the dramatic. Look, man. The carcass is finally branded by the sole claimant owner...

(McKAY looks)

McKAY: (incredulous) 'World'...?

DINGBY: Fire on fire, dear boy. There it is. 'World'. You have your answer. Much more than Atwell could possibly say.

TIMMS: Move him, McKay! Here's my shoulder!

COLVIN: And mine for pity, man!

McKAY: Take him, take him away.

(COLVIN, TIMMS, GILET and MILLINGTON hoist up the box. They leave. The others follow one by one.

TRUGANINNI gets up lifelessly. As she walks past McKAY, he stops her)

ROBINSON: Truganinni, will you stay here with me? A guest in my house, Truganinni. You can rest here as long as you like.

(After a time, TRUGANINNI looks up, nods casually, then shuffles out after the others.

McKAY follows.

Blackout)

2.

(Next day. The furniture returned to its usual place.
McKAY is sitting looking at the table.

Enter ATWELL)

McKAY: (rising) Mr Under-Secretary ... you've caught me unprepared. Where is Gilet?

ATWELL: I brought something of yours with me. He's helping with it. A good man, that Gilet. Have you thought of his parole?

McKAY: He's safe enough here. A servant of the state, but he's better as a friend of mine.

ATWELL: Yes, of course.
   (pause)
You're looking tired, Alexander.

McKAY: I tried to do something yesterday. A quip, a gesture; more than I should, I suppose. Today, I have a strong sense of failure.

ATWELL: Other people have never had your interest in the race, that's all. To them, the Tasmanian was an oddity -- King Billy, therefore, a show piece.

McKAY: (bitterness rising again) As vague as that? You know better.

ATWELL: Perhaps.

McKAY: Objects of lust, savages to hate or fear, then scavengers of contempt. In that order, the history of the Tasmanians. And now they are gone, objects of derision. Not even allowed to go to their Maker whole. A few dangling loose ends. About seventy-five years, that's all they could stand us. They simply laid down to die, Atwell, and I fancy that's an adequate commentary on us when all's said and done.

ATWELL: You're a funny man, Alexander. Still, your efforts do not go unnoticed. You're a humanitarian, and people are looking to you for that. As an official, I can say it with knowledge. By the way, you have Truganinni staying here with you?

McKAY: I am harbouring her, yes.

ATWELL: Watch over her closely. Mobs would claw past you just to see her now. Being the last, she's doubly unique. That makes people doubly insistent.

McKAY: I'll watch over her.

ATWELL: As we all know you will.
   (indicating intention of leaving)
Well ...

McKAY: What did you say you had for me?

ATWELL: I'll see to it on my way out. It was nothing important.

McKAY: (knowingly) If you have the coffin outside, let them bring it in.

ATWELL: (shrewdly) You've heard?

McKAY: Nothing. You've changed your manner. That could only mean one thing. Yesterday, I actually thought I could give him peace in the ground.

ATWELL: After yesterday ... I don't think I can bring myself to tell you.

McKAY: I am no dried-boned optimist. They can bring it in.

   (ATWELL leaves the room, calls, then re-enters.

   Enter GILET and another man carrying an empty coffin. They set it down, then leave quickly.

   McKAY goes over to look at it)

McKAY: Quite, quite empty. Did he ever exist? King Billy, the last hope, vanished.
   (fiercely)
I felt so sure I could prevent this. I felt I could ...
   (stops)
I can't even remember what I felt I could do. Maybe shame them.

ATWELL: The grave was found disturbed this morning. I was called. The earth had been removed and the coffin partly hoisted up. On the ground nearby, that skull, the substituted one. Everything around was saturated with blood. The constable swore he was asleep and heard nothing. I could have him broken, but what's the use?

McKAY: Where ...?

ATWELL: Where is the body? It may not even be in fat form by now. A trail of blood ran from the grave to one of the gates. But, for all purposes, King Billy has been snatched -- minus his hands, his feet, his skull, minus his dignity. What else ...

TRUGANINNI: AIEE!

(She stumbles into the room. For a moment she rocks, hugging herself, in a kneeling position, then fully collapses in a faint)

McKAY: My God, she heard you!

(They go over and try to pick her up.

Blackout)

3.

(The living room. A week later. McKAY and DINGBY)

McKAY: How serious is it?

DINGBY: My dear friend, I'm only a doctor, and a pretty crude one at that. I've helped to fashion the times but not once have I healed it. That's Robert Dingby.

McKAY: There must be something wrong with her, man.

DINGBY: (shrugging) The Tasmanoid has been going off like this for seventy-five years and we still don't know why.

McKAY: With Billy, it was diarrhea.

DINGBY: Choleraic diarrhea. With the others, mainly consumption. But these are only symptoms. It's the way the symptoms materialize and refuse to respond.

McKAY: She refuses food.

DINGBY: She's dying, Alexander.

McKAY: (stopping) Is that what you honestly think?

DINGBY: She's dying, I know.

McKAY: But what of, man, what of?
   (no reply)
I had to pick her up of this very floor that day. Atwell came to her feet. Bloody fool that I was. I tried to lift her from under the armpits. The only thing that gave was her dress. She looked like she was staring up at me, unblinking, spittle running from her mouth. She kept frothing and when she awoke, kept wringing her hands.
   (pause)
An hour later, probably more, she finally stopped. The other day, she went to go out into the street. There was that crowd still outside, waiting for her. When I heard the screams she made, Gilet had to haul her back. But that's not even over. That lack of movement in her legs.

DINGBY: Anything particular she talks about?

McKAY: (with shame) I can't seem to go in to see her.

DINGBY: You're doing enough, Alexander. Don't worry.

McKAY: Are you absolutely positive you can't help her?

DINGBY: Me? I'm one of those who has already done his worst.

319

McKAY: (suddenly fierce) Have you ever thought what it must be like to be a biological freak? A joke of Nature?

DINGBY: She is dying. The answer is there. Why should she act the tragedienne?

McKAY: You think that's what she's thinking?

DINGBY: What else?

McKAY: It's not necessary. Not here. Not in my house, Robert.

   (Pause)

DINGBY: I can't give you that guarantee, Alexander.

McKAY: I only wanted it confirmed.

DINGBY: It'll be as long as she sees fit.

McKAY: (suddenly) I want her story!
   (trying for justification)
 I want her story, Robert.

DINGBY: You think she will give it to you?

   (McKAY shrugs)

DINGBY: If she would tell it, I suppose it Could do you both good. I knew a minstrel once. He was always after stories. He'd sing them once and then never use them again. Sucked the goodness out of them, he said.

McKAY: (quiet determination) She must give it to me.

DINGBY: Bring her in here. It's bright enough and cool. And central; it'll be a part payment in return for you. Well, I'm off, dear boy. I've got an appointment with a certain Molly, currently of the Dog and Partridge. She uses better medicine than I could prescribe myself, and I really do need the cheering. You and your damn over-compassion, parches the throat. I think you're after a hounding for us all.

McKAY: (caustically) Before you go, how is your College of Surgeons going to feel about this?

DINGBY: I tell you frankly, there'll be some interest as before. Star attractions only last until the next one comes along. Back in London town, I can see the advertisements already starting to be put up. I'd rather be here. At least there's lamentation here.

McKAY: Yes, I am lamenting. I feel it's all my fault.

DINGBY: No, stop that.

(He turns to leave, stops)

DINGBY: She's got the death-wish, Alexander. With that story, don't wait too long.

(He leaves, McKAY sits silently for a while, then:)

McKAY: (calling) Gilet?

(GILET enters)

McKAY: Ask Truganinni to come in here. No, tell her and move her things in here.

(Blackout)

4.

(TRUGANINNI sits half-propped on a sofa. She is staring at the wall. Some untouched food is on the tray beside her.

Note: The shadow play of a large crowd outside can be seen through the window. Throughout this scene, the shadows get larger; they spread more and more across the floor towards her.

Enter McKAY. He does so tentatively. Though she hears him, she doesn't look around)

McKAY: There's food beside you, Truganinni.
  (no reaction)
There are some questions about food, but not about what it's for.
How are you feeling?
  (offering hand)
Would you like to try and walk today? Try. You don't you're your legs going, you know that.
  (a dismissive pause)
I said, would you like to try and walk, Truganinni?

TRUGANINNI: (into air, almost lullaby) A ridge of sand and animal droppings. If it was only me, I would be glad. If it was only me, I would dance on an empty belly. I would dance for my father.

McKAY: Try to walk. Outside, even when it's raining, people stand waiting for you. They'll give you cheer.

TRUGANINNI: (rocking) Oi... oi...

McKAY: What's the matter? They know you're in my house, so why don't you look out?
  (pause)
You're safe here. I'm here. Don't you know, want to know, me?

TRUGANINNI: (into air) At night, my father would light his fire at a place apart. My mother comes singing to him. I hear her scream, and deep by my stick I finger the yams...

McKAY: Here, your red handkerchief. You wear it when you're out walking in town. Remember.
  (then directive)
Just make yourself remember.

TRUGANINNI: If I was alone, I would dance empty-bellied. Hands on my belly.

McKAY: Truganinni!

TRUGANINNI: (languid) What do you want with me?

McKAY: You are a guest in my house.

TRUGANINNI: I know.

McKAY: Just try to get better.

> (TRUGANINNI begins to hum)

McKAY: You needn't keep yourself sick. What's the point? Not...
here. Why here?
   (she hums over him)
On your life, are any of us here running you down now?
   (she stops humming, thinks on that)
Am I running you down now? Is anyone here?

TRUGANINNI: (flinging question back) Why are you running us
down? Why are you running us down, white man?
   (just as suddenly returns to crooning)
A ridge of sand and animal droppings.

McKAY: Eat some food. Sleep, sleep.
   (gets annoyed at continuing no reaction)
Will-you-take-some- food?

> (He is about to give up, when:)

TRUGANINNI: (laconic) You have gone to trouble.

McKAY: No.

TRUGANINNI: The killing is finished with. You will tell me that.

McKAY: A few mouthfuls, and you'll be back to your old self. A
little pot of ale, hmm?

> (TRUGANINNI turns her eyes to the wall)

TRUGANINNI: The fire would be lit; though in the air would be...
whisperings sss sss.

> *(The shadows of the crowd outside swell; the people asking to
> see her become audible. She shudders.)*

TRUGANINNI: Don't let them in until I am far away.

McKAY: Don't stay sick or I must, Truganinni.

TRUGANINNI: Oi, they will come...

> *(Noise of crowd fades a little. In the lull...)*

McKAY: They wait outside all our doors. Eventually. One door to
one man. There shouldn't be more, Truganinni. My own will come
soon enough. Walk out from here. Don't let there be so many outside
my door.

> *(But she remains with face averted. He speaks to her of his own
> guilt; he wants her to understand)*

McKAY: Listen. Listen... there runs one of your women with a belly
bulge in front. I'm too young to know what it is. She can't escape so
she climbs a tree. I was only a lad and I shoot at her, laughing. And
then the scream. When I open my eyes, a foetus drops, bounces at my
feet... then her... I think it was my father's gun! *I think it was me!*

> *(He stops, shocked by the confession. After the silence that
> follows...)*

TRUGANINNI: What do you care?

McKAY: One day, they'll be waiting outside for me. I will die with
it.

TRUGANINNI: Who will care?

McKAY: Let me save you from this!'

TRUGANINNI: Will you make love to me, white man, give me presents? I am dirty down there; there has been plenty of company.

McKAY: Old woman, when your people were being shot at, I went out to try conciliation. You know that; you were with Robinson. I did my best to make it up what I did. But I swear I didn't do it just to send you all to die on that island. Nobody could say I did that.
    (pause, then)
But who would say that I didn't? Would you? Will you stand up for me and say that I didn't, Truganinni?
    (she refuses to reply)
If you won't, then nobody will. You know that. All right, old woman, I fired a bullet. But I was young. Don't you see? None of you ever said to me, all right Alexander McKay, you've made it up, go your way. *None.* Why can't you? Now. The last. Just say it. Will it kill you to say it?

    (He is drowned out by the mob outside surging again. The
    shadows inch towards TRUGANINNI. She moans)

McKAY: (heavily accusing her) What do you want? More of my ridicule than even King Billy's funeral? Are you wishing another Billy on me, old woman?

    (The crowd momentarily drowns him out. Now she is almost
    opening reversing things and pointing it out to him.
    He has to shout to be heard now)

McKAY: You should answer me something. I'm involved, Truganinni, but don't let all the plays end with me.

TRUGANINNI: (sing-song) My legs were not strong enough to keep them away. My mother is dead when she speaks to my father. The waratah is wild and the ferns, my ferns ... oi, why should I always be afraid? It is finished ago.

McKAY: (actually getting furious) I've asked you here; you owe me something. Those people outside know you're in my house. You must walk out of here!

TRUGANINNI: (outcry) Don't let them cut me up!

(The sound of the crowd rises to crescendo)

McKAY: Give me your word you will walk out of my house!

TRUGANINNI: Don't let them cut me up! Bury me behind the mountains!

McKAY: *Don't do this in my house!*

> *(Crowd noise and shadows cut off suddenly.*
>
> *TRUGANINNI cringes into her blankets.*
>
> *In the contrasting lull, McKAY waits for a reaction from her, gets none, then finally, with great heaviness, gestures disassociation)*

McKAY: So. The Tasmanians die...

(He leaves her)

> *TRUGANINNI begins to hum softly. The crowd surges again; its shadows envelope her while she is very alone.*
>
> *Blackout)*

(End)

BULLSH

(OR, THAT BLOODY COW)

The Yarns

BULLSH is based on the best-selling 'Australian Yarns' by Ron Edwards. First published by Rigby Ltd, 1974, and re-issued by the University of Queensland Press in 1996.

Individual actors are free to go their own ways with relating the yarns and relate them as is or reduce them according to their own rhythms.

Other works by Ron Edwards

Ron Edwards authored nearly 300 books as one of Australia's most versatile and creative authors and folklorists. His output includes works in fiction, nonfiction (on such topics as leather working, the wheat industry), sketchbooks, travel guides, folk lore including ballads, music and oral traditions. The list goes on. He was a fine painter and illustrator in his own right.

He founded and was the guiding light behind North Queensland's favourite publishing house, The Rams Skull Press in Kuranda at ramskullpress.com, from where a full list of his books can be got with many still in print.

The National Library of Australia and all major public, school and private libraries contain full catalogue details on Ron's work as well.

The Rams Skull Press remains the oldest privately owned publishing house in Australia. The business has been owned and operated by the Edwards family for over fifty years. The very first books issued under the banner of the Rams Skull Press were printed by Ron Edwards in 1950 and were a short run of books on a traditionalist's screw press featuring linocuts created by Ron.)

The Plays

Bullsh
Premiered at the Playbox Theatre, Melbourne, on 7 July 1978.
Director   Malcolm Robertson
Designer   John Beckett
Cast: Athol Compton, Cliff Ellen, Brian Hannon, Frederick Parslow,
John Wood

More Bullsh
Premiered at Playbox Theatre, Melbourne, November 1978.
Director   Malcolm Robertson
Designer   John Beckett
Cast: Cliff Ellen, Frederick Parslow, John Wood

Act 1

(The time is later afternoon, early evening. The shadows will grow and the sunset will eventually deepen to evoke a sense of something passing.

The noise from inside the outback pub is rising and falling as it does throughout.

But right now, out here on the pun's verandah, there is a frozen moment. It is centred on MICK and POP... but SANDY and PRICKY, who are also sitting out there, seem to be waiting expectantly too.

MICK is literally staring at POP's ear from only a few centimetres away. He is not inspecting it or touching it; he is merely leaning forward towards it, having just shouted into it and now waiting breathlessly for an answer – as though the ear itself would answer back.

While we wait we observe that SANDY and PRICKY are sitting in their places so comfortably that they are obviously in their time-honoured spots. POP, too, is seated in what is significantly the only chair of the verandah. Its throne-like height somehow typifies not only his age but also the greater length of time that he has been coming to the pub.

As the 'frieze' extends in time, MICK's expectancy for the answer becomes palpable; he seems mesmerised by POP's ear and cannot take his eyes from it.

POP clears his throat. It is a signal for even SANDY and PRICKY to look up. But nothing further comes. MICK drags his attention away from the ear and 'leans' forehead-to-forehead with POP to stare unblinkingly into the old man's eyes. All he gets is an unblinking stare back.

After this anticlimax, SANDY and PRICKY go back to their own thoughts again.

Finally, MICK can't stand it any longer. He yells at POP:)

MICK   Well?!

(This scares the life out of the other two, but doesn't cause POP to turn an eyebrow)

SANDY   Jesus wept!

MICK   (appeal) Give's a hand, you blokes.

PRICKY   (shrugs) He can't hear a word you're saying.

MICK   The old bugger's lying doggo.

PRICKY   Who?

MICK   Why didn't you?

SANDY   Why didn't we what?

MICK   (eyes upwards) Jeezwept. So why'd he ask me what I'm doing with the 'dozer here for then?

SANDY   Wondering that meself. Weren't you, Pricky?

PRICKY   Who?

MICK   (loses patience) Man'd get more sense out of...
    (indicates inside pub)
that mob in there and I can't understand a word of what the buggers are saying.
    (goes to stride off inside, but stops for:)
Tell me when Johnno lobs up, okay?

(and goes in. The screen door creaks as traditionally unoiled. It will be a sound that is a constant reminder that this pub is an old one that hasn't been touched by progress up to now.

Just as MICK disappears inside, POP comes to life with a

bursting vengeance, shouts after him:)

POP   Bring out 'nother three while you're at it, son.
   (to others)
Think he heard me?

SANDY   Dunno, Pop.

POP   (nudging SANDY with his foot as he does throughout) What?

SANDY   (shouts reply as he does throughout) Dunno!

POP   You never know if they're listening these days.

   (Verandah frieze again.

   *POP again clears his throat. The other two again look his way
   and then turn back when nothing comes out.*

   *But POP this time is actually winding himself for an absolute
   gush of words)*

POP   You wouldn't read about what someone was just telling me,
y'wouldn't. Goin' on about how they're 'dosing this place into the
ground tomorrow. That so? My old Dad, he first come here when I
was about ten, I reckon. Dyou think he could ever spit through a
snake's bum at fifty paces! That's another story. Course, I could
drink a bit more in those days. Started to taper off when I got around
fifteen. Met the old girl, what happened. Responsibilities. Drove a
man crazy, she did. That someone, he was saying some river or
something coming right through here. How come I ain't ever seen a
river wandering around here? Says they're going to turn this place
into a lake or something. Stuff having a lake. If I want a lake I go to
the dunny, don't I?
   (thinks seriously about that)
Who was saying this is the last day for this place? Says there's a big
mob of high-up poofs grogging on inside on account of the place
won't be standing tomorrow. Poofs! What's the flaming world
coming to if a bloke can't get near his own bar for high-up poofs up
from the city? You listening? If you two blokes listened instead of

333

yakking all the time you'd hear a few things. What's wrong with
you?... letting poofs take over a man's sacred place. Wait up.
   (rethinks)
Some bastard just told me that they're gonna 'dose the whole place
into the bloody ground tomorrow. What lying bastard would say that
to an old man? Thought that that young Mick was one of the hands
out of your place. What's he doing driving a dozer anyway? Don't
you teach them anything proper?
   (getting panicky)
I can't swim. I ain't gonna sit here in the middle of some great big
bloody lake with poofs floating all around a man.
   (finally stops)

SANDY She'll be oke, Pop!

POP (sudden revival) What's going on anyway...?

SANDY Last day, Pop!

PRICKY (hard whisper) Don't tell him.

SANDY Aw, he's got to know.
   (shout back to POP)
You'n'me, we've near done our dash, Pop, so drink up!

> *(But POP, deliberately or not – we don't know -- is no longer
> listening to him. SANDY turns back to PRICKY)*

SANDY Last day. Ain't it a fact.

PRICKY Even most of my mob's buggered off into town today.
Nice loyalty to God and country, that is.

SANDY (sadly) Aw, well, what can you expect?

PRICKY Who?

> *(They meditate.*

> *We now see that this sadness mostly explains the occasional
> periods of silence they have between them. This characterises,*

*too, their movements of annoyance when either a burst of
laughter or of singing comes from inside. One of these bursts
of singling comes now.*

*PRICKY puts his ear up against the window by his head. He
hears all he wants to and pulls away absolutely horrified.)*

PRICKY They're singing about Sydney, and that's only one of my
favourites, and I don't even know em. What's the world coming to?

SANDY I wouldn't let 'em get away with that!

PRICKY Who?

SANDY You.

PRICKY Bloody won't either!

SANDY Knew you wouldn't, Prick.

PRICKY (but stopping) What'll I do?

SANDY ('simple') Drown 'em out.

*(PRICKY stops at this, looks at SANDY for a shocking display
of bad taste)*

SANDY (long-sufferingly) You drown 'em out, not in-the-lake
drown them out. Cripes.

PRICKY Bloody will, too!

*(He picks up the tune from inside and sings the song loudly,
competitively. SANDY joins in when he can and claps time.
They take over the song:)*

PRICKY:
By the sluggish river Gwyder lived a wicked redback spider
And he was just as vicious as could be.
And the place he camped in was a rusty IXL jam tin.
So he was also just as sticky as could be

Near him lay a shearer snoring; he'd been on the beer all morning
And all the night before and all that very day
And the kooking of the kookers and the noisy showground spruikers
Failed to raise him from the trance in which he lay

When a crafty looking spieler with a dainty looking sheila
Came along collecting wood to make a fire,
Said the spieler, 'There's a boozer, and he gonna be a loser,
And if he isn't you can christen me a liar.
Wriggle around and keep it, honey, while I pan the mug for money
And we'll have some little luxuries for tea.'
But she answered, 'Don't be silly, you go back and boil the billy;
You can safely leave the mug to little me.'

She circled ever nearer, til she reached the dopey shearer
With his pockets bulging, fast asleep and snug.
But she didn't see the spider that was lurking there beside her
For her mind was on the money and the mug.
Now the spider wanted dinner, he was growing daily thinner
He'd been fasting, was as hollow as an urn;
She eyed the bulging pocket, he just darted like a rocket
And bit the spieler's sheila on the stern.

Like a flash she raced off squealing, and her clothes began unpeeling
While to hear her yell would make you feel forlorn;
On the bite one hand was pressing while the other was undressing
And she reached the camp the same as she was born.
The shearer pale and haggard woke and back to town he staggered.
He caught the train and gave the booze a rest,
But he'll never know a spider that was camping at the Gywder
Had saved him sixty-seven of the best.

(In the silence of the victory that follows, SANDY looks up and around the old building. He sighs:)

SANDY Aw, well, it's been a bugger of a place for leading a man astray when you think of it.

PRICKY (sadly) Ain't it a fact.
   (then forcing himself)

336

Not as bad as the Imperial at Chillagoe. Fair dinkum, I was standing
at the bar there once. I remember it was on a Satdee as right as rain…

*(MICK returns with a crateful of bottles carefully nestling in his
arms. They look at this appreciatively. But he huddles them to
himself protectively.)*

MICK (defiance) Mother's milk for the morning, orright?

POP (sudden fighting words) What're you doing 'dosing in a
working man's pub, ya mug?

MICK (ignoring him) Johnno turned up yet?

PRICKY Who?

*(This could be diversionary, because at this time SANDY
casually reaches for a bottle, opens it with a multipurpose
hunting knife)*

MICK Hey, hands off me breakfast!

SANDY No worries.

*(and hands the bottle up to him to have a swig. This largesse of
gesture is very hard to refuse even though the bottle belongs to
MICK. MICK has to give in and start an inevitable chain
reaction of passing around all his bottles. He doesn't realise
this as yet' for now, he sits and shares swigging contentedly,
while SANDY keeps the bottle supply going)*

MICK (justification) Johnno owes me boodle anyway.

SANDY We was just saying about worse pubs than this old bastard
ever was. Some were rough as guts in an autopsy.

(POP digs him in the ribs with his foot)

SANDY ('replying') Pubs as rough as the old lady's knees!

337

POP   Ain't they ever, an' I oughta know. Reminds me about the time Snuffler Oldfield's missus was giving birth. The nurse came out and said, 'You've got a baby, Mr Oldfield', then a bit later, 'You've got another baby, Mr Oldfield'. 'Christ, nurse,' he said, 'Don't touch her again! She could be full of them!'

(thinks sagely, before carry on just when they go to drink again)
That there bloody old Snuffler Oldfield was one of the Galloping Joneses breed; I can't remember whether or not he was a contemporary. There are thousands of stories about him. You know how they shift them from one character to another.

(goes on)
Here's one that I can remember. The cattle rushed every night and Snuffler used to be out risking his life while the boss and the jackeroos and all the silvertails were back in camp, safely up a tree. So one night away went the cattle again and the boss and all of them are up the tree. The boss said, 'My God, poor old Snuffler, he's out there amongst them'. The cattle turned and all raced back through the camp, under the tree, and the manager yelled out, 'Where are you, Snuffler?'
'One limb above you, boss.'

MICK   Yeah, well, talking of the rottenest pub… what about the old Landsborough at Camberweal? That must be one of them if you ask me, straight up. There was that time I was in a terrific blue there. Doug Harris was with us, he walks in and spots a fellow from behind the bar and he says, 'You were a mongrel provo bastard' and up with a bar stool and let it go at him.
Well, that was all the bar needed; they all just wanted an excuse to start! In the struggle I get knocked out through the swing doors, so I flies back in and as soon as I got in some buggerlugs hit me and out I flies again!
So I though next time I'm not getting caught like that, so I crawled in under the swing doors on my hands and knees, and bugger me dead if a fellow doesn't sink a boot into me. Rolled me over and then a couple of blokes walked all over me.
I got out through the swing door and I says to m'self, 'It's too rough for you in there; stay out'. So I watched it from over the top of the swing doors. Well, bugger me again, I reckon three times out of three those swing doors hit me. I wasn't meant to be in there.

(then indicating inside pub)

We ought to get in there. Some mad city toff in there's laid a tenner on the bar for whoever comes up with the best bit of bullsh. You blokes'd have no problem.

SANDY A tenner?

MICK A tenner.

SANDY Naw, not worth it.

MICK Not worth it? That sort of bullshit would get you that tenner. That's what I'm saying.

PRICKY Not even worth a man clearing his throat to whistle up McIlroy's prize bull to the sheep dip.

SANDY (agreeing) Flamin' insult, really. Where does a tenner go these days?

MICK Sorry I mentioned it.

> *(Pause)*

PRICKY Course a man could go in there and waltz off with it by telling them the one about how we used to hang on to those bloody buckjumpers.

SANDY You've never seen a buckjumper in your life.

PRICKY Didn't I b'jesus! When we used to train buckjumpers, we used to get on them in the yard and get them to buck, and after they'd bucked so long we'd jump off then and let them think they'd won. Rightio, so then we'd saddle them up again, or get on them with the same saddle and they'd buck and we'(d let then win again. At times you'd ride the nearly to the finish, and then you'd leave them, but never ever ride them right out – never ride them till they stopped bucking.
Of course there was a few of them there we didn't have to leave; they left us. There'd be an argument between the boys whether we'd left the horse or the horse left us. Course you'd never ever admitted you got thrown. You'd say, 'Oh, I slipped as I was getting off.'

We used to mount all the buckjumpers in the middle of the ring, and this is the way we used to hold them. We use to screw up one ear and get it in our teeth.

(with contortionistic display)

You'd have the other hand up round underneath the neck, and have the other ear screwed down; you'd have hold of the halter, the twitch down there, like with your hands and the rope. On hand up here with this ear screwed down, you have the other ear screwed up and in your teeth. See? Then you'd jump on the let the whole bloody lot go!

(shouting to POP's foot nudging him again)

That's no bull either.!

POP (getting in before accused of being irrelevant) This horse was a terrible horse to catch, you know. There were four or five fellow running around trying to catch him, running round backwards and forwards around the paddock.

The boss says, 'Do you know this horse?'

'Yes, boss.'

'Can you catch him?'

'I've caught him for the last twelve months, boss.'

'How do you catch him?'

'I got down on my hands and knees and I crawled towards him, and you know why I done that? Well, as I crawls towards him he's starting to think he might have hobbles on, and they must be pestering and annoying him and I was going to take them off. As I crawled closer and closer to him he just stood there and he's worrying about those hobbles, his feet are getting sorer. Finally I played around with his feet, nice and quietly, and then I grabbed him. Yelled out to the other fellows to get a bridle. No trouble, it was the only way to catch him, boss.'

MICK (getting up) Struth, if that Johnno doesn't get here soon, I'll be broker than when I was last looking in the mirror...

(With agitation he goes inside again. They watch him before)

PRICKY I heard about that Landsborough at Camooweal Mick mentioned. There was one like that, I reckon, around the Torrens Creek area. Can't remember its name, but I went to that last race meeting they had around that area. Won't ever forget that in a while Gawd!... during the afternoon Uncle Dick had been boozing up at the bar when he came back to our camp, tanked to the eyeballs. He said that some ringer had been threatening to beat him up. A bit after this he wandered out into the night and flaked out on the ground some little way from the tent. One of the aunts coming back from the toilet came across him lying there, and remembering what he had said earlier, jumped to the conclusion that he had been caught up with by that ringer.

'Poor Dick has been bashed up,' she announced as soon as she got to the tent. Uncle Bill, also with a few beers under his belt jumped up in a rage, 'I'll get the bastard that did', and charged out into the night. Heading across the flat he tripped over Dick.

'There you are, you rotten bastard', Bill shouted and started to put the boots into Dick's ribs, fist one side then the other.

Near morning old Dick was staggering around the camp holding his sides. 'Some bugger really got me last night and really did me over.'

SANDY   C'arn, they were just knocking you off the perch. I'll tell you how I got caught. We were in this bush pub, and everyone was talking about how much you could drink in one go. This fellow said, 'I'll bet anyone that me and my mate can drink a five gallon barrel dry in one go, me taking one long swig and then him'.

Everyone started putting money down and the publican handed over a barrel to the bloke. Instead of tapping the bung out he got hold of a hammer and knocked the whole top out. Then he took a long, long drink, but it wasn't that much. Then he said, 'Now I'll get my mate', and he went out and brought his horse in.

We all lost that bet for sure.

POP   What?

(SANDY ignores POP's boot nudging him and opens another of MICK's bottles.

As he is doing so, JOHNNO comes along. He is surly and worst for wear)

JOHNNO   Seen Mick by any chance?

PRICKY   Who?

SANDY   What happened to you, Johnno, y'old bastard?

JOHNNO   Would you believe it? Bloody snake. Come off me bike.
Seen Mick?

PRICKY   Mick who?

SANDY   Johnno, you get into more strife than Galloping Jonesy,
straight up.

JOHNNO   Who's he when he's home?

SANDY   Only Galloping Jonesy.

JOHNNO   Not the Galloping Jonesy…?!

SANDY   Same one.

JOHNNO   Never heard of him.

SANDY   You never heard of Galloping Jonesy?

JOHNNO   Never in me life.

SANDY   Aw, pull this one. It plays God Save the Queen.

JOHNNO   It'd want to do something useful for a change.

SANDY   Yeah, well… I'll tell you about Galloping Jonesy. He
walked into the pub in Georgetown one night and Treacle MacFarlane
was there. Everyone got out except Treacle, who didn't know him.
Galloping Jonesy said to him, 'When I walk into the pub everyone
gets out.'
Treacle said, 'Who are you, mate?'
'Galloping Jones, and who are you?'
'Treacle MacFarlane.'
'And you're not going to get out?'
'No,' he says, 'When everyone else gets out, I stay.'
'And why do you think you can stay?'
'Because I can fight.'
'You want to fight, mate?'
'Yes.'

'Well, you just met your Waterloo.'
Well, they fought for hours and hours, but they couldn't beat one another.

(He stops as though finished)

JOHNNO I don't get it.

SANDY Who said there was anything to get?
   (and then carries on)
He was a real joker, Galloping Jonesy was. One of the best. No one could put it over him. Even drunk he could take the whole bar on and they couldn't beat him, and to ride a bad horse and things like that they reckon he was terrific.
He used to punch cattle off one place, go past two or three places then sell them. That same night those cattle would be gone again and sold somewhere else. They reckon he was terrible. He didn't want the money or anything; it was just in him. If he saw an iron gate on a property while going through, that night he'd come back and the gate would be gone. If he saw an empty forty-four-gallon drum sitting there, even if it was no good for him, he'd go and pick it up.
One time ago they handcuffed him, because he had killed another man's cow for beef and the coppers rode onto him. So what they done is they cut the brand out to take as evidence. That night, taking him into town, they was sleeping there, the police and the tracker fellow. Galloping Jonesy, he gave them a few rums and when they was sound asleep, he went off and got another hide and he came back and took the police hide and left the fresh hide there, all rolled up, and he put it in the bag and everything.
The next day they took him into town and tried him for stealing. Anyway they got through the evidence and they pulled the hide out to show the brand, and it was one of Galloping Jonesy's own brand!

POP (suddenly lucid) Galloping Jonesy?! He didn't even rate! There used to be an old chap at Mossman, Danny, and he was a terrible strong man. Every now and then he'd get on the grog and he'd say, 'Now well look for a bit of fun'. He'd look out and there'd be…

(He stops there. They wait but nothing more. Finally:)

343

JOHNNO (not impressed) Mike around did you say?

PRICKY Who?

JOHNNO I could use the few red cents he owes me.

SANDY He just went inside looking for a tenner.

JOHNNO (brightening) What'll you have when I find him?

SANDY (indicating bottles, coyly) Well, we were trying to save these for breakfast…

JOHNNO Say no more. Mick'll come good.

(He goes to go inside but is stopped by:)

SANDY Tell you what, Johnno, while you're at it in there tell 'em the one I told about Galloping Jonesy. You never know how many tenners are floating around in there.
   (as explanation)
Big knobs. More money than you could shake a red-bellied at.

JOHNNO (catching on) No sweat.

(and hurries inside)

PRICKY Why don't you go in and tell it yourself?

SANDY Me? In front of a tenner? A man's nerves'd shatter.

PRICKY (the realist) Yeah, the bloody shakes. They always come at the wrong time.

SANDY Any rate, a man wouldn't even understand what them city big notes are on about half the time, so how are they gonna understand what we're on about, you tell me that.

PRICKY (now really depressed) You don't know if that tenner's bullshit or not. The sooner they flood the joint out, the better.

344

(Long pause)

SANDY (brooding) Mind you, some lucky bugger ought to rescue that tenner before the tide gets it. How would you reckon this one would go…? Tom Doyle, he was elected to the Kanowna Council. The matter before the house was government aid to have the local water supply dam enlarged as it was too small to supply the needs of a growing town.
Tom was on his feet. 'Yes, it is too small; I could piss half way across it'
Then came the voices of all the other councillors, 'Mr Doyle, Mr Doyle, you're out of order!'
'Yes, bedad, and if I was in order I could piss the whole way across.'

PRICKY Might be in with a chance. Course, you might have to compete with me telling the one about the mad Irishman Michael Cody who had made a bit of money on the goldfields and he had a new hotel built at West Northam. Northam is about sixty miles east of Perth. This time he'd been in Perth doing business and was standing on the railway platform. The Kalgoorlie Express was just ready to shove off and he was discussing some matters with the brewers.
The guard blew his whistle and waved his flag but old Michael was still talking to these people when the train went off. He shouted, 'Stop the train! Stop the train for Michael Cody of the
Grand Hotel, Northam!'
However, they didn't stop the train.

SANDY You're right. He was a bit of a character, alright. But do you know the greatest character I ever come across? Fred Silas's wife.

PRICKY Whose Silas's wife?

SANDY Fred. Fred Silas's wife. She used to come out on the bus. She was a little skinny sort married to a half cast called Fred Silas and she was very proud of being Fred Silas's wife. She never called herself Mrs Silas, she was always Fred Silas's wife. Well, that old bus, it's a wonder they didn't have to put elastic sides on it, the amount of people it used to carry. Nobody had any cars those days;

we were always broke. Coming home at night it would have all these
tribal fellows and drunks and Fred Silas's wife.
I remember one night, she was standing up there, drunk, and says,
'Case anyone here don't know me, I'm Fred Silas's wife'.
Oh yes, everybody knows her, but nobody wants to say, the state
she's in. So she looks around and she sees Bernie Stone: 'That you
there, Bernie?'
Well, quite a few of them were sober this night, I don't know why,
and she says, 'You going to have a drink of wine with me, Bernie?'
'No thanks, Daphne.'
'Don't call me Daphne. I'm Fred Silas's wife.'
'All right. Fred Silas's wife.'
She says, 'You won't drink with me, ay? You too stuck up, ay?
Yeah, well, I could tell a few things about you Bernie Stone.'
Then she started dragging up his past to all the bus. Everyone's
trying to make himself as small and inconspicuous as possible. When
she'd finished with old Bernie, she looks around and there's Wally
Peters. 'That you, Wally Peters? You know who I am?'
'Yes. Fred Silas's wife.'
'Have a drink with me, Wally?'
'No, no thanks, Daphne, I don't feel like it.'
So she started on (poor old Wally's history and we thought it would
never end. Then she saw Rex Jones, 'That you there, Rex? You
going to have a drink with me, Rex?'
'My bloody oath I am,' says Rex, 'Gimme the bottle!'

POP   What?!

SANDY   Real characters, Pop!

POP   Real characters? One comes to me mind alright was the old
bastard I met at the post office. The postie had told me that he owned
Ned Kelly's plough, so I asked him about it. 'Are you the man who
has Ned Kelly's plough?'
'Yes, that's me and would you believe it, it has a wooden blade. Now
some people wouldn't believe that.'
So I says, 'Do you know any songs about Ned Kelly?'
'Songs? Well, I've got a muzzle-loading six shooter of his; have you
ever heard of one of those?'
'I haven't. But do you know any songs about Ned?'

346

'And I've got an old Roman sword belonging to Ned Kelly, about this long, with an old English string handle. Now would you believe it.' At this point old Jackson, who had been listening to all this, and had never seen the other bloke in his life, shouted out, 'Tell us about those songs your old man sung about Ned Kelly when he came home drunk!'
The other bloke with Ned Kelly's wooden plough just stared at him for a bit, and then went on to tell us other Ned Kelly wonders he owned.
A few days later I see him again and I go, 'Have you remembered any songs about Ned Kelly yet?'
'No, but they might be in my car; I've got all sorts of things in there, sandsoap and things like that old Ned swore by...'

SANDY   Yeah, but he was nothing compared to a

(He stops when MICK comes back out and casts a sorrowful eye at the dwindling supply of bottles)

MICK   Johnno come back yet?

PRICKY   Who?

SANDY   That tenner gone yet?

(MICK shakes his head forlornly, sits down to a swig)

SANDY   As I was saying about that Ned Kelly character. He was nothing compared to a bloke I used to work with nature. His best idea was that of walking from Cairns to the tip of Cape York; I suppose it would be a bit better than five hundred miles. He said it would be no trouble; he was not scared of a bit of exercise. He got all his stuff ready for the big trek, and then found that no one would drive him the two miles out to the main road, so he gave the whole idea away and caught the next train south.

PRICKY   While you're on about on the track and wives, you remind a bloke of the old Afghan camel driver and his mad missus I once heard about. He was called Galloping too. The Galloping Ghan. He was fairly well known in northern New South Wales and southern

Queensland; all around that area. His territory ranged out to Burke, and the fellow who told me about it came from Burke.

Galloping Ghan's wife was a very good looking sort, and a fellow she'd known for some time came by and she offered him tea and they finally ended up in an immoral embrace on the couch. Old Galloping G. walked in on them, and his wife caught sight of him and she shouted out, 'Rape! Rape!'

He said, 'What for you cry when I see your big arse lift up?'

(sails on regardless of others objecting to the bad taste)

Then there was this old coot called Bloody Old Bill, too. His real name was Norm Brown. No idea why they used to call him Bloody Old Bill. Anyhow, he was a great one for fighting too, especially with a bit of O.P. in him. I recall one time there was a bit of a party going on, dancing and that, and in came Bloody Old Norman Bill full of good spirits. All the woman and kids go out of the place very smartly, and then he threw all the men out, and then one by one he threw out every bit of crockery, all the plates and cups and pans, and then he started on the furniture, all the chairs and tables and the sideboard, the lot.

Finally, there was nothing left in the place but the old wood stove. He tried to grab it, but it was red hot. So there he was, nothing at all in the place but him and the stove, and the stove had him beat. It was about the only thing that ever tossed him.

MICK   Jeez, you speak a lot of bullsh.

SANDY   I don't know about that.

POP   (as though suddenly remembering MICK)   What's he doing going round saying he's gonna 'dose me pub down?

MICK   (stung)   Shit, I've already told him a hundred times.

PRICKY   Who?

SANDY   Told you he don't hear a word.

MICK   (agitated)   I dunno where that bloody Johnno's got to.

PRICKY   Who?

SANDY He's just been here, as a matter of fact.

MICK Where?

SANDY About where you're sitting, I reckon. Matter of fact, he just went inside looking for you.

MICK (suspiciously) I didn't see him.
   (then cunningly)
Who's shout anyway?

> *(When all falls silent, he knows he might as well get up and go inside to look for JOHNNO)*

SANDY Hey, Mick, while you're buying, nice of you, I'll share the tenner with you if you hit them with the one about the pub with the bell and the mad landlady with the broom.

MICK Go in and tell it yourself.

SANDY Naw, I wouldn't know where to start yakking.

MICK (sudden shout) For crying out loud, did you see that?

PRICKY Who?

MICK Bloody big rat size of e backside of a few barmaids I know!

PRICKY Been here all afternoon, that has.

SANDY Thought it was a bit of rat's turd on the ground at first, but it turned out to be the rat without the turd.

PRICKY We was saying them
   (indicates city slickers inside)
in there must've brought it with 'em. It's too small for one of the local variety…
Years ago I was riding around the Coolgarra country, and Jimmy Stone and I came on this old camp. In the distance you could see all these tins gleaning and shining, and when we got closer we saw thousands of old jam tins and syrup tins stacked up neatly.

We were talking to the old boy there and he said, 'The price of tin's going up. There's to be a big shortage and that's why I'm saving all these tins.' Silly bugger.

We looked around a bit and there's a kangaroo rat hanging by the neck. He'd been hanging up for a fortnight by the smell of him.

'You been having trouble with kangaroo rats?'

'Yes,' he says, 'Yes, they're a trouble all right, them bloody things. All night long sniffing and snorting around the camp. All you can hear is thump thump, squeak squeak. I tried poisoning them, but they're too cunning. I tried shooting them but they dodge bullets, they do. I didn't know what to do about them. I managed to catch one. I give him a fair trial. I tried him and found him guilty of jumping around the camp all night and keeping me awake. I sentenced him to death and I hung him.

'See that big blackboard up there? Can you read what's on it? KANGAROO RATS BEWARE. DON'T LET THIS HAPPEN TO YOU.

I hung him up there and that night thousands of them came hopping around, squeaking and thumping. Then they just stopped, and they started to read that notice on the board. The minute they read it they just wheeled around and took off, and you could hear them thumping over the ridge. They haven't annoyed me since.'

MICK   Fair dinkum you mob'd make the biggest damn liar in the world spit chips, you would.

SANDY   Never met him, but I was once in Blinman in South Australia at the old copper mine. I was installing some machinery and I met an old Irishman, Mick Carrick, who was a great stretcher of the odd yarn or two. He had been a bullock driver and one evening at the hotel, I put a couple of pints of beer into old Mick and this is the story he told me:

'I had the best team of bullocks that ever put their necks into a yoke. I was carting wool one trip from Bullcamatta in Hergott Springs. It's a long track and on the way I had to cross Coopers Creek. Well, Coopers Creek in flood time is impossible, you just simply can't go past, but at this time it was only eighteen inches deep.

'So we arrived at the southern side of Coopers Creek and I pulled up the bullocks. I said, "Whoa, me boys, whoa now; you've got a job in front of you". I walked into the water and it was just about up to me knees. I went back and walked around the team, and mind you, the team of bullocks I had there were the best team that had ever put their necks into a yoke, like I said. By God, they were a fine team of bullocks.

'Well, I went around and I told each bullocks and there were twenty-two of them in the team. I told 'em just exactly what I wanted of them. I goes up to the off side leader, Big Baldy, a marvellous bullock, a real friend of mine, and I stood off and gave a little bit of a crack with the old whip. I never lashed my bullocks; I'd just drop the lash onto them; they didn't need any more than that.

'I shouted, "Come on, old boys, gee old Baldy" and they put their necks in the yoke and they entered the water, and they pulled.

'I walked alongside them, and I shouted to them, telling them what a difficult job they had to get through the water. Eventually we came up on the other side and I said, "Whoa, me boys, steady now, have a spell!" I turned around and I looked back, and you may not believe it, it's no bloody lie, but that team of bullocks of mine had pulled Coopers Creek ten chains off its bloody course! That's the godsbold flea-bitten truth, that is. They were a damn fine team of bullocks, they were.'

(SANDY cracks another bottle without asking, much to MICK's disgust)

MICK Hey, fair go!

SANDY (diversion) If you catch the thirst going around
    (indicates the racket inside the pub)
in there, Mick, you could always tell 'em the one about the wind at Goldsmith's Creek. There weren't any rats; it was too windy.

MICK Oh, bull.

SANDY No, straight up. It was terrible windy place that Forsyth. When I was there a few years ago, I mentioned it to Pat Haigh, and he said the wind was even worse a few miles further out at a place called Goldsmith Creek. According to him the wind was so strong it used to blow dogs off their chains, and a man could only work about an hour a day.

'Why would that be?', I asked, expecting some scientific answer and Pat Haigh said, 'Because he spends the rest of his time chasing his hat'.

MICK   Listening to you lot worse than trying to get me loan back from Johnno. Inside, is he...?.

(He goes to go off inside)

SANDY   (stopping him)   Don't forget breakfast, Mick!

MICK   What about breakfast?

SANDY   (tapping MICK's now near-gone bottle crate)   When you donated this, you said remind you about yer breakfast stash.

MICK   (sourly)   Stash? I'd need a bank vault.

PRICKY   We're just saying.

(MICK goes off inside.

JOHNNO comes out almost ridiculously soon after MICK has gone in. He stands and, in unison with them, watches the movements of the rat off the verandah)

JOHNNO   (finally)   Seen Mick?

SANDY   He was just this minute askin' about you.

JOHNNO   Well, he'd better front up soon. I need to wet the whistle badly.

(SANDY magnanimously motions him to sit and help himself to MICK's stash. JOHNNO needs no second asking)

JOHNNO   Ask bloody Mick for a small ale and you wouldn't see a rain cloud for years

SANDY   That tenner gone yet?

JOHNNO   What tenner's that?

PRICKY   (fierce whisper to SANDY)   He's taken it off!

JOHNNO (regardless) You wouldn't believe how much lying's going on in there. There's so much bullsh, flooding'll only turn this place into one big dunny drain.

SANDY   Just goes to show what money does. Better off without it.

PRICKY (toasts to:) To free beer!

(There is a pause to savour the taste of it, then:)

SANDY   They might come another tenner if they heard about the old chap who used to be out our way. Now there was a terrible liar for you, if ever there was one.

POP Eh? What?!

SANDY Liars, Pop!

POP (getting in, gleefully) Don't give me liars, son! You remember what a rotten liar that George was? It didn't matter what you said or did, he had done it before you and better. Like that there time when we were talking to him about the saw, one of those saws that have wheels attached, and you walk them up to the tree.
He had never heard of one in his life, because it had to be explained to him in detail, but having once grasped what it was all about, he straightway became an expert. A few minutes later someone remarked how dangerous these saws could be if the blade broke while they were going; in fact a bit of the saw could take a bloke's head off with no trouble at all.
So right out of the blue George says, 'Yes, that happened to me once when I was using one of those cows of things, and a piece went into my forehead right there', and he pointed to the middle of his forehead and said, 'Can't you see the scar?'
His head was as smooth as a baby's bum and we all said we couldn't see a thing.
'Look,' he said, jabbing with his finger, 'Right next to where I got shot with the .303 bullet'.
We all said, give's us a break, George, we couldn't see that either, but it didn't worry George… 'Ah,' he said, 'that's the wonders of plastic surgery'.

JOHNNO   If Mick turns up tell him I'm looking for him inside, orright?

SANDY   (after him) You tell 'em that one Pop just said.

> *(There is another pause while they look expectantly at the pub's door after Johnno has gone inside. But there is no unusual burst of laughter that he might have told one of their yarns for a tenner)*

PRICKY   If he told it, it went down like a dose of cod's.

SANDY   Bugger probably forgot the punch line or something. Driving dozers does that to a man's brain.

POP   What?!

SANDY   (picks up conversation to PRICKY) How'd you say you went at the Torrens Creek races that time?

PRICKY   Go? That flamin' horse was alright. It would've walked it in if that skinny looking drongo of a jockey hadn't broken down in the straight the first time he tried lifting the whip. Y'know my old Dad always claimed that the only bloke who ever made money following horses was the ploughman.
When I was a bit of a kid the old man was ploughing in the paddock and this joker came along. He was looking for a bloke who was reputed to be very strong. The old man was ploughing out garden patch which was a swamp about two to three acres long, and a good one too.
The old man said to the fellow, 'Yes, he lives about three miles in that direction' and he lifted up the plough in one hand and pointed with it.

SANDY   Yeah, you can talk about being riding and going astray. There was that time Vic was going to take a horse and follow in the tracks of Kennedy the explorer. He got into all his cowboy gear and got himself photographed with somebody's old hack, gazing romantically across the plains, in someone's back yard. He managed to get the photo into one of the Sydney papers. It was real explorer stuff.

As you may know Kennedy started off from around Cardwell on the east coast and more or less followed the coast up all the way to where he was killed.

We asked Vic whether he would be starting right from Cardwell, and he said no, he would be starting from Normanton. Well, Normanton is five hundred miles to the west, and he was going to head straight up the middle of the peninsula from there, so he really wouldn't be anywhere near the track taken by Kennedy. So we asked him why, if his expedition was to follow in the footsteps of Kennedy, he was going five hundred miles to the west, and the silly bugger said it would be easier riding out there!

Anyway once he got himself in the papers that was enough. He didn't have to make the trip then.

> (MICK returns this time. He is visibly getting desperate. He can't find JOHNNO; he is running out of money; he is out of his depth with the city-slicker developers inside; his bottle supply for the morning all too obviously dwindled. He has a good whine:)

MICK   Jesus, what a bastard of a life. Johnno won't show. You can't get near the bar for blokes speaking with plums in their north-and-souths. Every bastard's trying to make a bloke do funny turns or something. A couple of the pricks are flashing the big ones into Shirl's shell-like, and she put a man on a promise tonight. A man can't even buy her a beer to settle her down while bloody Johnno's avoiding a man like the bloody plague. To top it all, the beer's gone warm as mother's milk in a heat wave   Life stinks!

PRICKY   (after pause) How'd you go?

SANDY   How's that tenner going in there?

MICK   (surly) What tenner?

PRICKY   Who?!
   (then to their disgust of him keeping saying that)
Hey, Sandy, you could get Mike to go in there and tell 'em about old Chicko.

SANDY (perking up) Rightio! Here's one, Mick, for the tenner and Shirl!

MICK (suspicious) What about the bloody warm beer?

SANDY They'll lash you out with buckets of ice with this one!
   (now with MICK's attention:)
Old Chicko was a travelling magician who used to go from country pub to country pub all over Queensland, all over Australia for all I know, doing a variety of ancient tricks and passing around the hat. As a rule the publicans didn't mind letting him have the use of the lounge for half an hour or so. It was a bit of entertainment for the drinkers and cost them nothing.
Some of the tricks were so ancient that they started to collapse before he got through them.
The best story I knew about him happened one evening in the Redlynch pub. He was busy pulling strings of dirty hankies out of an apparently empty tube when the false lining of it slid out onto the floor. He looked at it sadly, bent down and picked it up and stuffed it back where it had come from, 'I'd be buggered without that.'

MICK That's not going to get any tenner.

SANDY Hey, they're from the big smoke. What'd they know about a man being on Shirl's promise?

MICK Be buggery, you're right! Here goes...!

   (He launches himself inside again)

SANDY He's going to murder that Johnno when he finds him.

POP (renewed burst) You gotta get him before the mug comes to 'dose a man's only pub into the ground!

SANDY Mick is!

PRICKY Who?

SANDY Don't you start.

(then)
He used to be a bit of the old wild Irishman, Mick did, before the
sheilas got hold of him. Shame really. The trouble is blokes don't
take sheilas as they come.

PRICKY   Who?

SANDY   All I'm saying is there's no doubt about the way women
can get you into strife, especially if you get mixed up with too many
of them. A bloke that I know… nickname's Hoppy… took up with
this Chinese sheila at the meatworks. They're sex mad out there.
They were going along all right till Hoppy's wife gets to hear about it.
Someone had tripped over Hoppy and this Chinese sort under a
mango tree along the road. Was his missus mad.
Hoppy came in for lunch next day and she bangs the plate down in
front of him and nothing else.
'Where's the knife and fork?,' he says.
She just gives him a dirty look and says, 'Why don't you try
chopsticks?'

   (POP queries him with a nudge of the foot again)

POP   What?!

SANDY   Strange sheilas, Pop!

   *(It is JOHNNO who re-emerges this time. He hurries in from
   around the side of the pub. He could be running from, or
   looking for, MICK)*

JOHNNO   You blokes wouldn't be pulling a man's pisser about
Mick, would you?

PRICKY   Who?

SANDY   (really disappointed with JOHNNO's lack of beer)
Don't tell me you couldn't get near the bar neither?

JOHNNO   Mick's not in there.

357

SANDY Don't tell me some other bugger's won that tenner.

JOHNNO A bloke's looked high and low in there. He's not even behind the bar up Shirl's skirt. Hope the greasy mug's fingers turn green and drop off. If they don't haul me off for vagrancy, the mad house'll get me. Bloody Mick.

PRICKY Who?

POP (jolting to action) Me? Well, I'll tell yer if you want to listen…I used to be a hydroambulationist. You can ask what that is and I'll tell you it's walking through water and I'll fight any sod who says it ain't. It is something entirely new that I brought out myself. You've got to see it to believe it. And you know what? I appeared at the Adelaide Show once and I gave a six hour show and asked for 48 quid and they gave me 50. The first act I do is walking through water reading a book. Next I carry an umbrella and a hat in the other hand, then change hands and walk backwards. Next I walk sideways with a mouth organ, then I walk the other way breathing in and out. I said I'd walk across Bass Strait in forty hours but no one dared challenge me…

>   (JOHNNO doesn't stay to listen to any more of this. He exits
>   trying to catch MICK around the other side of the pub)
.

POP (undeterred) I walk in water and it comes just above me waist. I bend my head slightly and start squeezing a few notes out on me mouth organ, and the water acts as a megaphone. I play 'When I Grow Too Old to Sleep' and 'There's a Long Trail Awaiting', and several others I could mention.
Who asked what's the diff between treading water and walking through water? Treading water requires great manual exertion, the legs going out sideways. Walking in water the way I do requires no exertion at all.
I can pirouette on the tips of my toes in any depth of water, lay on an angle in any depth of water, turn north, east, south and west, kneel in salt water and don't sink, and also various other items too numerous to mention. I will not divulge the secrets. I keep them in the family.

>   (MICK comes out through pub's front door; takes a doleful
>   look at his near nonexistent supply for the morning, has quick

look down sides of the pub for JOHNNO)

MICK Mongrel, that Johnno. Someone said they saw him lurking out here.

PRICKY Who?

SANDY Anyone knocked off that tenner yet?

MICK I've posted scouts on every door and every flaming window in there. I've swung from the light so I could cop any bird's eyeful of the bludger. Now they want to charge me for it. I said you'd be bloody lucky, cocko, I ain't got enough to scratch m'bum with, let alone to fix any bloody crook light fitting probably broke before I climbed on. And that bloke who copped it underneath, I ain't paying for any ambulance; he shoulda known how jumped out of the way like I did. Okay, I said, charge me for manslaughter but wait til I finished those few lousy beers that bloody Johnno owes a man. Life stinks!
    (pauses)
Y'know, I know Johnno's not in there, but it's getting like I'd swear he ain't in there. Knowing he's a bit deaf, I even asked Shirl to whisper his name aloud. Shit, who can't hear a foghorn like her lest he's not wanting to?

SANDY Tried to dunny out back?

MICK Course I tried the…
    (stops, thinks)
Bejesus, you might be right!

(He hurries off around the other side of the pub to JOHNNO)

POP We had this stockman working here, Johnny Colombo, and I sent him out to find a mare that had escaped. I'd forgotten all about him, working around the yards, but in the evening he finally got back with that mare there.
'You found that mare all right then?'
'Yes, boss. I found her way over there. Didn't you see the smoke signal I sent up to let you know I'd found it?'

Didn't I see that smoke signal? That bloody smoke signal burnt off most of the Gulf country and we fought it for four months.

(JOHNNO bursts back onto the verandah from the side that MICK has just left by)

JOHNNO   Don't tell me I missed him again!

PRICKY   Who?

JOHNNO   Any of you seen Mick come by here?

SANDY   You notice if that tenner's still there?

(But JOHNNO pauses only to take a quick swig of MICK's bottle he left behind before dashing off around the other side)

SANDY   (shout to POP)   Chinaman, was he?

PRICKY   Who?

SANDY   (still to POP)   With the mare? Nothing's off like Sam Wong.
     (but POP has gone 'off' again; even so)
Remember him? That time my Wendy first meets him? She turned up at his house looking all prim and proper and clutching her big black bag which looked as though it might have been full of copies of the Salvo's 'Watch Tower', but actually contained her tape recorder. Sam must have taken her for a Jehovah's Witness, and the conversation went something like this:
'This where Sam Wong lives?'
'It might be.'
'Do you know if he's at home?'
'Don't know.'
'Listen, are you Sam Wong?'
'No.'
'Bullshit.'
'Come in.'

(MICK comes bursting back in from the other side of the pub).

MICK   I'll kill the mug, so help me!

PRICKY   Who?

> *(He goes to dash off again, but stops by his supply, and with no hope:)*

MICK   At least I know you blokes have the decency to replenish a man's life blood when you see it drained off…

> *(He takes off)*

SANDY   (after him) No worries, Mick! You just snag that tenner and Bob's your uncle…!

POP   (about MICK) Here, what's the dill going to 'dozer down me pub for?

SANDY   A dam, Pop!

POP   Damn what?

SANDY   A dam lake!

POP   What flaming lake? Funny thing is I was talking to some codger not long ago and he was on about a lake or something. He was going on about a missing river around here or somewhere. I dunno. I never heard about a missing river around here. What a thing, to knock down a good pub for a missing river.

> *(There is a silence, while they ponder the passing of the pub.*
>
> *There is a burst of singing from inside. PRICKY hums along to it sadly and then sings along)*

PRICKY
Oh, where is the lady whose dark eyes
I so often kissed and caressed?
She is sleeping under far-distant skies
With her head on some other man's breast.
Though she said my life she would ere share,

It seems she's forgotten our love so soon
But a man can't care when it's so hard to keep square
On the banks of the Reedy Lagoon.

> *(Renewed silence. The three of them remain static in contemplation and take no notice of the following sequence around them:*
>
> *MICK and JOHNNO – both of them madly running – dash in and out in a series of foot-banging, floorboard-rattling near misses. This starts with:*
>
> *JOHNNO dashes out of the door, sees MICK isn't on the verandah, turns and plunges back inside.*
>
> *MICK dashes around from the right side of the pub, up onto the verandah and into pub through the door.*
>
> *JOHNNO enters from left side of pub and hurries inside by the back door.*
>
> *MICK dashes out of pub door and hurries around the left side of the building,*
>
> *JOHNNO dashes out of the pub door and hurries around the right side of the building.*
>
> *MICK dashes back from around the left side of the pub and runs off around the right side of the pub.*
>
> *JOHNNO dashes in from the right side and run in through pub door, then a split second later comes back out of door again and hurries around the left side of the building.*
>
> *Etcetera.*
>
> *PRICKY languidly breaks the others' silence, indicates across the yard)*

PRICKY   I reckon that might be a local rat after all. Or is it a dog?

SANDY   What's its tail like?

PRICKY   Like a pig's, I guess.

SANDY   What's it sound like?

PRICKY   Like a bucking bronco I once had, I guess.

SANDY   Aw, pack it up.

>   *(MICK comes back, livid)*

MICK   You're all a lot of mongrels.

PRICKY   Who?

MICK   Johnno ain't around here at all.

SANDY   We was only trying to help.

MICK   (at depleted beer) Help? You're termite-ing a man's breakfast. You're denying him his heart starter. You have him whizzing around like a loony while those city-ites are in Shirl's pants. Life stinks! The whole pack of you galoots deserve to get bulldozed tomorrow. No, I tell you what… I ain't waiting for tomorrow!

>   *(He dashes out)*

SANDY   (after him) I take it that tenner's gone?

POP   What's he doing?

PRICKY   Who?

SANDY   He's going to 'doze the place in, Pop.

POP   Toldyer I dreamt about some snake 'dozing a man's pub in. How much of a sneaky animal can you get?

>   *(But they sit there placidly, without even looking up, when the*
>   *bulldozer starts up. It is put crashingly into gear and then*

becomes louder and louder until its approach becomes deafening.

Fade out)

(End Act 1)

Act 2

(By contrast, only the screeching of cockatoos.

POP, SANDY and PRICKY are where they were.

Suddenly, all hell breaks loose again. MICK comes crashing in flat out from left side of building, dashes across the verandah, disappears around the right side of the building.

JOHNNO follows madly -- almost, but not quite, on his heels.

Then JOHNNO comes crashing in going flat out from the right side of the pub, crosses the verandah and disappears around left side of the pub.

MICK follows madly – almost, but not quite, on his heels.

JOHNNO comes back flat out from the right side of the building across verandah and disappears off around left side of the building.

MICK follows madly – almost, but not quite, on his heels.

MICK comes flying back from the right side and careers past them to off around the left side.

JOHNNO follows madly -- almost, but not quite, on his heels

They are flagging, though.

It all goes dead silent again.

Finally, MICK comes back in, takes a beer, sits, swigs, then:)

MICK   Got you going with that 'dozer back there, didn't I?

SANDY   How'd you say that tenner was going?

MICK   What tenner?

SANDY   That tenner

MICK   No tenner.

SANDY   Knock it off.

MICK   There was never no tenner.

SANDY   The real shitheads!

PRICKY   The dirty rotten city-arsed dingoes!
  (then)
Who?

SANDY   They made me cough up me best yarn for nothing!

PRICKY   Same here.

SANDY   Bugger it, I was going to tell 'em about Glen Broughton too.

PRICKY   Who?

SANDY   Not who.

PRICKY   Who's that one, then?

SANDY   Not who!

POP   What?!

SANDY   (losing patience) The bloody mozzies, what else?

POP   (nodding sagely) There used to be a lot of pigs in among the mangroves and salt pans back of the farm. One day I was poking around I came across a hut like one of those New Guinea ones. It was built up in a tree, and there was this old joker digging around all the trees and all he had on was a waistcoat.

366

So I said to him on account of only having on this waistcoat, 'What's the idea of the waistcoat?'

'I've got to have somewhere to keep me matches,' he said.

That did it. I asked him how he handled the mozzies there.

'Well', he said, 'there's three ways you can deal with them. The best way is to keep still and let them get their tusks in and then when they've had a decent feed they'll leave you in peace.

'Now a lot of people get jumping about and all that and it gets the mosquitoes even angrier because their tusks get stuck jammed and keep breaking.

'I reckon the best way to deal with them is to go down to the swamp and roll round in that black mud. When that stuff dries on you, it's like an armour plate, and the mosquito gets his tusk into it and can't get it out and he pulls and pulls and ends up pulling off a wad of about two inches square. Well, when that mosquito gets free he'll fly back to his mates and warn them off you, and that way you'll be left alone.'

MICK (surly admission) Yeah, well, when I said there was no tenner it was fifty not a tenner.

SANDY Joking.

MICK They're city buggers, they wouldn't know the difference.

SANDY (craftily) Well, I was saving up the one where there were three of us, sleeping in a row, when this big boar pig, he walked down the pad and come straight down past my feet, past the middle bloke, and he come right around and looked at the joker on the end. He looked straight in, close on the mosquito net.

I heard, 'Go way! Go on, git!' I heard this; I'd been sound asleep and I thought what in the hell goes on here? I woke up and this fellow on the end, he wasn't game to move, but the bloke in the middle, he said, 'Hey, Les, you better wake up'.

I had a .32 there with me. When I rolled over I could see this pig and he's looking into the net down the end. He was a huge bloody thing. This bloke would say, 'Shoo!' and that pig just walked around a bit then came back and looked in the net again. I thought this is something unusual for a pig; this ain't right. I loaded the rifle and stood up and put one into him. He took off and stopped again, so I put the torch onto him and walked up and put another one into him, and he fell down.

About twenty minutes later back he came, the same bloody pig. He did. He came back and kept looking at this bloke through that bloody net. I thought that's funny. So I put the torch on him and put another couple into him.

It was the same pig, but I don't know why he ever came back. He'd come down along the pad and if he'd wanted to have a look at anybody, I was sleeping right by the entrance. But he walked around me and around the other fellow and got to the bloke on the end, straight up.

He was standing there hitting his tusks nice and slow on the bed and looking into the net. Next morning he was laying there and he had four holes in him.

Can you beat that?

PRICKY (not to be outdone) That's all right about that, but for 50 smackeroos, I might trot out that one about that Nelem. He was a clever goat, he was. One time when we were all living on St Pauls...

> *(He is irrevocably interrupted by JOHNNO creeping back in backward from out of the front door. He casts sneaky looks around both sides of the pub and relaxes until he sees MICK actually there)*

MICK Bastard!

JOHNNO (recovering shock) What's your game?

MICK A man ought to job you!

JOHNNO What's he on about?

MICK Hand it over.

JOHNNO Hand what over?

PRICKY Who?

MICK The spondoolix you bludged off me.

JOHNNO   You hand over the spondoolix you bludged off me.

(There is a real danger they will actually come to blows, but this is shouted down by PRICKY who suddenly hears singing inside. He listens with his ear to the wall while they wait on him, then shows absolute outrage… almost to the extent of rising to his feet.)

PRICKY   They're doing it again!

SANDY   Who?

PRICKY   Not who! They're taking a man's song! Who's the stoolie?! Who's the loud mouth!?

SANDY   Who?

PRICKY   Only me one about Charlie Mopps, that's all!

SANDY   Go get 'em, Prick.

PRICKY   Bloody will too!

(He climbs shakily to his feet and sings loudly and defiantly straight at the window. While he does so, MICK and JOHNNO break off and join the drinking circle, but with backs to each other)

PRICKY
A long time ago, twas way back in history
When all we had to drink was nothing but cups of tea
Along came a man by the name of Charlie Mopps
And he invented a beaut brew with the name of hops.

(chorus)
Oh, he should have been an admiral, a sultan or a king
And to his praise we will always stand to sing;
Look what he's done; he's filled us with good cheer,
God bless Charlie Mopps, the inventor of beer!

Oh, the Oceanic, the Barrier Reef and the Federal Hotel

One thing's sure, it's Charlie's brew they all sell
So come on me lucky lads at ten 'clock she stops
For five short seconds let's remember Charlie Mopps!

(chorus)
Oh, he should have been an admiral, a sultan or a king
And to his praise we will always stand to sing;
Look what he's done; he's filled us with good cheer,
God bless Charlie Mopps, the inventor of beer!

Well, Charlie he died, he went to Heaven's door
Up to old St Peter, said, 'Pete, what's the score?'
St Peter looked at Charlie, said, 'Who the hell are you?'
Charlie said, 'Charles Mopps'; St Peter cried, 'Straight through!'

(chorus)
Oh, he should have been an admiral, a sultan or a king
And to his praise we will always stand to sing;
Look what he's done; he's filled us with good cheer,
God bless Charlie Mopps, the inventor of beer!

(He gets boos and derisive laughter from inside)

SANDY   Buggers don't appreciate fine music.

*(He drowns his disgust with opening another bottle of beer,
swigs, hands it on to JOHNNO. JOHNNO goes to have a
guzzle but MICK snatches the bottle away)*

JOHNNO   Bash it up your bum then.

MICK   'Bash it up your bum'. Nice and charming.

(POP stirs)

SANDY   (almost alarmed) Hold it!

MICK   What?

SANDY   Pop moved.

MICK   I didn't see it. You, Pricky?

PRICKY   Who?

> (They wait on POP but nothing comes before JOHNNO cannot hold his tongue any longer)

JOHNNO   I said bash it up your quoit, and I meant ram it into your dyke!

POP   (unexpectedly again) You talk about pulling the sorts. I was in a pub in Katherine, and a bit of a brawl started between a couple of blokes. In the middle of it, a girl who must've favoured the other bloke raced up to the first mug and started to kick him in the shins. He swung around and went to punch her, but one of his friends standing near said, 'You can't do that, you must never hit a lady', so he shook his head and turned his back on her.
She ducked outside and next thing she'd come back in carrying a long metal sign advertising Dunlop rubber. She swung this around her head and went to whack him, and the poor bugger didn't know what to do until his mate said, 'I think it would be all right to hit her now!'

PRICKY   (not to be silenced) Alright, you don't want to hear about Nelem the goat, but did old Alf ever tell you about the fellows that got bogged?
He said out in front of his place were three blokes bogged there for six weeks with this old truck. I reckon that after a fortnight I would have given it away and walked out.
Those poor huggers were starving and they were packing up this truck and revving it back and forwards, building logs under it and jacking it up, but the bastard of a thing still wouldn't move.
Do you know those Estonians up there? There was a big family of them, big women you know, and there was this one woman and she decided to go to Mareeba, walked in from Julatten, must be about thirty miles, to do her shopping.
When she was in Mareeba, she walked around looking for bargains and she bought a wood stove. They must weigh about two hundred pounds, but she just put it up on her head and decided to walk back to Julatten.
Coming back she saw these three drongos who had been bogged for six weeks. She said, 'What are you hanging around here for?'

371

'We're bogged.'
'Right, well I'll give you a bit of a hand.'
She reached up with one hand, lifted the stove off her head and put it on the ground and she said to this fellow, 'You, you miserable little rat, you get in and you steer it.'
'Do you want me to start it up too, missus?'
'No, dopey, I'm going to lift the wheels up and wheelbarrow it out.'
The other blokes said, 'What will we do?'
And she said, 'You stand back and encourage the other bloke.'
Then she reached down with her big powerful arms and grabbed the truck and there was a sucking sound and she lifted it straight out of that mud and wheelbarrowed it right back onto dry ground.
And one of those who was listening to old Alf's yarn said, 'God, she must have been a two-ton Tessie walking all the way from Mareeba with a wood stove on her head and then wheelbarrowing a truck out like it hadn't been stuck in there for six weeks'.
Old Alf said, 'Aw, that wasn't half of it. I didn't mention the three bags of spuds she'd bought and had on top of the stove.'

POP (daggers at MICK) Too much noise and too many machines around the country these days. Mug larrikins.

SANDY I've been thinking the ghost of John Brown ought to be worth a fifty, Mick, split. Whatcha reckon…? You know how all them boundary riders' huts are all haunted because in almost every one of them at least one boundary rider has committed suicide.
The poor buggers all commit suicide… well, not all, but it's a sort of professional hazard of being a boundary rider, like. They all knock themselves off. That's why most of the huts are haunted.
This bagman one time went into a boundary rider's hut and he was fooling around, unpacking his gear and whatnot in the dark and there was a storm on The next thing, he bumped into someone in there.
That was enough for him; he tore outside and camped out in the rain.
Next morning he met a bloke walking down the road with his swag and he said to him, 'Where did you camp?'
'Oh,, I had a bastard of a camp out in the rain. I went into that bloody boundary-rider's hut up there and there's something in there, I'm telling you.'
Well the first bloke said, 'Yes, I was in there and it frightened the seven bells of hell out of me too! What time were you there?'
'About eight o'clock.'

Of course they found out they'd scared one another.
I don't know whether that originated from a true story or not, but I've heard it polished up. In this version the bloke was getting undressed in the hut and this ghost said, 'I'm a ghost of John Brown' and all this sorta stuff and went on, 'There is only you and me here. Only you and me are here, whoooo.'
And the other fellow there said, 'Yes, and when I find this other bloody boot you'll be here on your own!'

JOHNNO   (out of patience) What dyou mean the dough I owe you.

MICK   Don't give me that.

JOHNNO   You owe me.

MICK   You owe me, you mean.

JOHNNO   Hey, I was the one chasing all over this joint after you!

MICK   Bullsh, I was on your hammer!

JOHNNO   I got calluses on me feet to prove it!

MICK   You'll have a thick ear on your head to prove it if you don't watch out.

JOHNNO   (warning) Mate…

MICK   (ditto) Mate…

PRICKY   (breaking it up, to SANDY) Why don't you get Pop going on Kidman again, Sandy mate?

SANDY   Gawd no, they'd shove that fifty back into their kicks and you wouldn't see 'em for dust.

PRICKY   For old time's sake, like. Town's going to be too far for him. A man might never hear him going at his Kidman again.

SANDY   What a glutton for punishment.
   (but even so to POP)

373

Kidman, Pop!

POP (chuckling) Old Kidman, eh? Don't get me started on him.
Struth, they say there was only one time Kidman ever got taken in in
all his life That was when this old Chinaman came along and Kidman
took a liking to his horse.
'Will you sell this horse?'
'Yes, I sell him all wight, but he no lookee too good.'
Kidman rode around him two or three times.
'He looks all right to me. I'll buy him.'
'All wight, but he still no lookee too good.'
So Kidman gave the old fellow five pounds, and took the horse home.
Next day he came back and he says to the Chinaman, 'Hey, listen,
that horse you sold me is blind as a bat.'
The Chinaman says, 'I tell you he no lookee too good.'

SANDY (loving it) You wouldn't believe it, wouldyer?

PRICKY Who?

JOHNNO (back at MICK) I'll pay you next week.

MICK What're you going to do, row it out to me after they've
flooded the place?

JOHNNO What're you mean?

MICK There won't be any next week here.

JOHNNO Bloody hell.
    (then)
Then don't come the raw prawn about paying me next week.

MICK I wasn't going to pay you next week.

JOHNNO That's all right then. None of youse could row your way
outa a paper bag.

SANDY No need to get stroppy, Johnno.

JOHNNO Tell 'em to keep out of it, Mick.

374

MICK   (to SANDY and PRICKY) You heard me mate. No need to get down from yer high horses.

JOHNNO   (dutch courage) LEAP OUT THE FIRST BASTARD!

   (No one moves)

MICK   (proof positive) Weak as water.

JOHNNO   (sitting back down) Not worth a man muddying his boots.

MICK   (down at JOHNNO) That'll be another tenner you owe a bloke.

JOHNNO   Come off it. What for?

MICK   (winking at the others) For saving your good looks.

PRICKY   For saving who's good looks?

MICK   Come to think of \it, that'll be another tenner for saving on the ambulance you would have needed.

JOHNNO   (rolling sleeves up) Right!

MICK   (ditto) Right!

   (They stride off to 'go around the side' to fight.

   SANDY and PRICKY watch them go with mild interest)

PRICKY   Who?

SANDY   (answering) I'll lay you Johnno's tenner on Mick.

PRICKY   I'll lay Mick's tenner on Johnno.

   (SANDY notices POP stirring, and brings PRICKY's attention to it.)

375

SANDY (whisper) Might be anotheree about Kidman.

POP (instead:) 'Late for Koorboora'? Gawd strike a light, I know
how that saying got started, ya mugs. We were mining at Koorboora
and we used to meet in the evenings. There was Dick, he was the
'mayor'. I was up in Otto's old place and Wilfred was in his own tin
humpy, and every night we'd all congregate at one house, usually
Dick's. As mining fields go, they all take turns to entertain at night.
Any rate, Dick was comparatively young then; he was only sixty-five
or so. Wilfred the same and I was thirty. Wilfred would come down
with his hurricane lantern about half past five or six o'clock and then
we'd sit and talk till about eight.
Of course Dick would be up at four in the morning, coughing and
smoking and drinking tea. You could hear him all over Koorboora.
There was nothing left there, only bare stripped-out country, and
these few old tin humpys.
So at about eight at night Dick would say in his cultured old school
teacher's voice…. he would never insult anyone outright, he
wouldn't'… he'd say, 'I'll just take a little look at the time'.
Of course we all knew what was coming. He'd go and make a great
noise getting ready to kip down, throwing plates around and shifting
billy cans, and of course we're all there waiting. Eventually he'd find
the clock, 'Ah,' he'd shout out, and that was it. Out he'd come and
say, 'You wouldn't believe: it's eight o'clock, boys! My word that's
late for Koorboora!'
And that was the signal for everyone to leave.
    (has to pause in wonder)
Dunno why I started on about that…

SANDY 'Late for Koorboora', Pops.

POP What about it?

    (But, anyway, there is a cry of pain and outrage off.

    *MICK comes back helping JOHNNO who is holding his head
    and dragging his feet. He helps him to his possie, puts a
    refresher bottle in his hand)*

376

MICK (an explanation) Poor bugger only goes and trips over that bloody big rat. He steps back and bang over the bastard thing he goes and hits his head on the 'dozer. That's the trouble with driving a bloody bulldozer, them dirty rats following you everywhere. They can't leave 'dozers alone, those bloody rats can't. You can tell the real trouble makers in 'em too… they're the ones with pig tails.

PRICKY Who?

MICK (as though he asked) Not stuck on their heads, stuck on their bums.
　(then, thought)
Hey, anyone see bloody old Wally Jenkins in there pissing away in a corner?

JOHNNO (sitting up) His pay day today.

MICK He owes me a bob or two. No wonder he started shaking like a cur when he saw me coming.

JOHNNO He owes me too.

MICK Don't come that.

JOHNNO He bit me last week

MICK He bit me last month

JOHNNO He bit me a year ago.

MICK Bullshit!

　　　(It looks like they are going to start up again. But PRICKY
　　　inadvertently comes in with the show-stopper:)

PRICKY Who?

SANDY (adding to urgency) Knowing Wally flamin' Jenkins, he could be in for that fifty. The way he can spread the bull, I'd be a bit worried… but then
　(meaningful at MICK and JOHNNO)

I wasn't in the hunt for that tenner like somes I know, either…

MICK   Sandy's right! That mongrel-on-the-sly Wally bloody
Jenkins…!

(He and JOHNNO dash inside.)

PRICKY   (all innocently)
Oh, the pretty girls of Bowen were handing out their duds.
I longed to have a chat with them so I made a beeline for their tubs,
When some curly children saw me and soon they raised my dander
Crying, 'Mother, quick, take in your duds; here comes the
Overlander!'

(chorus)
So pass the billy round, boys, don't let the pint pot stand there
For tonight we'll drink the health of every Overlander.

> *(MICK comes haring back from around the left side of the
> building. JOHNNO comes haring back from around the right
> side of the building.*
>
> *MICK points him to go around the left side of the building,
> while he hares off around the right side of the building.*
>
> *They come back around to the verandah, panting but empty-
> handed.)*

MICK   Did a skinny looking redheaded bludger with pockets
longer'n his arms choof around this way?

PRICKY   Who?

JOHNNO   Goes by the name of Wally or Stingy…

PRICKY   Who?

MICK   Bloody Wally bloody Jenkins, who else? Cripes, what's up
with you?

SANDY   Oh, might you be talking about Wally Jenkins?

MICK   Hand the dill over!

   (SANDY and PRICKY point off in different directions.

   MICK takes off around the left side of the pub, while JOHNNO
   takes off around the right side of the pub.

   SANDY and PRICKY wait patiently for them to finally emerge
   together, but still empty-handed, from the front door.

   They are wiping fresh froth off their lips)

SANDY   (jealously) Where'd you get that?

JOHNNO   (very coyly) Somebody's buying in there.

SANDY   Why didn't you stay?

JOHNNO   They weren't buying us.

PRICKY   (hopefully)   Any mention of us out here?

MICK   Dunno. I'll go and see…

   (He and JOHNNO goes back inside. They come back out a
   moment later, but with wiping more fresh froth off their chops
   again)

MICK   (mock apologies)   Naw, you're better off out here.   The flies
are terrible in there.

SANDY   (roused) I've a good mind to have a fling at that fifty.

PRICKY   Who?

SANDY   Me.

PRICKY   (relieved) Thank Christ, I thought it'd gone.

SANDY   That was the tenner. The tenner went off.

MICK   There weren't no tenner, right?

PRICKY   (irrespective of that)   I was worried someone wouldn't get in with the one I heard not so long ago. Mind you, I wasn't there but all the others were there and they tell the tale. They went into the pub and Allan was across the bar, and now and then he'd stare at this Polish bloke. I don't think he'd ever seen this Polish fellow before, but this character was looking at him the wrong way or something. Anyway Allen got drunker and drunker and said, "I'll belt this mug'. All of a sudden he raced around to this bloke and he said, 'Come outside, I'll have you!', and he pulls out his tobacco and rolls a cigarette like going outside was the easiest thing in the world. He puts it in his face, lights it, and he blows smoke into the other fellow's face, going, 'Come on, come on'.
The Pole says, 'No need to go outside' and Allan said, 'All right, I'm a gentleman. I'll give you first hit. Come on, I'm a gentleman!' Next thing 'BANG!', down went Allan, that cigarette splattered all over his silly looking moosh. The Polish fellow jumped on Allan and was bashing the living daylights out of him and the publican had to pull him off on the threat of no more beer.
As soon as Allan could get up he said to his mates, 'A great lot of mates, you lot are; wouldn't give a man a hand'.

SANDY   Naw, that's not as good as when old Carl gets hit by that pig.
    (to PRICKY)
You tell me that one?

PRICKY   Who?

SANDY   Well, listen and learn something. There was this 'ere pig that was bailed up and broke away from the dogs and come straight down the ridge. It was wet weather and Carl slipped on a vine and the pig hit him and the tusk went into his arm and laid it open to the bone. Carl had to go into the hospital and he's waiting in the out-patients, you know how they make you wait and wait.
Finally Carl says, 'I've been sitting here and there's blokes coming in with little scabs on them and pimples, and women with warts and things like that, and one thing and another. They are treating them and treating them, and I'm sitting there, drip, drip, drip, a bit pool of

blood. The bloody old dragon of a matron walking around there, been drinking vinegar all last night for sure; you could tell by the look on her face. Hour after hour I'm still sitting there and the pool of blood's getting bigger and bigger. At last a girl comes over to me with a book and she says, 'What's your name?'

'Thank buggery. Name's Carl Arn.'

'What's your father's name?'

'Otto Arn.'

'Mother's name?'

I told her.

'What's her mother's name?'

I told them the family history going back for five hundred years and signed a lot of papers and one thing and another and they asked me was I married and I said, 'Yeah, can't you see the look on my face?'

'Why did you marry? And what's her name? What's her father's name? What was her mother's name?'

She goes back through that side of the family for three hundred years and the pool of blood is getting bigger still and I'm getting weaker and weaker. In the end I just lost me bloody temper and I stood up and started waving my arm around splattering up their nice clean bloody floor and I bloody shouted, 'You mob of mongrels in here; isn't there a bloody doctor in the joint who cares what a real bastard of a wild pig is watching'n'thinking?'

That really got them going and in a few minutes they had five doctors running around giving me drinks of water and had me stitched up in no time.

Like I said, you've got to open your mouth at times or next time a pig comes at you what're you going to do? Nothing! Nothing's gonna stop it if it thinks all you've got is sitting there in your own pool of blood. It's not right to let pigs think they can play the merry hell like that.

MICK (suddenly pointing out) There he goes!

>(JOHNNO leaps to his feet, goes to dash off, but MICK grabs
>him first)

MICK (calling sweetly) Hey, Wally...? Good to see you, Wal...

JOHNNO Did you see that?!

381

MICK   Bloody hell! There's nothing to that Wally Jenkins, but I never seen a man jump over a bulldozer like that.

PRICKY   I ain't ever seen a rat chasing a man jump over the bulldozer, either.

SANDY   It mightn't been the rat.

PRICKY   It might've been a pig, after all.

SANDY   Naw, pigs can't fly over bulldozers like that.

PRICKY   What about a pig's arse with a lot of rat up front?

SANDY   Yeah, that'd be a different matter…
   (then)
Where were we?

   (Silence, before:)

POP   'Olympics'? Talking about the flamin' Olympics and long jumps, I was working on Strathmore Station and Stan Forwall the head stockman asked me if I could drive a truck. Well, I had driven an ordinary truck… kinda… but he asked me if I could drive a blitz wagon. I thought it'd be pretty similar, so I said yes.
Now there was this mob of young jackeroos just took on and a heap of pack saddles to be shifted out to the twelve-mile camp just over the twelve-mile creek. I thought I'd have a bit of fun with these wet-behind-the-ears jackos. They were all sitting around the blitz there scratching their heads over what they were looking at.
I walked around that thing two or three times looking like an expert, looking at the tyres and clicking my tongue and shaking my konk, and that sort of got them a bit more worried.
I said to one young fellah, 'You know what this is?'
'No.'
'You've never seen a blitzer before?'
'No.'
'Any o' youse?'
'No.'
'This's a motor car come lorry come truck come tractor, orright?'
'We still ain't ever seen one.'

Anyhow, after a bit of trouble I get the old bomb going. Stan told me she had no brakes and he said when I come to the twelve-mile creek to put her in reverse when I had to stop if I couldn't find any soft tree around there, like. So I loaded them young jackos and the saddles in the back and got started.

I couldn't find any reverse Stan was talking about but I thought what the buggery there's got to be soft trees around the twelve-mile camp since he mentioned it without being asked.

Off we go. We were going along the track and all the jackaroos started to sing a bit. I thought I'd show them getting so cocky and confident in me driving. So I ran over this big tree root, went in the air five or six feet and come down with a biggest thump you ever seen.

I heard a lot of yelling from the back and tried to pull up but there was no brakes, was there?, and I only managed to pull up four hundred yards down the track and I said, 'What's all the yelling about?'

'Willy fell out,' one of them said.

This young Willy had been bounced out all right and he'd taken two or three pack saddles with him. I said to him, 'What's wrong with you?'

'I fell out.'

'There must be something wrong with you falling out like that.'

'I dunno what happened.'

'Well,' I says, 'don't let it happen again.'

So we started off again and this time got to twelve-mile creek without him falling off. That creek really had steep banks back then, and I thought cripes, no brakes, now what? Then I had an idea and I shoved it into four-wheel-drive where you don't need gears, not in those days… you just stick it into four-wheel-drive and go into neutral. Anyway, while I was trying to do that we took off down the bank. We didn't quite break the sound barrier, but we must have come near to it. Bang! Crash! Bounce and bash! And then halfway up the other bank I hear all this yelling and then the blitzer stopped just before the top and started to roll back down. I looked through the back window and all I could see was that silly little Willy buggerlugs and a heap of pack saddles all in an untidy heap in the middle of the creek below me. I thought I was going to hit him because I had no way of stopping. I've never seen anyone scatter like it; that kid scooped up all the pack saddles and got out of the way, and the blitz just see-sawed back and forth, up one bank then the other, till finally she stopped in the middle of the creek. Was I mad and that young'un Willy was just the excuse I wanted!

I got out and shouted at him, 'What's wrong with you?'

'Dunno.'

'You're always falling out and making me stop to pick you up!'

'I dunno why. I just keep falling out.'

'You going for the Olympic long jump or some mad thing?'

'No, sir.'

'Well, there's nothing wrong with this truck and there's nothing wrong with my driving. Now get back up in there or I'll start driving as rough as bags and then you'll be really sorry!'

So that got all the new jackos going. They all climbed out and started pushing and got that old blitzer up that bank and they kept pushing her all the way into camp. When we got there, I shouted, 'Whoa up!' and they did.

And that's how I got to twelve-miles without having to resort to any soft trees.

> *(MICK and JOHNNO come back to join them. They are even more forlorn about things)*

JOHNNO   Have to admit that Wally's got legs.

MICK   Come pay days, he's grease lightning.

PRICKY   Who?

JOHNNO   (cunning) Old Shirl put you on a promise, did she?

MICK   You had yours last week!

JOHNNO   Easy on… Just thinking, once upon a time one of Shirl's promises used to be worth a few of the old folding matter.
   (even more slyly)
What'd you reckon it'd be worth now?

MICK   (catching on) Raffle it, you mean?

JOHNNO   Just sayin'. Knowing those dorks in there are from the city and ain't got any sense of taste or smell left.

MICK   Let's go!

(They take off inside again)

SANDY   That wasn't bad, Pop, that one about falling off trucks. Got me thinking about that family who had that little mining show and Joe the youngest was a lad about eighteen. He was on with a girl at the Glacier Restaurant in town, a few miles away and they used to go into the dance on Saturday nights.
Well, Joe had very sweaty feet, and water was scarce. One night he picked up the girl and she said, 'Oh, Joe, you smell badly. What is it?'
'Oh,' he said, 'me socks I suppose. I've got sweaty feet after a six mile walk and there's not much water to wash socks.'
'Well, Joe, go down to the store and buy a new pair,' she said.
So he went down and it was open and he came back again wearing these brand new socks, and after a while during the waltz she started to phew-whiff again and she said, 'Joe, what did you do with the old pair of socks?'
'I've got them in my pocket,' he said.

POP   (suddenly piping up) I took out me teeth and put them on the bedside table to give the cockroaches something to play with. In the morning I rolled over and had a look at the clock to see whether it was time to get up. But not having my glasses on I couldn't see it properly. Still half asleep I reached around and found my teeth and stuck them in, and then had another look at the clock. I still couldn't see the time.
'Shit,' I said to m'self 'I'm going blind.'

PRICKY   That's all right about you being robbed blind, Pop. What about me? I was just about to make a move on that fifty with the one about that time in the mines. A bloke coming in above where anyone might be working would sing out, "On top!' to let everyone below know he was there. If there was anyone below they were supposed to yell out, 'Below!' Well, that's what they were supposed to sing out, but what they really used to sing out was 'Arse'ole!'
One day this old chap was bring down a couple of lady visitors to look at the workings and when he got in he shouted out, 'On top!, and none of you blokes sing out 'Arse'ole!' cos I've got a couple of sheilas here with me.'

SANDY   Yeah, and it would've served them right if you had've told it, too, mate.

PRICKY   You just have to blink and they whip things out of sight these days, let alone a fifty. Ain't that…
    (MICK and JOHNNO return shaking their heads in disbelief)
right, Mick?

SANDY   (about MICK) What's wrong with him?

JOHNNO   Shirl's gone and half the bar's gone missing too.

MICK   Life bloody stinks!

PRICKY   Who?

MICK   (thought) Hold on, she can only be in the cellar out back!

JOHNNO   How come?

MICK   It's the only place room enough for her to get 'em in a long enough queue…!

JOHNNO   The rotten hounds!

MICK   (war cry) Bastards, that's my betrothed back there!

   (He charges off, followed by JOHNNO.

   The bulldozer is heard started. Gears engaged. It shakes the earth as it is driven past, and then a crashing of the back part of the pub being dozed in)

SANDY   I guess you'd say that fifty's no longer up for grabs.

POP   (hearing it) Is it tomorrow already? Don't think I won't sue the bloody dogs onto 'em first! You can laugh, but we were up at Stratford pub one night and one of the blokes with us was that Peter, you remember him. We used to call him the man with the magic thumb. No one could see anything wrong with it but he used to be off work for weeks with it on the strength of a doctor's certificate about his thumb being crook. Lucky bastard.

We'd be talking about what a wild bloke old Tiger could be and a bit later in came the old possum himself. We could see Peter was a bit toey about him when he joined us, and so someone gave Tiger the drum to act up to his reputation for a bit of a lark.

He was a great old ham of course and he started in to rant and roar as if he was going to pull the place down at any minute. After a while Peter got a bit of dutch courage back after staying quiet ever since Tiger'd come in… and he started correcting somethingorother Tiger was saying.

Tiger shouted back at him, 'Don't you answer me back or I'll come around to your house and pull your nose!'

Peter thought he was fair dinkum and said, 'Come round to me place, mate, and see what's-what. I've got a savage dog. A Doberman, and one word from me and he'll tear your throat out!'

Well, a week or two later we were over at the Knob and Tiger remembered the incident and said, 'Let's go round and see this savage beast then.'

We found out where Peter's house was and drove around and when we go through the front gate this medium small hairy Heinz dog comes up wagging its tail. Peter opened the door to see who it was.

'Where's this savage Doberman who's going to tear my throat out at one word from you? ' Tiger shouted.

'That's it,' Peter said, 'At least it's part Doberman, and it's very savage.'

'Well, let's see you give the magic word,' shouted Tiger.

'Attack!,' cried Peter, and the dog wagged its tail.

'Kill!' shouted Peter and the dog jumped up and down in lick Tiger's face.

'The trouble is,' said Peter, 'I've forgotten the word, but if I can remember it, this dog will tear your throat out.'

SANDY Bugger it! I forgot my one about the dogs.

PRICKY Who?

SANDY That German up at the Daintree. My old man went up there one time and though he'd never seen him, the moment the old chap came round the corner with his bandy legs… three wild pigs could have gone through them at one time; his legs were just like boomerangs… my Dad knew him.

My old man said, 'That's the bloke Jack's always talking about. We'll have a yarn with him.'

So we go over and this old boy's pushing this enormous wheelbarrow and on it he's got a jam tart.

Well, I've seen tarts that Auntie Alice used to make; they use to make them into sulky wheels, but this one was bigger. You've never seen a jam tart like this sticking out over the side of that barrow there. Gigantic it was.

He's got this old hat on and a bit of a straggly beard. My old man and he said g'day and Dad said he was up here campaigning for the council elections, and the old bloke with the barrow said, 'You're just the bastard I wanted to see.'

And he started in on what was giving him the shits about the district… I forget what it was and didn't care then at that age. All I know was as soon as he started talking, these thirteen or fourteen little dogs… little yappy things… you could choke them with one hand… well, as soon as he got up a storm talking to my old man, those bloody little dogs, they sort of divided and started running around in circles, sort of, yapping, yapping, and then they'd turn back and make a dash for that wheelbarrow of his making for that great big jam tart he had on it. But that old bloke never missed a breath or one word; he just kept on picking the little dogs off the tart and throwing them off, throwing them off, throwing them out and off… and they'd all be hitting the ground and licking the jam off their chops and then they'd come back.

How he could talk so loud and fast and still control his left and hand hands throwing these dogs out of that barrow, I don't know. But finally he stopped in the middle of a sentence saying he couldn't stand there all day yakking because he had to go before 'these bloody dogs of mine', he said, forced him to abandon the wheelbarrow and go for a cardboard box or something to put the jam tart in…. 'A man already had to go and take it out of the back of the ute and put it in this barrow because it's got so small'. And he said the shearers down at the shed he was taking it down to were a picky lot when it came to his jam tarts and they got real shirty if his dogs ate more than their fair share.

Gawd knows how big that jam tart was to start with, but as I said it was even bigger than Auntie Alice's sulky wheels even at that stage. I dunno how many of those yappy little bloody dogs he had.

(They sit in silence again.

*There is another bout of laughter from inside, which cause
PRICKY to roll his jaundiced eye to peer through the window)*

SANDY   That mean the fifty's still going, y'reckon?

*(As if to answer, MICK and JOHNNO come back very dirty.
They ascertain no beer left for them in the stash, and don't
bother to sit)*

MICK   You buggers don't care about a man's morning breath.

SANDY   Shirl?

MICK   (justified) She was just stringing them along.

SANDY   Still going through with that raffle then?

MICK   Shit, I forgot about that raffle!

*(with renewed hope, he and JOHNNO dash back inside yet
again)*

SANDY   (after them yet again) Try to get that fifty boosted to a 100
to make it worth a man trying…

*(But there is immediately angry shouting from inside, followed
by the unmistakable beginnings of a fight turning into a general
brawl)*

SANDY   A 100 must've got their goat up. Pity. For a 100 I might
come out with how I was once tootling along Wild Dog Creek. You
heard it? Of course you ain't. Keeping the best for last. Anyway, I'd
been talking to the old fossicker about bush ballads when I noticed
three wallabies slowly hopping up the gully towards the main camp,
moving on all four legs in the ungainly manner they adopt when
feeding.
We were sitting outside the old man's hut; he had upended an old
fruit box and I was sitting on an engine block. The wallabies showed

no fear or even surprise at our presence. They only stood swaying slightly to have a good look at us, and then resumed their feeding. I expressed surprise at their tameness.

The old fossicker said, 'Well, you see, they all know me. When there's no one else around, they come up and talk to me.'

'You mean they grunt and that sort of thing?'

'No, no, they talk proper like, you know, just the same as the dog.'

(The fight inside is now going full swing.

SANDY picks up the last bottle. They take last swigs from it dolefully)

PRICKY   Last one.

SANDY   (philosophically) Tempus fugit.

PRICKY   Who?

SANDY   Last day too. Almost forgot about that.

PRICKY   Real pity, that.

SANDY   Wasn't a bad old bastard of a place, when you think of it. Few years, you'n'me, Pop, here, eh? Got in a fair blighter of a rut under this bloody verandah, we did, I spose

(MICK and JOHNNO re-emerge all bloodied)

SANDY   What happened?

JOHNNO   (scandalised) Shirl only goes and puts the boot into him.

PRICKY   Who?

MICK   Bloody life stinks!

(and huffs off. JOHNNO follows.

In the hiatus that follows, SANDY holds up the last bottle; there is not even a drop left)

PRICKY   Coming tomorrow?

SANDY   Naw, couldn't stand to see even a coat of paint taken off the old place m'self.

PRICKY   (sympathetic) Know what you mean..

> *(SANDY rises to leave. He is so 'wedded' to his spot over the years that when he gets up a piece of the verandah's floorboards comes away with him. He puts it back reverently and then walks off not realising a bit of it is still stuck to his backside.*
>
> *PRICKY shrugs his turn too, and:)*

PRICKY   See you one day, Pop.

POP   What?!

> *(When PRICKY rises, the old Fosters sign he has been leaning against all these years breaks up. He hesitates, looks down at it, shrugs, and leaves it fallen and busted there.*
>
> *POP seems to doze a moment in the evening light. Then he just carries on with:)*

POP   A chap and I were going around looking for bloody propositions in West Australia gold fields. If you give a man a bob or two in those days you could take an option, and you and he sign that and it's legal. Now you've got his property for twelve months, and if you sell it he's on vendor's commission. Everybody's happy most times.
I might sell it for ten thousand quid. Tell a hell of a lot of lies, but the man I was with was prepared to do that. He was a new chum too. I lost a lot of money, but. I was a bloody mug of course. Anyway, this chap and I went to this town and we took a room. It wasn't part of the main house; it was set away a little. We put some biscuits and bread and other things in the room and went out. When we came back home there'd been a bloody cow in there and it had eaten all the bloody stuff and shit on the floor and went out.

I thought, 'What a bloody cow.'

Dunno if you know this, but the cow's got wonderful brains, and any new chum that comes there a cow like that bloody cow knows a new chum's breezed in and no matter where you come in the town it knows where you, the pushover, is at any given time, night or day. She knows you don't understand that and she comes and robs you and shits there just to let you know what a pushover you are.

Well, we went away from that dead-end town and come back in a couple of months, and we had all out food in the car – spuds, bread and biscuits. We stopped at the pub and when we came down next day that same bloody cow had been at the car, unlocked the doors and pulled the stuff out and done a lot of damage, including leaving her shitty calling card under the steering wheel.

She knew we were back! Wonderful brain, wonderful!

So I went to Thursday Island not long after. It was my first time there which made me a new chum, see, and I had a camp in the bush and there was a bloody cow come there knowing I was a new chum of a pushover and wouldn't know what's what with bloody cows!

But I did, didn't I?

I put some wire round the camp but that bloody cow still got through and ate everything and knocked everything over, and shit on the floor of course just to show me who's boss.

So I put a proper fence up, but the bloody cow got in again and does the same thing including the dirty doings on a man's floor.

I says to myself, 'I'll fix that bloody cow'.

I put the fence up again but this time I left a big gap so the bloody thing could come sailing on through… and I'd know where *it* was. So I hid in the camp willing to wait for as long as it took for that bloody cow to get in and think it's got the better of a bloke. This time that that bloody cow was going to get a two-by-four right between the eyes, right smack on that wonderful brain.

Well, I hid myself away and played possum until finally I see that bloody cow coming. So I braced myself.

I had a bit of fence post with a knob on the end like a club and I was going to do that bloody cow in or half do her in anyway. Didn't matter to me. I was sick of being shit on.

But, you mightn't believe this, that bloody cow went round the camp and she's pressing her head through the wire, not succeeding there, and moving on to another place and pressing her head through the wire again, not succeeding, then moving on to another place… going round and round that fence and every time going past the big gap I

392

left for her to sail on through. One time she's even got her arse-end inside the gap trying to get leverage to get her head through the wire from the outside.

So then she starts pressing her weight against the wire here and leaning against the wire there and still going round and round past the gap I'd left for her to sail on through. One time she tried to lean her weight where the gap was and nearly fell on through, but on she went to try another place. Talk about cunning. See what a wonderful brain that's no mug...?

Any rate I'm still waiting and hiding in there. I was thinking to myself just keep waiting her out and when she cottons on to the gap being there and she sails on through, boy, is she going to get it right on the noodle, wonderful brain or no wonderful brain.

But do you know that bloody cow kept sticking her head through those fence wires and leaning her weight against them and walking past the gap I'd left for her to sail on through, until she gave up and wandered off.

Clever, you wouldn't read about it.

And the thing was I never did get a go at that bloody cow.

(Fade to blackout)

(End)

∞⊙✕⊙∞

CASS BUTCHER BUNTING

Introduction

The resurgence of interest in Australia drama during the latter years of the last century produced a crop of young dramatists who enjoyed considerable success in their depictions of contemporary manners and mores, sometimes treated seriously, but most often seen from a mildly satirical viewpoint.

Bill Reed's 'Cass Butcher Bunting' is wholly serious but it is only contemporary in so far as it deals specifically with characters of the post-war – and now international-terror-driven -- generation. They and their dilemma could be transferred to any time and place without loss and the overriding theme of the play, the fear of being trapped in a situation of imminent destruction, is basic to all living creatures. The play is brutal and shocking and it is unremitting in the demands it makes of its audience. That it is fa removed from the popular idea of 'entertainment' goes without saying. Its importance as a contribution to Australian dramatic writing is quite another matter.

The play begins with an explosion and a cave in down a mine shaft. Three miners are trapped there; Cass, the local golden boy, sometime star football player and medical student, now an ordinary worker in the mine, drug dependent and complete cynic; Butcher, the average product of a small mining town, inarticulate, unimaginative, who thinks that the best life can offer is a new motor car; and Bunting, an old-time miner with the typical miners' 'hump', lonely and taciturn with an obsession about the welfare of cats. The play explores the reactions of these three men to the disaster that has befallen them and the fate which awaits them.

Both Bunting and Cass have been injured by the explosion while Butcher suffers nothing more serious than shock. Cass's pain does not seem to result from the effects of the cave-in as much as from the apparent loss of his drugs for which he searches between severe bouts of withdrawal symptoms that become more painful as the play proceeds. Bunting's injuries are critical and he dies during the course of the play. He never regains full consciousness but moves intermittently between a near-catatonic state of total incomprehension and delirium, during which he shouts barely decipherable ravings about cats being mutilated or destroyed in a variety of extremely sadistic ways. Bunting's words bear no relationship to the continuing dialogue between Cass and Butcher; they function as disturbing, almost surrealistic interjections of the single theme of human brutality to cats, a specific example of man's inhumanity to animals – but probably more so as a metaphor for the happenstance violence-in-disaster visited up the three men and, of course, upon their lost miner mates.

Man's fundamental inhumanity to man is a major theme explored in 'Cass Butcher Bunting'. Bunting's ravings are reminders that in the modern world this inhumanity is most often expressed in cruelty to animals. The exchanges between Cass and Butcher and their varying reactions to each other can be seen as subtle revelations of aspects of this theme which Bill Reed has explored in a situation as near to the extreme as can be imagined.

The setting of the action deep in the bowels of the earth places so-called civilised man back in a primordial situation, in a closed-off cave, his only weapons rocks and stones, his battle against impending death, his companions two work-mates. Butcher, the ordinary man (average man? Everyman?) responds to the explosion with shock, rising panic and then optimistic practicality – he tries to make contact with the world outside by persistently tapping on a pipe which runs through the mine. Inarticulate and unintelligent as he (intelligently!) thinks he is, he looks to Cass for explanations and support. They grew up together, went to school together until Butcher, like his father before him, went to work in the mine and Cass, unlike his father, went on to scholastic and sporting triumphs. He then became Butcher's personal hero and the proud boast of the township.

Cass, on the other hand, having found himself to be undistinguished, if not an abject failure, despite all the promise he had before him... and having grown past the township's narrow horizons through his sheer excelling abilities... is trapped at a time when he metaphorically has his tail between his legs. He and Butcher are now work mates and it made clear early on that Cass automatically takes command and stills his own fears in an attempt to help Butcher gain control of his rising terror. His repeated requests to Butcher to cool it have some effect. But this is only temporary; Butcher's agitation would be soothed by Cass's admonitions were it not for Bunting's unpredictable bursts of raving and contagious panic.

It becomes clear that, underneath their lifelong relationship there has existed a genuine and deep-seated incompatibility. Cass's highly-cultivated imagination – revolving around his own inflated image of himself – gave him such an exaggerated idea of his own abilities that he eventually failed when he faced the competition of the larger world and retreated into drugs. After the disaster they find themselves barely surviving, he comes finally to see how death is to be accepted, if not actually wished for. He pierces the façade which makes the work-a-day world bearable and acknowledges his dislike for a mate who, he finds himself really believing, is dull-witted, unambitious and damned by his inability to change:

> CASS: *Butcher, you've always been without poetry. It's... not only that I never liked you, Butcher; it's just that I don't want to die with you. Just don't come near me'.*

Then there is Butcher's grievance which is also released and cannot any longer be held back:

> BUTCHER: *You took away the only female I ever wanted, bastard. You hitched her up and then, bastard you, you ditched the only woman I ever wanted, and I vowed I was going to get you one day. Bastard.*

Their imagined terrors are exacerbated when the dying Bunting begins to inhale and exhale deeply and loudly, to almost theatrical proportions as though he was burlesquing respiration. Butcher goes berserk and tries to batter the senseless Bunting into silence without regard for the consequences, but his efforts are entirely ineffectual. It is important to notice here, in the light of later events, that Butcher's violent attack on Bunting is not an act of malice but an act of terror. He believes Bunting is using up far more than his share of what little air remains and he is overwhelmed by the imminent fear of death by suffocation.

Cass's injuries from the first rock fall and the increasing intensity of his withdrawal pains have made it virtually impossible for him to speak. However, after Butcher has for a time become the sole focus of attention for the audience, Cass lapses into a 'trip' and hallucinates, moving the play into a whole new dimension as the audience experiences Cass's mental state with him. During this section, Cass mixes reality with fantasy in nightmare proportions; there is, predictably, no logic to the action, no anchor for an audience to attach itself to.

One thing is clear: Cass or Bunting succeed in killing Bunting during one blackout by bashing his head in with a large rock. This puzzle is never resolved with any certainty in the text and so adds a special piquancy to the dialogue in the closing scenes.

After his 'trip' Cass enters a halcyon, painless period but has lost his power to dominate Butcher. Their verbal sparring, always potentially dangerous, is now reduced to the physical level as they arm themselves with rocks to keep each other at bay. Until this point their exchanges of mutual abuse have been stilled before they reach the stage of physical assault by ominous signs that the first explosion will not the last. Rock falls, small provocative needling have become more or less diversions to pass the time.

Bunting's death provides a new diversion. Their 'requiem' for him is as dramatically unconventional and as convincingly realistic as the rest of the play. It shows two fellow workers paying their last respects to a third by giving a cool and sardonic account of him. There is none of the heart-rending veneer of sentimentality so beloved of our early balladeers and fiction writers, none of the platitudes essential to the funeral as a social occasion.

The 'requiem' for Bunting during which Cass and Butcher were in agreement and were, moreover, united in mood and attitude has shown that, in spite of their obvious and apparently irreconcilable differences, they have something indefinable in common. In an unconscious desire to strengthen this bond each is moved to justify himself and his life to the other, to explain his successes and failures. In a way, each offer a requiem for himself. This leads to an unspoken but real understanding, forgiveness and acceptance. When they hear the approach of the final catastrophe and recognise it for what it is, they move together and, in a final gesture which boasts of their proud membership in the brotherhood of man, wave their penises in defiance of death. Thus they die brandishing the ultimate symbol of the life force, ironic as it may be under these circumstances.

400

The complexities of 'Cass Butcher Bunting' do not immediately reveal themselves and, in any case are by no means contained in the dialogue; at least a third of the text is taken up by what are technically known as stage directions, but here these are equally important to understanding as the dialogue. In performance, sound, light and action share equal importance with the spoken word. This divergence from orthodoxy is an essential ingredient in a drama which shows, among other things, that inescapable inarticulateness and natural reticence, along with pride that is undeniable, are major barriers to mutual understanding even among those who have as much in common as Cass and Butcher.

This point is reflected in the dialogue itself which is repetitious and thin, intended as it is, to express feelings rather than ideas and to show that language can often be a very real barrier to communication. Bunting's sporadic outbursts do not advance the action, are rarely complete sentences, but do in general show man's need for warmth and companionship. Butcher who speaks most of the dialogue is more a man of action than of words and has a very limited vocabulary which consists largely of expletives and obscenities. Try as he might his attempts at communications are usually vague and groping; he is the victim of limitations of which he is unaware. Cass, although highly intelligent, is hampered by pain and his own drug-withdrawn escape into a world of fantasy he finds inexpressible.

Although 'Cass Butcher Bunting' is a full-length play it does not observe the usual conventions of act divisions; rather it is divided into 26 sections of varying length, most of which are indicated by blackouts. The play could run continuously or could be broken by an interval or intervals.

In the original production at the Alexander Theatre the play ran continuously without the section endings being indicated and a normal interval at the end of section 11 gave the impression of a play in two acts. This fluidity in the overall dramatic structure reflects the relative unconventionality of the play.

The play works, as suggested earlier, on a number of levels. It may be seen simply as a straightforward drama about a disaster in a mine shaft or, as one reviewer claimed, 'a powerful expose of a restricted mining community which is as claustrophobic and as destructive as any rock tomb'. It may, as the playwright replied to a newspaper interviewer, be 'about *dying* not death'.

Unarguably it is in the face of impending and inevitable death that man, with nothing more to lose, can step out from behind his everyday mask and reveal his needs and his weaknesses, acknowledge and accept his failures. Between the simple social comment suggested by the reviewer and the distinction of 'getting through' more than the acceptance of death put forward by the playwright, lie a number of layers of meaning which the individual member of the audience or the reader will find for himself.

Mary Lord
General Editor
Monash New Plays series
Monash University, Melbourne

The Premiere

Winner of the Alexander Theatre Playwriting Competition 1976, CASS BUTCHER BUNTING was first performed by the Alexander Theatre Company of Monash University on June 16 1976 with the following cast:

Cass   Hamish Hughes
Butcher   Burt Cooper
Bunting   Tom Lake
Production design and directed by Peter Williams
Lighting and special effects by Bill Akers
Set design by Graeme McGuffie

Act 1
1.

(The stage is dark. There is an atmosphere of damp dust, of unhealthy and depressing depth.

Sound grows slowly, just as heavy work on stage becomes more and more perceptible through the darkness. The sound somehow encapsulates the very internal crashing insistence of technology.

Two or three 'lighting flashes' allow the set to be assessed. What the audience can discern is a coal face in one of the deep crosscuts of the pit. The three men working there are doing so evidently in an unusual part of the mine since they are cramped so uncomfortably. It is as if they want to get the work there over with quickly so that can get out of that 'pocket' they've been assigned to work in.

Rather than diminish, the sound of the mine increases to a crescendo until a sudden contrasting silence. Then shouting from far away. Then a shock wave of a deep explosion pushes upwards and through. Then the sound of the rock falling in everywhere and the shaft caving in.

The cave-in fills the whole theatre, continues, then stops abruptly. Silence. Then there is nearby moaning before a renewed silence that quickly become claustrophobic.
The stage is now pitch black. A long pause before a scream breaks through, replaced then by what sounds like a monotonal raving, low and incoherent. It is coming from BUNTING.

Thin and even-disorientating lighting allows the audience to pick out and follow the men, even though they themselves remain in a terrifying total darkness. The audience sees that BUTCHER is the liveliest, at this stage, of the three. He is groping around... but only really near himself and obviously in too much shock to do much else as yet. Any purchase he can

*make on the rock around him he clings on to for a moment as
though it could be a life saver.*

*BUNTING is sitting up against the rock face away from
BUTCHER. He can be seen and heard to be in an incoherent
but transfixed state.*

*CASS is stretched out flat, almost as if he had been neatly laid
out there. He is so still he could be unconscious, for any who
cannot see the wild rolling of his eyes.*

*Suddenly BUTCHER screams again; this time it is more
forceful than the outcry that came through the pitch blackness
earlier; this time it is more measured, more an expression of
anger.*

CASS rolls his eyes over to BUTCHER's direction and:)

CASS (strangely languid) Yes?

BUTCHER *Who*?

CASS Cass.

BUTCHER *Where*?!

*(Butcher tries to grope towards Cass. It proves an unsuccessful
attempt. Cass does not help him by talking so as the other man
can be guided to where he is; nor is Butcher keen to 'launch'
himself out into the pitch blackness. Butcher gives up the
attempt, begins to shake)*

BUTCHER Fucking hell, Cass.

CASS Yep.

BUTCHER *Jesus.*

CASS Yeah.

BUTCHER You alright?

CASS   You alright?

BUTCHER   Chrissakes, Cass.

CASS   I know.

BUTCHER   *Where are you?*

CASS   (sotto voce) In my tomb.

BUTCHER   What?

CASS   (harder) In my tomb, Butcher.

BUTCHER   Jesus.

CASS   Stay still.

BUTCHER   (not comprehending) What?

CASS   Still. Stay still.

BUTCHER   What?

CASS   Jesus. Stay still!

> *(Silence, while Butcher tries very hard to suppress his mounting hysteria. It is all he can do to keep himself from crying out again. Cass, even though he is just as fearful, forces himself to lie back again)*

CASS   (crooningly) Stay still stay still stay still. Stay still, Butcher.

> *(This has a calming influence on them both. Butcher manages to calm himself such that only his breathing comes through shallow and irregular. Relative silence, which makes Bunting's outburst all the more alarming)*

BUNTING   Cats! Catscatscatscats….!

(He drops suddenly to mumbling. Both Cass and Butcher have frozen with alarm)

BUTCHER   What was that?
  (no answer)
Who's *there*?
  (gets no reply)
Bunting? You alright, Bunting?

(He forces himself to crawl towards where he thinks Bunting must be, guided by the latter's mumbling)

BUTCHER   Bunting.

BUNTING   (suddenly) Cats barbed tried writhing wired barbarous barbed wiredaround. Yes.

BUTCHER   (overcoming fright) Cass, it's Bunting.

CASS   Yes.

BUTCHER   He's sitting up like a zombie.

CASS   Keep it level, Butcher.

BUTCHER   What's going on?

CASS   Absorb it, Butcher.

BUTCHER   Fuck that.

CASS   Get to know it.

BUTCHER   FUCK THAT!

(Pause. But Butcher's agitation only increases because of it; he can't withstand it any longer)

BUTCHER   I wanna know what happened. I wanna talk about it. *Cass*.

CASS Stay still first. For a bit.

BUTCHER You hurt?

CASS Don't, Butcher.

BUTCHER *Cass!*

CASS (explodes) Look...!
  (checks himself)
Still, stay still, see.

BUTCHER What're you on about?

CASS It's happened, see.

BUTCHER I know it's bloody happened, Cass.

CASS No, it's happened, Butcher.

BUTCHER Christ, man, what's bloody happened?!

CASS (calmly into air) Haven't you always known it was going to happen, Butcher?

BUTCHER *What?*

2.

BUNTING (lyrical burst) Cats set alight in the phone box the kero tin left charred alongside of. Cat gut spasm on the poison laid. Yes.

BUTCHER (spooked) Jesus, what's he saying?

(gets no answer back from Cass who is holding himself 'in' for all his might. In the heavy silence Butcher tries to crawl over to Cass, but he cannot locate him, even though he misses him only narrowly. Cass does not help, nor, again, is Butcher too keen

on doing too much groping around blindly)

BUTCHER   Cass, I'm trying to find you. Say something. Where are you, Cass?

> *(He stops to listen for Cass's breathing, but Cass deliberately holds his breath in a hunch about what Butcher is trying to do)*

BUTCHER   Cass, you breathing?
  (no reply)
Don't leave a man alone, Cass. *Cass*. CASS!

> *(Butcher's hysteria is visibly rising again. It bursts out when he traces the rock stratum to find out how low it is over his head. He only just manages to stifle another scream for help.*
>
> *Bunting joins in as though joining in singing.   His babble takes over. Butcher tries to move towards him to stop him, but cannot and can only cover his ears.*
>
> *Bunting stops his maddening screeching suddenly)*

CASS   Cool, Butcher, cool. Roll your mind around it. Try consuming.

BUNTING   (again frightfully) Cats of kittens of cats drowned they were. Inrush a lungful, why dontcha? Come halfdrowned in the sea of waves. Wave to the kitty, dontcha? Cats swimming by the side of the ship trying to crawl up a steel side. Hull it's called and them cats did I see. Yes.

> *(stops just as suddenly. Pause)*

CASS   Alive, Butcher. Simple.

BUTCHER   You call this alive, Cass? Cass?

CASS   Not so simple. Not so simple, is it, Butcher?

BUTCHER   Listen, Cass, mate….

CASS   Alive, Butcher. Still in the here's-me.

BUTCHER   Cass, you've got to listen to me.

CASS (simply) No.

BUTCHER   Chrissakes, Cass, where are you?
  (no reply)
It's not much to ask, Cass. Just let me touch you. Cass…

BUNTING (burst again) Half cat half nothing. Nothing half of
nothing. Left, dontcha know. Like it was sawn in two. Yes. There
in front of me around the back down by the side lane by the club
rooms there. Its two back legs and half a body is all thatssall. Oh.
Yes.

BUTCHER   SHUT YOUR ARSE!

> *(He swings a back-hand swipe in Bunting's direction this goes
> nowhere near the other man. Controls himself before turning
> to CASS's direction)*

BUTCHER   You think I'm weak as piss, Cass.

> *(Cass is seen to open his eyes suddenly, as though he has just
> seen how low the rock formation is hanging over his head. He
> reaches up repugnantly just as Butcher had and is better able to
> relatively calmly trace the surface with the back of his hand.
> 'then he too panics and is barely able to control himself before
> he cries out. It comes as a gurgle)*

BUTCHER   (listening hard) Cass…?

> *(Cass finally manages a strangely croaked and bitter laugh.
> This makes Butcher angry)*

BUTCHER   You reckon I'm as weak as piss. Who're you, Cass?
  (then weakly)
Chrissakes, all I want to do is feel you.

CASS   Bunting.

BUTCHER   Bunting?
   (turns to Bunting's direction)
Bunting… all right now?

> *(He gropes his way over and this time manages to find Bunting. He traces the old man's face with his fingers. Bunting neither moves or changes his expression as Butcher probes what he can now discern as a large gash on Bunting's head)*

BUTCHER   Blood, Cass. It's gotta be blood.

CASS   Sure.

BUTCHER   I think he's hurt bad.

CASS   Shit, man, it's showing clearly. We can't see it showing clearly, Butcher.

> *(Butcher shakes Bunting hard. At least it gets Bunting to turn his head towards Butcher, but his expression can be seen to be unchanged)*

BUNTING   Yes. And in the market, cats. Stalling kittens. Day old, yes. A dollar going. Buy the kid a… and at the end of the day did I see him fling it into the furnace out back. A giggle it was.

BUTCHER   (strained) He's not going to be any help, Cass.

CASS   A help? Bunting? (snorts) You'd be lucky.

BUTCHER   Let me touch you, Cass.

CASS   Still. Stay still's better, Butcher.

BUTCHER   I ain't that big time, Cass.

CASS   No.

BUTCHER   (outcry) JEEE-SUS!

CASS (ditto) YES!

    (Pause. They both have to control themselves again)

BUTCHER I have to talk about it, Cass.

CASS Yes.

BUTCHER *What happened?*

CASS Your lamp work, Butcher?

BUTCHER (bemused) Must've lost my cap. Yours?

CASS Must've been the way I fell. Here's a question, Butcher…
could I have fallen any other way if I'd tried?
   (no reply)
Bunting's?

    (Butcher grunts the logic of that, gets back to Bunting and
    gropes around for his helmet. He can't find it)

BUTCHER Can't find it, Cass.

CASS (amused) Ask him.

BUTCHER (seriously) He wouldn't know.

CASS (laugh) That right?

BUNTING (burst) Ears cut off the tabby. Wasn't it howling and
and. Yes. I went to it but it died. But dead. Oh, yes.

BUTCHER He's giving me the shits, Cass.

CASS Give it slack, Butcher.

BUTCHER You can talk. What areya, subhuman?

CASS Subbed.

BUTCHER   You tell me what happened.

CASS   Is there a hurry? No hurry.

BUTCHER   Fuck that, Cass.

CASS   I want to hurry, mate. No hurry. We hurry we die quicker.
Butcher, just shrug and live now.

BUTCHER   Up yours too.

CASS   We hurry, we go down screaming, Butcher.

BUTCHER   Don't talk to me like an idiot.
   (thinks on that, then angrily)
Don't talk to me like a fucking child, shithead.

CASS   We hurry, we…

   (stops, losing control almost)

BUTCHER   (premonition) *Jesus.*

CASS   (gagging) We hurry it, Butcher… subhumaned… animals…
asking a no god, yeah… for everything, Butcher. Mind leavings…
dro… dross, Butcher.

BUTCHER   (stopping up his mouth) Uh.

CASS   It's always been com… coming, Butcher. It was…

   *(Butcher can't hold his gagging any more. As soon as he starts
   up, Cass's panic likewise wells up. He literally joins in outcry
   with Butcher and their outcries threaten to turn into full on
   screams until they exhaust themselves. They sound like two
   animals in the abattoirs.*

   *As they slowly get themselves under control again, they enter a
   new stage of how the situation is what it is and how it is
   inescapable for the time being.*

414

Cass regains his senses first and half sits up with great difficulty, but then has to lie back in pain.

All this time, unheard but now heard, Bunting has been mumbling away and now bursts out again:)

BUNTING   The greyhounds were given stolen cats. Practice runs did I see. Cat claws pulled out so no hurting the doggies. Grey and killing they were. Yes. And wire meshing tied around the cat's body and it, yes, tied that time to the mechanical hare. Ha ha what a giggle, eh. The greyhounds, they tear a lot and doesn't that cat not stop twitching. Twitching. You seen twitching? And you see that little girl one time wrench right off part of the head of that kitten? I did. Clap, clap. Yes.

(He fades back to mumbling. Butcher stays with the side of his face against the rock wall. Cass suddenly remembers something and gropes for his pocket. It has been ripped off. He heaves himself up as best he can and gropes around for whatever he was after from his pocket. He has no success)

BUTCHER   What're you doing?

CASS   Looking.

BUTCHER   Cut it out. It's getting on my nerves.

CASS   Get stuffed.

BUTCHER   (sotto voce) All I say was the flash, Cass.

CASS   There was a flash alright.

BUTCHER   You hear them talk about it, but…

CASS   I don't want to hear that shit, Butcher.

BUTCHER   Big man.

CASS   Yeah.

BUTCHER Always the champion.

CASS If you say so, Butcher.

BUNTING (reburst) That cat, oh yes. That cat was crucified on a fruit box. Nails for its front paws and one both back ones and that cat's blood on the footpath. Blood bath blood path. Did I see.

BUTCHER We've got to shut him up, Cass.
  (Cass doesn't answer)
We never got any warning.

CASS Matter?

BUTCHER It matters, Cass. To me it matters.

CASS We're alive.

BUTCHER That's why it matters!

CASS (thinks about it, then) I'll pay that.

BUTCHER How long, Cass?
  (no reply)
Come on, how long we've been down here?

CASS Too long, what dyou think.

BUTCHER Listen, Cass.

CASS Too wide and long. All the colours going. It's been too long, okay, okay. Maybe I should've rolled down the schoolyard and tumbled straight on down into here. Y'reckon that would've been quicker and cleaner, Butcher?

BUTCHER All I'm talking about is I don't want to die, Cass.

CASS You'll die.

BUTCHER *Not like this*!

416

(Blackout)

3.

(During the black out, the audience feels the essential claustrophobia that the three men are experiencing. Bunting's mumbling takes of a new dimension of a whispering paranoia that Butcher in particular has been reacting to. Through this, each one's breathing, every little movement they make becomes heightened and magnified... sounding boards)

CASS Butcher, don't you find it strange... that you can't see a thing... yet you've got to fight to close your eyes? Jesus, Butcher, it's a cruel threat, isn't it? A kilometre of it up there.

BUTCHER Cut it out.

BUNTING (almost normally) In the arsehole of the cat, yes, pieces of glass still out. Jags. Didn't it jag ya? And nice kids normally, they were sticking their tongues out at me. Here kitty-kitty, here.

BUTCHER Old dope.

CASS Even the vestiges of colours, go. You noticed, Butcher? No colours and you can hear yourself all the more. How grey, like, you are. But your... *thing*... keeps factorying on. Here we are here, earthed. No living function at all anymore, Butcher, and we're still churning it all on. How's that for ho bloody hum?
    (no response; gives bitter laugh)
Cat got your tongue, Butcher.
    (then)
Bunting was always pissing on about cats, wasn't he? Now he's bombing out in true Alice in Wonderland style. Name of that cat? You don't know, Butcher. I don't know, but you don't *really* know, right? Listen to me, man. Who bothers to talk when we're alive?, and then we get... nearly not alive... yeah, nearly not alive, Butcher, and all we want to do is talk, talk.

BUTCHER (fiercely) I'm not going to die like this, Cass.

417

CASS   (monotone) Good.

BUTCHER   There was an explosion first. You hear it?

CASS   Roll on, roll on.

BUTCHER   Don't go getting like Bunting on a man, Cass. You hear it, I asked.

CASS   Yeah.

BUTCHER   So it must have been a blower. They must have let the gas build up. The stupid dumb bastards!

> (He smashes the palm of his hand into the rock, then tries to 'melt' into it)

CASS   Cool, Butcher. Stay still.

BUTCHER   Don't keep talking to me like that, Cass. You ain't my bloody old man.

CASS   Alright.

BUTCHER   Cass... I'll take most of it, but this isn't right. This is...

> (He is starting to make himself sick)

CASS   Say it, my friend.

BUTCHER   (near choking) ...fucking horrible.

CASS   Yes.

BUTCHER   *Horrible*, Cass.

CASS   Yes. Say it, Butcher. Get it off your chest. You gonna alter it by saying it? Because you might, Butcher. Try, homo sapiens.
God in your fingertips, snap snap. You're a magician come down the human line, Butcher; you're got the magic puff of smoke at the end of

418

the millions of years of us clawing up.   So, go on, God's choice, pull
the caper out of the stinking rabbit hole.
    (equally as surprising as Bunting's outbursts)
BUTCHER, YOU BLOODY LISTEN TO ME!

BUTCHER   What's wrong with you?

CASS   You ever sat and watched a sunset hummmm at you,
Butcher? Like it was melting, oozing at you,,, cornball stuff like that?

BUTCHER   We going to just sit here?

CASS   For a while.

BUTCHER   I'm asking what're we going to do.

CASS   For a start, mate… we, yeah, we spout wings, right? We
spout scythes. We spout scything wings, Butcher. We buzzsaw off.
We disproof Nature.

    (He makes farting noises)

BUTCHER   I'm coming over to you, Cass. If I don't feel you, I'm
going to be sick.

CASS   It's just shock, Butcher.

    (Unexpectedly, he doubles up with pain to his stomach)

BUTCHER   Cass…?

    *(He starts to go towards Cass, but freezes when the ground
    begins to shake. From seemingly everywhere at once, there is
    a rumble that comes from a fearful depth. It grows until at its
    very crescendo Butcher is screaming along with it. Cass is in
    too much pain to react. Bunting, however, seems aroused by it.
    He talks his mumbo-jumbo loudly through it)*

BUNTING   Oh, yes, found out didn't I how he had smashed the
mother cat's head in with a hammer and yes thrown it out with the
rubbish. Did I see. And then that an put the kitty-kitty down the

lavatory alive and I took that madman to court over shooting cats through the back legs. Crawling along. Dragging their whatnots.

(A second rock fall crashes in around them.

Blackout)

4.

(Finally, a sneeze. Instant better lighting up, although the men are still in pitch black.

Cass sneezes a second time, then a third. The dust is resettling. We see how only BUNTING has remained where he was and unperturbed. Butcher re-emerges almost reluctantly from beneath scoria. When he has recovered enough to grope around again, he manages to find Cass's feet and gets kicked off.

Cass begins to laugh drily.)

BUTCHER   You alright, Cass?

CASS   Call me champ, Butcher.

BUTCHER   You'd be fucking lucky.

CASS   No, Butcher, you're not reading me. Here's the upper crust of his god-sized space ball falling in on little old Cass and all little old Cass wants to do is sneeze in the championship round.

BUTCHER   (craning his head) Listen.

CASS   If I'd sneezed first, you could have blamed me for the whole dumbdown cave-in, Butcher. But sneezing after, I'm playing at a little tin god. You see, Butcher? Give the champeen a bit of a giggle…

BUTCHER   (still hearing something) Quiet.

420

CASS You've always been without poetry. Here we are. The whole earth come down on us, blind and black like so you can feel it, and Butcher's still working away on Butcher's feeble little hopes. We stuff that, Butcher, old son. The thing of me still wants to sneeze, see, Butcher. Let me tell you about sneezing.

BUTCHER I heard something.

CASS That's not the point. Sneezing...

BUTCHER (feeling it on his face) I've got air!

CASS Sneezing might be thought to be clearing the old snoz...

BUTCHER Cass, air!

CASS (deliberately over him) ... of little irritations.

BUTCHER (hearing something now) Hold it!

CASS (but going on) So a kilometre o rock fall is a minor irritation, comes in that category, see, Butcher.

BUTCHER (with bare belief) TAPPING, CASS!

CASS (singsong) I hear youse knocking but youse can't come in. Just some old bones rattling, Butcher.

BUTCHER You crazy?!

(He find a rock, begins to tap back urgently)

CASS (mockery of a shout) Can't come in. Can I come out?

BUTCHER Shut it, you fool!

(and tries to listen to responses to his own tapping. At least in himself, he becomes more and more confident that he is getting responses from above and begins to get more and more confident)

421

BUTCHER (excitedly) Hear that?

CASS I sneeze hard enough, Butcher, you think I could clear all the passages from here to eternity? See the headlines: 'Cass Sneezes out the Sniffers'.

BUTCHER There. Hear *that*?

CASS I sneezed. I wish a sneeze. Butcher, I sneeze a wish. I am the very champeen of my mind, Butcher. This setback I regard meaningless and temporary and meaninglessness temporariness, Butcher, and…
    (same careless tone)
I think I've been hurt bad, Butcher. Boo hoo.

BUTCHER (unheedingly) We're getting through, Cass! You little fucking bottler!

CASS (audible smirk) Butcher, you will never die.

BUTCHER Start tapping. Get at it, Bunting!

CASS Bunting, he says.

BUTCHER Get at it, Cass!

CASS Tap, tap. Okay? Forget it, man.

BUTCHER (convinced about getting results) Oh Jesus, they're there, Cass!

    (But Cass has gone back to lying as still as he can)

BUNTING (somehow understanding, but tapping like a child and setting his rhythm of his words to it) When I went around didn't I the fat Greek was giving away kitty-kitties to the children in his shop. When after did I see them throwing them onto a roof and all those concrete drives below. They lay there.

BUTCHER Shut up shut up shut up!

(Blackout)

5.

(Butcher is still tapping but is now having difficulty keeping it up as his illusions fade. CASS looks as though he is sleeping. But he comes to start to shake violently. Butcher keeps looking venomously in Cass's direction as though the other man has been the cause of the tapping not being successful.)

BUTCHER   (not realising Cass incapable) Take over, Cass. God damn you.

> *(Cass manages to sit up, managing a grin, but his voice is trembling)*

CASS   If He existed, wouldn't you reckon he would have damned me already, Butcher?

BUTCHER   They're still answering, Cass. Getting nearer, on the right tack…

CASS   Maybe they know the way of the damned.

> *(Butcher has to drop his rock, rests)*

CASS   How long have you been doing that?

BUTCHER   Yeah, pretend away, matey. Your turn.
   (no reply, finds this one strange)
You've been moaning. You hurt?

CASS   Nothing to you. Bunting?

BUTCHER   He's still giving me the willys.

CASS   His right to one third of the worm hole, Butcher.

BUTCHER   Yeah, well…

(then)
He always was off his rocker a bit. Useless.

CASS   (calls) Bunting?
   (but nothing)
Useless, how?

BUTCHER   (hotly) Useless as a pisshole without the hole but a
bloody side wetter.

CASS   I'm useless too, Butcher.

BUTCHER   (quietly) I don't know what you're playing at, Cass.
You could be hurt. You might be bludging on a man. I don't know.
What can I see? I'm burning up alive too. I'm bloody suffocating
here, but at least I'm trying.

CASS   (claps ironically) You're a wonder of human architecture,
Butcher.

BUTCHER   Up yours too, sports star.

   (resumes his tapping. Relative silence)

CASS   Mind you, you've got the air there, Butcher. Say you didn't
have the air. Air's a funny thing. You try touching it, Butcher.
Better. You try touching without it. Way I figure is we only rate…
Butcher only rates…because of something we can't touch, Butcher.
'Air.' Say it. Roll it around your tongue. 'Air.' That's you you're
not saying. Why aren't you saying it, Butcher? Because it sounds
bloody stupid, right? Well, that's you that you not saying, Butcher,
because it sounds stupid. You getting frantic because you can't get
enough air or enough you, whatcha reckon? Same thing, or what?
Butcher?

BUTCHER   At least I'm tapping, mate.

CASS   We suck in air, Butcher, or does air suck us out?

BUTCHER   (fiercely) *I'm getting out of here, Cass!*

CASS The air in here not good enough for you? You not good enough for yourself in here? And useless Bunting, Butcher. And useless *me*.

BUTCHER Stuff Bunting and stuff you, Cass. Just get over here and keep tapping.

> *(He can't see that Cass has another spasm of pain and can't stop grunting over it. Butcher stops, listens, lays down rock, crawls towards him)*

BUTCHER Cass?

CASS Keep away from me.

BUTCHER What's wrong? What can I do?

CASS It's... not that I never liked you, Butcher. And it's not that I can't seem to get away from you. It's just that I don't want to die with you. Just don't... come near me. Not much to ask.

> *(pause. Butcher absorbs this statement. Even he realises how it changes being together in horror to going back to their old animosities. He crawls back to his space)*

BUTCHER Big man.
  (Cass laughs)
I can take you apart with one hand, bugger you.

CASS But I always got the pats on the back, didn't I, Butcher?

BUNTING (not knowing how timely the burst is) Frequently. Didn't you see? Frequently in the rubbish bins alive. Barely, I thought. I think. Tied to a brick. Gagging. And the grey tab hanging from the fence tied by the legs. Long time before I got there. I said... I said... didn't I...?
  (then clear shout)
Boys?! You there?!

> *(This startles the other two)*

BUTCHER Bunting...?

(But Bunting only resumes his mumbling to himself)

BUTCHER Bloody hell
  (then shout in Bunting's direction)
STUPID OLD SHITHEAD!
  (then to Cass's hard laugh)
Cass, let's get along in this. I don't mind telling you, I'm packing them.

CASS Of course you are, you goon.

BUTCHER *Jesus, it's so black!*

CASS (monotone) You've got your tapping. You've got your air. You even think you touch, feel, smell both of them. Butcher, you're going to be alright.

BUTCHER Help a man out, Cass.

CASS You know why you're going to make it, Butcher? Because you'd do anything to survive. I mean we all do, but you come right out with it. See, you know what I think, Butcher? I think you haven't got enough imagination not to survive. Tap, tap. Knock on wood.

(But of course, Butcher can't see Cass tapping his head as illustration)

BUTCHER (hardening) Yeah, alright, big sports star. But I'm the one calling them in. Tap tap yourself, smart arse.

CASS Say, Butcher, apart from recently, you ever had a doubt in your whole life? No, really.
  (no reply)
Thought not. A doubt's three-parts of an idea, right?, so where you ever going to dreg up a doubt, mate?

BUTCHER You know what I think, Cass. I think you're a gutless wonder.

426

(Cass starts to laugh at him again but this time it hurts, and then he begins to shake epileptically)

CASS (surprisingly) GOD, NO!

(He scrambles around as best he can looking for what he has lost from his pocket again)

BUTCHER (hiss) You sound like a rat. *Cut it out!*

(Cass manages to take hold of himself reasonably enough, but carries on searching while he talks)

CASS I am a rat, Butcher. I've been scurrying to this for a long time. I've lost something, see. You, you've got your tapping, Butcher. You've got some sort of cavalry thundering down to Butcher's rescue. You know, if it wasn't around the corner for you, you'd wilt, Butcher. Always the same. Never-change Butcher.

(He gives up the search, lies back tenderly.

Pause)

BUTCHER (quieter) You tell me what else can we do, Cass.

CASS I guess you're doing it.

BUTCHER I'm asking your opinion, Cass.

CASS (now teeth chattering) I guess you're going to sys… systematically search around this tomb, see what you can come up with.

(Pause)

BUTCHER I can't do that thing, Cass. You do it, Cass.
    (no helping reply)
I'm not *touching.*
    (then)
It's up to you.

CASS Me? I've lost something, Butcher. It's my reason, see.

BUTCHER What's that mean?

CASS You lose reason, you lose the moving part, Butcher. Simple.

BUTCHER I don't dig you, man.

CASS (sloppily tries to sing-song) Don't dig me, Butcher. Dig me out.

> *(Butcher waits for him to go on, but there is nothing more. He resumes his tapping, then stops to listen, and pulls his head away from the rock face quickly)*

BUTCHER Jesus, no…!

> *(Another rumble grows. This time it advances more quickly. At its height, Cass and Bucher can just be seen screaming through it, and Bunting mumbling manically aloud.)*

BUNTING They shaved the cats. Well, didn't they? They lopped the cats from lopping. They wrenched off the cats. They strapped the cats up so they could never lie down. Did I see. Oh, you bet…

> *(Even his voice is finally swamped out*
>
> *Blackout)*

6.

> *(We hear whimpering as the earth shaking recedes. It is Butcher. Finally, the lighting resumes)*

CASS Butcher?

BUTCHER (barely) Uh?

CASS Shove that whimpering, Butcher.

(Butcher's reaction to this insult is almost simultaneous. His fright gives way to anger and hatred of Cass, even though the latter is now is constant pain through both injury and obvious withdrawal symptoms and, compared to Butcher, is increasingly finding it hard to hold his nerves)

BUTCHER   Who's whimpering, mug?

CASS   You were.

BUTCHER   I hat your stinking guts, Cass.

CASS   That's it.

BUTCHER   I'm not kidding, bastard.

CASS   Nice of you.

BUTCHER   I've always said that one day I was going to do you.

CASS   You wanna play toesies for it?

BUTCHER   (seemingly the only thing he can think of) You took my woman away from me, *prick*

(This makes Cass laugh openly)

BUTCHER   You're a mongrel, Cass.

CASS   You're a comedian, Butcher.

BUTCHER   You smart pisshead.

CASS   You're a cunthead, Butcher. You've got shits for brains.

BUTCHER   So help me, Cass, I'm gonna see you laying on your back.

CASS   You dummy.

BUTCHER   You… suckhole.

429

(Cass lightens the situation with a dry laugh. In the dark all this aggression has been ineffectual but at least it has provided a necessary catharsis to bring them back to the reality of their situation)

CASS   Tubes cleared now?

BUTCHER   Yeah, well, you still took away the only female I ever wanted, bugger, you.

CASS   I'll bite. Who was that?

BUTCHER   Carol, and you'd better know it now, Cass.

CASS   Carol.

BUTCHER   You heard me. Shithead.

CASS   Yeah, but which Carol, Butcher? There's been Carols. Oh, Butcher, there's been Carols.

BUTCHER   That's right, big shot, play around with it. You married here and you ditched the only woman I ever wanted whether you liked it or not, and I vowed I was going to get you for that one day.

CASS   Oh, that Carol. She dropped you like a steaming pile of crud, didn't she?

BUTCHER   You've got it coming, mug.

CASS   What did you reckon you'd done, Butcher… paid a deposit on her? Put her on lay-by? The idiot box, her, a new three-bedroomer, new vehicle… all one neat bundle of joy, Butcher? You reckon you were capable of that, Butcher.

BUTCHER   Better'n you, bastard.

CASS   She might have wanted an achiever, mate. Not you. An achiever, see. Me, Butcher. After all, what else are we higher animals here for, or haven't you cottoned on to that in your old age?

(Butcher growls)
We're here to have to achieve, Butcher. It ain't easy. We're here to
think it out, and thinking it out's a real bugbear, believe me. We have
to carry the load of thinking before we can go the lay-by escape
hatch, son. You can go around looking like a bloody rooster with
your latest lay-by thingo on parade but we've got to do the heavy
brain stuff lifting. Like now, Butcher, right"

BUTCHER   What're you on about,?

CASS   Now. Who's gonna think us out of here. It's called the fly in
the ointment, Butcher.

BUTCHER   Like always, you're farting not yakking.

CASS   *More, don't you see, dopey?* Who's going to have to take it
on if we don't think our way out of this?

BUTCHER   Bugger you, you bugger.

CASS   Well, well... *that* Carol. The love of my life as I remember.
So what's the beef past the old post, matey?

BUTCHER   IT MATTERS NOW!

CASS   (stops to think on that, conceding) Maybe. No. No, it
doesn't.

BUTCHER   (conclusive accusation) You did her down, prick.

CASS   (suddenly anguished) *Yes.*

   (Blackout)

7.

*(This scene played in total darkness without lighting even for
audience.*

Cass's breathing starts to become stentorious over Butcher's tapping and Bunting's babbling. Cass's voice, too, is noticeably starting to thicken)

BUTCHER Hot. Cass, you stripped?

CASS Yeah, maybe.

BUTCHER I'm burning up here.

CASS I know.

BUNTING (burst) Cats. Didn't I see them in cartons for the rubbish tip dumped! Yes. And scratch, scratch on the cardboard, oh yes! And when I turned that corner that cat had its back leg tied to its head. Running away from me sideways on threes!

BUTCHER (spooked again) CASS?

CASS Still here, Butcher.

BUTCHER Not like this, Cass. I don't want it like this.

CASS Tap. Function. Tap them up even though they don't know it, mate. Get 'em up from the depths of hell.

BUTCHER You could tap with me, Cass.

CASS Shit, you want me to hold your hand?

BUTCHER *A man's not a human being down here!*

8.

(Lighting returns.

Butcher and Cass are not stripped as best they can, since it has become so fiercely hot down there. Cass is doubled up. Though his movements are of someone in agony, they also begin to take on a sleepy, surreal quality, previously only indicated occasionally by his voice)

BUTCHER   What's wrong with you?

CASS   Butcher, how much 'soul' you reckon you've got left in your bones?

BUTCHER   Knock it off.

CASS   No, I'm asking. It ought to be important, mate. No sight and all that. 'Souls'… you 'soul'… Butcher, ought to be singing hallelujah and busting to get out. What's the point of carrying one around with you all your life if it doesn't do what it's supposed to when the time comes? 'Come out soul and explain yourself!' Butcher. Butcher. Butcher.

BUTCHER   Shitsake, what?

CASS   You know where my 'soul' is right now? Crabbing around in my skin trying to hide, Butcher. *Cringing.* Crawling around in fear like it never asked to be dumped in this world. Digging its claws in. Mate. Mate.

BUTCHER   Oh, Christ.

CASS   Christ? Yeah, you're right. I'm not saying that Christ didn't have it the worst, Butcher, but at least he had the sky to look up into. At least he had something sorta… noble… to fall back on. At least he had something to melt into. Who'd want to melt into any of this? You're right, soul! Stay where you are!
   (impatient pause before:)
When we go where's the rosary, Butcher? No rosary, mate. No shiny little coloured beads. When we flip out, we're gonna go filthy and greasy and grimy and shit all over us and not even our souls wanting to associate with us. *Animals.* They won't come down to get us. They'll decide it'd be too embarrassing if they found us. They'll say to our families: stay with any recent photos.
Dirty, butcher.

BUTCHER   (new urgency) Cass, I want to tell you something.
   (doesn't wait)

433

I don't know what happened to you, Cass, but I want to tell you something… that I'm not getting any tapping back. I dunno now if I ever did.
   (still no reply)
All I saying is…
   (but can't spell out any defeat; get angry again)
You talk to me, big sports star. I don't know what's happening, but I'm not getting any tapping back anymore if I ever did.
   (waits, listens for Cass, for tapping, for anything)
CASS!

   (Blackout)

9.

(Through the intervening blackness…)

BUNTING   (light-headedly) Cat did I see dragging a rabbit trap. Gnawing at its back leg on the go. And cat legs putrid in rat traps. And the weight slung around kitty's neck so it couldn't lift up its head. Oh, yes. Didn't even get across the road. No.

BUTCHER   SHUT THE FUCK UP!

   (There are unmistakable sounds of Butcher crawling over to Bunting and shaking the older man violently. It is a murderous rage, finally abates.

   Lighting returns. Butcher has fallen away from Bunting and is still panting with frustrated violence.)

CASS   Keep off the poor old bugger, Butcher.

BUTCHER   You gonna stop me?
   (but then remorse)
Bunting…?

   (He now retraces himself to Bunting and traces his face with his hands, purring for quietness)

CASS You're going to try to do us both in, Butcher?

BUNTING (whine justification) There's no tapping anymore, Cass.

CASS Butcher to the end, is it? Might is right, right? How does it go?... the weakest imagination, the strongest hold-on? That you think you can means you're too dumb for words, matey.

(Butcher is stung to crawl back to his 'space'. There he defiantly resumes his tapping, his listening)

BUTCHER They're around, Cass. Small fall. Setback.

CASS Crap.

BUTCHER I'm telling you, Cass.

CASS Crapulence, Butcher.

BUTCHER Help me tap, you prick!

CASS Mate, can't you see I'm trying to get it over with, not drag the laugh-on-us out. You're a goon, Butcher.

(Pause)

BUTCHER (fearful whisper) How many you reckon?

CASS This section at least.

BUTCHER No, how many in all?

CASS This section, has to be at least a hundred. Both shafts? How can guess?

BUTCHER Jesus.

CASS Does it help to know how many of us, or not know, Butcher? Because one way or another it should help. Answer?

BUTCHER I'm coming over to you, Cass.

435

CASS No, you don't.

BUTCHER Put out your hand. Tap or something.

CASS (relapsing) Go and get... tapped yourself.

BUTCHER That last fall get you, Cass?
   (no response)
Hey!

CASS (coming back) Aw, wise up, man. I got hurt. I think I'm
even bleeding pretty badly. In there. In. Feeling bruised. So what's
that, Butcher? I've lost 'em. I've lost my life's balls. Trying not to
go berserker, see.

BUTCHER (stopped) You were supposed to be cured.

CASS They call it drying out, Butcher. If I'm bleeding how am I
dried out? Cured. I am ham. That make you Shem and our daddy
Noah? We gonna float on out of here, Butcher?

BUTCHER (something to be contemptuous about) Weak as piss,
you, and a liar.

CASS You tap, Butcher. But watch out. Withdrawal symptoms,
mate. *I might withdraw*. Poof!, outa here in a puff of smoke. Oh,
yeah, I'm going to suffer... lost it, can't find it. Rock Squashes Ice.
I...
   (suffers pain)
Uh... Butcher?
   (recovers)
Like that, Butcher. Icy old me. Ice gives you the shits shivering.
Butcher, I can hear you tut-tutting from here. You've always been an
old hen, Butcher. What're you at church, deacon?
   (now having to fight pain again)
Don't you... worry about me, son. This hooked-up friggin' *front
thing* that spritzes around the world as me... you oughta see how you
know it's rotting every fucking day, Butcher. Rot, rot. You.. you tell
me how this down here... in here... how it's much different. Lumps.
Lumps bumming out, like a sack of potatoes, son. Lumpy and soft

squashy. Your type, Butcher, you'd call it the life that lives. My kind calls it the botfly process. My kind… we're legion, Butcher.
  (depressed, Butcher stops tapping)
What's wrong, pal? Tap turned off?

BUTCHER (monotone) They're there.

CASS Cock, and you know it.

BUTCHER You've got a head full of meat, Cass.

CASS No, no. I get it. I do. They've got to be up there for the Butchers of the world, right? I know what goes through that tiny little brain pan of yours, mate… mirages. No imagination, they have to be mirages. All's trudging across the endless plain, right?

BUTCHER You'll get yours, big sports man.

CASS (taking threat seriously) Butcher, it might be the Butchers before any other shithead, but don't get any ideas, pal. I might be going to suffer but I've…
  (passing pain makes him take different tack, laughs)
Hey, I was going to say I've got my beadies on you. Laugh, Butcher.

BUTCHER I ain't laughing.

CASS What worries me. Especially when you realise we're not getting any more air in here anymore…

  (Butcher reacts. He gropes for a place he has known air's been getting through to find Cass is right. The last rock fall…)

CASS Now will you believe me about the tapping?

BUTCHER They're up there!

CASS Sure they are, and you stick with that. Me, I just sort of figured it was some other poor bugger close by and after that last fall, Butcher, he ain't tapping so well anymore.

BUTCHER Shut your filthy gob.

CASS   Watch out for that imagination, Butcher.

BUTCHER   Watch out for the eebie-jeebies, junkie.

CASS   Don't waste the air, son.

BUTCHER   FUCK YOU, THEY'RE UP THERE!

(Blackout)

10.

(Through the blackness, almost inevitably, Bunting's rambling rises to domination)

BUNTING   (accelerating) Cats! Tacks driven into paws, were there. Hobnailed in pain and roaming with. Cats! Bellies slashed, guts trailing, did I see. Spasms of cats. Where they lay dying bellies going up and down, up and down. Does the pulse go last? Get out. Move away. Flies on cats. Big blowies going the cats. And cats blown. Half buried before the licks of fire could be licked out, you bet. Didn't I see. And the little tabbies with their teeth pulled out. Pliers. Toy hammers. Tweezers the whiskers. Tweezer the whiskers. Dontcha. Cats dead at a bloke's feet torso tourniquet'd. Poetry in motion. Oh yes and yes cats.

(He fades)

BUTCHER   Thank buggery. Useless prick. Cass? You still in the land of the living, dopeboy? Cass. Cass. Cass. Even your name has always pissed me off. You know, Cass, it's curious, Cass. You talk about not going out anywhere near me, but the feeling's mutual, junkie. I don't mind too much not cottoning on about the air. But now *you* pointed it out, I'm having a hard time holding myself back from panicking. I could turn into a raving fucking lunatic. Not… in front of you… bloody Cass.
   (rocks back and forth, holding himself in)
If you weren't here, Cass, I would. I would let myself go. And you know what? I know it'd be the juiciest, *suckery* feeling I'd ever have

in my life. No bull, Cass. Just drop myself over the side and let my nut loose. But as long as I can hold out, I ain't gonna do that. Not in front of the mighty Cass. Not to give the great Cass the satisfaction. And, too, because I know that'd be the end of the line and I don't know about you, but I'm gonna live. So fuck that for a lark and fuck you, Cass.

>*(Pause. When he knows he isn't going to get a challenge from Cass, he goes back to tapping, until…)*

BUTCHER   How much air you think we've got? You wouldn't know, you weak piss. Come to think of it, it's just coming home to me how much I've always hated your guts. As long as I can remember… bloody Cass. Cass, the big footie player. Cass, the great headlines man. Champ of champs bloody Cass. And what? All you did finally was flunk out. Smoke it n' dope it Cass. You even run away from your own wife. *My* Carol, bastard. You got had up for dope-arsing y'self and get thrown in the boob, that's all you ever did. Big man Cass. Gonna bring the great wide world down. What'd you ever even finish? I would've given my eye-teeth to have been paid to go to university like that. But you, you crawl back here a deadbeat, a useless fucking *drongo* with his tail between his legs… yet it's still poor Cass. Everybody make room for our shining boy come home. Give the champ his father's job; set him up because he's been injured boo hoo. You've always had it made, bastard, and I've hated you for it. And I'll tell you this, big man…. I'm gonna see you go down first.

CASS   (barely)   You'd be lucky.

BUTCHER   Now I know why I said I'd have you as my side-winder. I've been sweating on the opening to have you, bugger, you.
   (pause)
Y'know, my old man spent forty shitty years down here, Cass. Same as my Grandpop. When I was a kid, I'd roll in shit just to smell like my old man then. I'm talking about all *this*. It's always been in my flesh. Now I'm underneath it. You figure that? It's rolling in me.
   (madly)
Prickhead, I would've made my Carol happy!
   (half controls himself)
And I'll tell you this, mate. Apart from a broken toe, the only thing that got at my Dad finally was the dust, and only then in his ripe old

age. And it's gonna be the same for me. And you listen to this, big shot… I never ever wanted to be away from this town. I hate it out there. This is my dust, see, and it's going to take until my ripe old age, too.

(then)

Yeah, you can go all quiet, bugger, you. I hope you're having a hard time of it. I just hope you stay alive until they get here and see the great sports star as he really is. Shit, I can smell you from here. What I think, Cass, is you've shit yourself, like, not even fit company for a man. And I'm gonna be around to tell 'em how the mine didn't get the great Cass but the junkie stuff did. Whimpering. Run away, run away. Bye bye, Mister Number One on the dais.

(snorts)

Superman.

(pause)

God, I'm dry.

(has sudden appalling thought)

God almighty, what if they flood!

(Blackout)

(Suggested end of Act 1)

Act 2
11.

(Lighting returns slowly through:)

BUTCHER   Cass?
   (is immensely relieved even to get a grunt for a reply)
Must've drifted off. I don't want to drift off. Don't let me drift off
again, Cass. I don't want to have to wake up again. I don't want to
be near this… this, flying off the handle, most likely. Mate. Cass?
Okay? You hear me drifting off like Bunting, you say…
   (then)
You had to bring up about the air, didn't you? Bastard, you. I'm no
coward, Cass. I'm…
   (stops himself thinking along those lines, then:)
Listen, what dya reckon's wrong with Bunting? Why's he gone all
quiet? Hey! Bunting!

> *(He crawls over to the older man, shakes him, but Bunting
> doesn't stir. He puts his head to his chest, feels the head
> wound. Nods, then crawls back to his own space)*

BUTCHER   His bleeding's stopped. Dunno what it is with him. At
least he's not giving a man the shits. What's wrong with the old goat.
You ever hardly heard a word out of him normally, Cass? Like they
used to say, you should drop him down the shaft instead of the lift just
to clear his throat. Crapping on like that. Cats. Jesus. We end up
down here and Bunting turns out to be a fucking loony. How would it
be ending up like that?
   (remembers another grievance)
Don't give me all that crap about me chasing material things, bugger,
you. I mightn't be as pouncy clever-dick as the great Cass, but at least
I know what I want. Me, I'm never forgetting the first time I got
myself behind the wheel of my first new car, mate. I can still smell
the smell of that real leather. Okay, it wasn't real leather. I don't
give a stuff. It smelt like real leather. Like my old man used to say,
'Don't feel it, smell it'. I had to scratch and scrimp to get that smell
of leather, Cass, and it'll never leave me. I don't care what the great

high'n'mighty Cass says that smell was worth every penny. What it did, see, what it did was it made me feel like I belonged. Yes, mug, bloody ads and all the hype. Who cares? If that's the way it goes, that's the way it goes, big sports star.

(stops until further thought)

Where'd you ever belong, shithead? All you could ever do was light up and draw it into your lungs. Even when you come back here with your tail between your arse cheeks, you tell me you ever belonged...

(gets nothing in return)

And get this, big-timer... what I reckon I want most back is that smell of leather. So, okay chasing things... you tell me a better guide for getting through the day-to-day gunk, mate. Big ideas man.

(Suddenly Bunting begins to breathe laboriously. His breathing in and out becomes so rhythmically belaboured that it becomes alarming. He keeps it up, and it becomes obvious he is doing not so much deliberately but just as blindly-brutal as his rambling outbursts. Butcher lasts out, until:)

BUTCHER   KNOCK IT OFF, IDIOT!

(But Bunting doesn't stop, rather seems to increase the annoyance. Butcher loses control. He scrambles over to Bunting and tears at the old man's head as if he would dash it against the rock. He wrenches; he heaves; he pushes and pulls; he pounds until Bunting suddenly falls silent and Butcher can return to his space)

BUTCHER   (but still panting with rage) How're we gonna stop him, Cass? I tell you, I can't...

(then)

I'LL KILL YOU, YOU OLD BASTARD!

(and finally)

Cass, you ought to say something to me, Cass. I don't want to be alone like this. Not down... not down *here*.

(He bursts into a bout of frenetic tapping, then stops almost immediately. He sits back, and, in an odd gesture since he cannot see anyway, sits with his face in his hands. His voice is now deeply imploring)

BUTCHER Bunting… don't. I'm asking you, old man. Stop. Stop it, see. You're using up the air, Bunting. Bunting, I know you're sick. I'm sick too, Bunting. I can't help you. I don't want to move around, see… and I admit it, see… and, fuckit, Bunting, you've got to stop.
    (and)
Cass, you still there? Cass, you make him stop. Alright? *Alright*? Cass, see, I don't think I'm going to be able to…
    (simply stops)

CASS   (painful effort) Hold on.

   (Butcher starts to hear his voice, gets a blessed kick of reality
   from it, comes back sniggering)

BUTCHER That's my Cass. That's the prickhead. What's the big dramatic act for? Well, you hold on yourself, junkie, cos I want them turning up their noses at the very stink of you. Big man. Useless to man or beast. Okay, somebody's got to go something and that's got to be me. Okay, big shot. Okay…

   (He forces himself to explore as much of the pocket they are in
   as he is able. It is extremely repugnant for him to be doing so
   and, against all his sense crying out as they are, it is also an
   extremely brave thing for him to do. In order to keep himself at
   the task, he keeps attaching Cass:)

BUTCHER Champion bloody Cass. Perfect man. World-beater. Hot shit. The golden goose's piss. Example for us all. Drag yourself up by the bootstraps like the champ's doing. Lick Cass's boots. That right, champ?...

   (By sheer good fortune he locates a helmet in the rubble.
   Madly he puts it on, tries to lamp. It works. It floods the cavity
   with precious light.

   For a moment, Cass struggles to his elbows to see what it is,
   then falls back. Clearly he has the shakes which are causing
   him great pain through his internal injuries.

   Even Bunting shows a momentary interest, then goes back to
   mumbling to himself.

443

This is a solidly quiet moment of disbelief, and relief.

Then Bunting spoils it by resuming his exaggerated breathing in and out...

Blackout.)

12.

(At its highest, the area is probably less than two metres high, and even this does not extend very far. It seems that the cavity they are in does extend fairly extensively beyond this, although the light from the helmet doesn't allow the blackness out there to be penetrated.

The effects of the helmet light are not all a blessing. Any movement is played grotesquely against the side walls of the rock... frightening in their circumstances, and only serving to accentuate the oily, we nigrescence of the rock.

At least one prop can be seen clearly to have splintered badly, while another, which is taking the main weight of the hanging wall above them, is clearly shaky.

At the beginning the very definition of their situation fills Butcher with fear and loathing. Finally, he adjusts to the new perceptions as much as humanly possible, trapped down there like that. He has got himself able to search around but he finds nothing which could help them.

He can now confront Cass and Bunting. The former, he stands apart from but 'over' and then merely turns away. With Bunting, however, the sight of the older man with his head wound and his oscillating, annoying half-rambling, half-mock-breathing makes Butcher's rage at him even more hard to contain)

BUTCHER   You're trying to use up the air, aren't you, you old bastard? Why would that be?

(He gets himself to turn away from Bunting, goes back to Cass, where he can snigger)

BUTCHER   Cass, you look disgusting. Take you nowhere, my friend.

(Cass tries to raise himself to what is evidently a threat, but cannot make it. Sadistically, Butcher bends over and presses down on Cass's stomach. Cass cries out in great pain. Immediately, over this, Bunting's artificial breathing takes on surreal proportions)

BUTCHER   (over Cass, hypnotically) Cass. Cass. Cass.

(Blackout.

Then almost immediately, lighting back on. Cass could have blinked. Indeed, for a split second, the cavity is filled with hallucinogenic lighting effects. Then return to 'normal' lighting.

CASS   (as though nothing had happened) Here.

BUTCHER   (still mesmerically) Cass. Cass.

CASS   Here.

BUTCHER   (into a hiss) Casssss…

CASS   Whoooo?

BUNTING   (taking up the slow rhythm, but very loud) Breathing for the cats!
   (sucks air in and out)
Yes. Doing it, doing it. Suck…
   (sucks air in and out)
suck. Meouw, pussy pussy.
   (laughs hysterically)
Breathing for the cats. Did I see.
   (sucks in air, lets it out. Theatrically)

445

(Etcetera.

Cass begins to sway to the rhythm that Bunting is setting. Only after realising this, does he try to break its hold but still struggles unsuccessfully.

The audience now begins to see from Cass's p.o.v. His body is now in wave motion. His entreaties to the 'outside' have the figure of Bunting slowly and waveringly begin to merge into that of Bunting. They seem to melt in with each other at the far end of the area., except that Bunting's tone has become more bullish and mocking, more deliberately malicious. His sucking in and out of the precious air in there takes on an edge of malevolent defiance and of knowing precisely what he is doing.

Cass looks like he is trying to bring them closer and push them away one and the same time, and...)

CASS   Come in, come in.

BUTCHER   Cass, stop.

CASS   Come... *in. What?*

BUNTING   (starts up madly again) Breathe for the cats.
   (sucks in the air madly once more)
I'm doing it. Did I see.

BUTCHER   (driven to distraction) Bunt... tinggggg.

CASS   Here.

BUNTING   Breathe for the. Cats! (gulping the air) Srrrrr. Srrrr.

BUTCHER   Hunt... innnnggggg.

CASS   Come in

BUNTING   I'm doing it, yes.

CASS   WHAT?!

(Blackout)

13.

(Return of lighting effect from Cass's point of view, but slightly less hallucinogenic. Pervading all, Bunting breathing becomes less crazy and more as though he is truly having trouble doing so. For a moment Butcher and Bunting cannot be seen, then they seem to emerge from out of Cass's body. Again he is trying to hold them in while trying to push them away. They are mocking him.)

CASS   Make streel. Who streel. (chokes back a giggle) Streeled. When cushion cuscus. What's a streel?

BUTCHER   Dummy wants to know what's a streel.

BUNTING   Meouw, meouw. I'm doing it. Yes.

CASS   (enjoying the playacting) A streel, Butcher, is a rrrrr of steel.
   (changes tack)
Yes, come in, come down. Shitheads…

(fade to blackout)

14.

(Butcher and Bunting are feeding from Cass who is now in a position of a sow feeding its young. Colours play across them and have a peaceful effect, one of contentment. Cass's arms are flung out widely in a come-one-come-all gesture.

At first Cass is comforted but this soon changes. He starts to honk like a pig, initially softly. But then Butcher's piglet noises become more aggressive, more brutishly going at the teat. Cass's noise rises in alarm. Bunting's kitty-kitty meouwing follows Butcher in aggressiveness intent.

447

The lighting effect flickers even more cyclically until a peak is reached, when Cass doubles up and tries to get away from the other two, tries to escape from them, but is held back from doing so.

Blackout)

15.

(Cass sits dead still. Sitting by him in yoga fashion are both Butcher and Bunting.

All is silent.

They seem to loom above him. The silence becomes agitated, even deadly.

They remain like this for as long as can be borne. Then each begins, starting from deep down, a moaning which builds up into a sort of cacophonic unison. Butcher's is one of anger and bursting violence. Cass's is one of a rising spasm of pain he cannot hold back. Bunting's is a mixture of sad cat sounds and the infantile.

When they are at full pitch...

blackout and sharp silence)

16.

(Return lighting to laughter just beginning to bubble out of all three. One more Butcher and Bunting are leaning over Cass. He is making initial little flurries to get up but without any obvious impediment. His attempts increase in frequency as their laughter at him increases.

Now Butcher and Bunting are physically restricting him,

egging each other on to do so. They seem to be smothering him.

There follows a series of lighting 'cut-outs', even of strobe effect, during which the laughing, now openly menacing, is in crescendo. Cass is even screaming but silently. After each, Butcher and Bunting take up new positions which express their outrageous intrusions on Cass. Butcher sits on Cass's head; Bunting bites his legs; Butcher kneels on his neck; Bunting bites his hip; Butcher slithers down his torso while Bunting does the same the other way. Butcher twists his arm; Bunting twists his leg; Butcher has his finger in Cass's ear; Bunting is pinching his nose...

... until a last quick cameo showing Cass being held by the arms and legs while he struggles frantically.

There is a frieze on this.

Then Bunting's exaggerated sucking air in and out rises even more malevolently. Cass opens his eyes. Above him, their faces are accentuated by the lighting to be repulsive, reptilean.

Cass lets go with a scream finally.

Blackout)

17.

(Cass is now on his own. Bunting and Butcher have withdrawn and sit in the shadows away from him. When they speak to him, their voices are strangely, as though they were coming through a vacuum.

They talk in monotone. Even when Cass doubles up in pain, he does so with a kind of deliberation and tonelessness that indicates his mind is floating free of the reflexes of his body.)

BUNTING Meouw.

CASS   Pain here, Butcher. Where are you, Butcher.

BUTCHER   Where's Cass.

CASS   Come in.

BUTCHER   Cass, there's more than meets the eye.

BUNTING   (dry laugh) Here, kitty-kitty.

BUTCHER   Doing what, Cass?

CASS   What?

BUTCHER   Don't do it, Cass.

CASS   Must. Save us.

BUTCHER   Must you have did done, Cass.

CASS   Have to, you know.

BUTCHER   More.

CASS   No more. I can feel things through here, Butcher.

BUTCHER   Any meaning?

CASS   Is there a flicker see corner sight like?

BUTCHER   Corner site shopped, Cass.

CASS   Let me go just because I did.

BUTCHER   You did.

CASS   Let me go, Butcher.

BUNTING   (derangedly) Cat got your tongue?

BUTCHER   Bunting, Cass.

CASS (agony but still drily) Bunnttinnnggggg…

BUTCHER What I said, What can Cass see? Bunting bloody breathing like that.

CASS See. Uh. See. A long coming. Edges black. Disgusting.

BUTCHER Bunting breathing it all away.

CASS Yes. Butcher?

BUTCHER Cass? Listen. Bunting. Cass, listen.

CASS (agitated by strangely monotone still) Butcher. Your face. I know it was me. Flesh, where it moved, where you put your mouth on me with those talking maggots. All bloody hhhheavinggggs, Butcher. Maggots, see. Let me go as I did it, now…

BUTCHER Smart arse… any meaning?

CASS (childlike) Let me go.

BUTCHER Nobody said about Bunting.

CASS (breaks the expressionless) BUNNN… TINNGGGG!

(Blackout)

18.

(The lighting is now suddenly flickering in colours and confusingly. It bombards the three of them with each other's silhouette.

And then, seemingly impossibly, the three silhouettes come violently together. The impression is that one of them… certainly either Cass or Butcher has leapt up and launched himself onto the other two. The three silhouettes form a violent struggling mass before quietening in movement, drawing apart

451

again, then merging again, this time slowly.

One thing is definite – one of them is struggling with one of the others, while the third is trying to separate them.

Lighting dims.)

BUNTING   (deranged, repeatedly, but going to gurgle) Cat gotcha tongue? Cat gotcha tongue?...

19.

(Bunting's suckings of air comes hard, then suddenly stops altogether. One of the figures moves guiltily away from another. The first figure slides down to the ground. The third figure remains looking on, not moving. The second figure looks to be suddenly dry retching.

Blackout)

20.

(Butcher's silhouette remains motionless behind Cass, who is now back in his 'normal' position. Cass begins to trace something on the rock above his head, but having done so suddenly tries to knock it away. It is though whatever it is falls to the ground dangerously by him. He cringes, but then seems to notice something else on the rock above, sits up, tries to knock whatever it is away too.

The lighting starts to become more profuse, reminiscent of cockroaches and centipedes scampering on the rock, on himself. The effect begins to invade Cass. His panic now is open. He cries out. The cry is pathetic.

Butcher's silhouette detaches itself from the wall and he comes over to hold Cass down. Butcher slaps him, not without a good deal of pleasure in it.)

452

CASS (clinging on) Such a dread, Butcher.

(He tries to struggle away from Butcher and, even though his actions are still disabling, he now starts to show that the climacteric is beginning to pass.

Blackout)

21.

(Lighting is even and 'real' again. Cass is still doubled up but is relatively in charge of himself once more. Butcher is back in his old place and has resumed his tapping, this time with a morose and near hopeless cadence.

The body of Bunting is off to one side... obviously deliberately moved to there.

Once again, there is a growing rumble in the mine. It mounts in intensity and proximity.

Cass noticeably braces himself. Surprisingly, Butcher is able to laugh at him, even as this next rumble threatens to come down upon them.

It passes)

BUTCHER   You can tell me now, Cass.
    (gets no reply)
Nothing to say, Cass?
    (still nothing)
You're a real fucked-out case, aren't you, Mister First-past-the-post.
Hey, Cass! I'm glad I've seen it.

CASS (without looking up) How long?

BUTCHER   You sniveling like a wimp? Who cares?

CASS They'll come again, Butcher. Question. Do I hope there's enough time for them to come again?

BUTCHER There'll be time. I've got the light and they're sure as shit coming, bonghead. You're gone this time, Cass.

CASS Slit open, am I?

BUTCHER Like a fucking mullet, mate.

CASS (looking about) You wonder where we getting the air from, Butcher?

BUTCHER What're you on about?

CASS We should be gasping like your mullet by now. We should be in for it. Must be fresh air coming from somewhere.

BUTCHER (excitedly) You're right!

(He casts around again but still can't find any air source)

BUTCHER Doesn't matter where it comes from.

(He resumes his tapping. It is then that Cass notices Bunting's body set apart. It is startling)

CASS What's wrong with Bunting?

BUTCHER Yeah, play the idjit, bugger, you.

CASS What's going on?

(Since Butcher is not forthcoming, Cass raises himself enough to be able to crawl over to Bunting but, before he gets halfway, Butcher throws a rock at him. Cass stops, then starts again. This time Butcher throws a large rock directly at him)

BUTCHER Don't try it, mug.

CASS (hiss) You tell me what happened, Butcher.

454

BUTCHER   You tell me, hot shot.

CASS   (can now muster up menace) I said, explain.

(Butcher leers at him as though he knows something about Cass now and is keeping it to himself. Then he finally shrugs so-what:)

BUTCHER   Old buggerlugs keeled over in my arms. The story I'm sticking to, see. For the time being, Cass… for the time being.

CASS   Just keeled over like that.

BUTCHER   You know it, pal.

CASS   You were going at the poor old sod before I went out.

BUTCHER   So what?

CASS   And now we've got plenty of air.

BUTCHER   Who was to know about that then?

CASS   I'm going over to look at him, Butcher.

BUTCHER   You've done enough damage, you fucker.
   (pause, then speaking with a blackmailer's equivocation)
He kept sucking our air in and out. No reason except bloody-mindedness. Maybe it was… what d'you uni smart arses say?... extenuating circumstances. Yeah, pull this one. But you're right, who knew about the air still coming in then?

CASS   I didn't say…

BUTCHER   (over him) I'm not saying one way or the other. Only he gasped then lunged at me. I held him. What can a man do? Then he rallied, like, as though he was seeing me for the first time. You listening, Cass, you prick? You'll laugh at this. He said something about cats down the old mine shaft. With a straight face that was.

Then he slipped down me. The least I could do was let him down, Cass.

CASS Is he dead?

BUTCHER Don't come that act.

CASS Dead, Butcher?

BUTCHER Comedian.

CASS So Butcher's making sure he at least's getting out of here, right?

BUTCHER I've got the light, Cass. I got the legs. Flooding holds off and we're gonna be alright. I'm pulling you through to answer a few questions, you weak turd.

CASS Not so weak. Don't tell me, pal.

BUTCHER Who'd want to bother, Big Man.

CASS So everything's jake because Butcher says it's jake. All we're supposed to overlook is the small fact that Butcher has...

   (He stops)

BUTCHER (hiss) Has what?

CASS You know it, Butcher.

BUTCHER You say it.

CASS Don't try anything.

BUTCHER I did Bunting in. That what you're saying?

CASS You said it, Butcher.

BUTCHER YOU DID BUNTING IN, CASS!

CASS   (stunned, before…) No.

BUTCHER   Tell him you didn't then.

CASS   No way.

BUTCHER   Tell him a second time.

CASS   (frantic on the possibility) No way!

BUTCHER   (leering) Make it a lucky third time, bastard.

(Cass goes to spit an answer back but finds he can't do so. Instead, he picks up a rock threateningly)

CASS   Not so weak, Butcher.

(Butcher picks up his own rock and they threaten each other

Before this can happen a gob fire spontaneously starts in the rubble, which both men know could lead to another explosion at worst or using up any limitation on the air they might have left. Quickly, they both cooperate in shifting the rubble, exposing the fire and putting it out.

There is a small moment of incredulity before each picks up his rock again and back off warily from each other.

Blackout)

22.

(When lighting returns, Cass and Butcher have resumed their places but remain with rocks to hand. Occasionally Butcher taps and receives a mocking laugh from Cass, who gets in turn an up-yours finger.

Another rumble comes, but this time they are getting used to hearing them far away. It quickly passes)

CASS Scared, Butcher.

BUTCHER Not of you, sports star.

CASS I'm scared, Butcher, but that's only because I've got an
imagination to imagine a no-morrow on the next horizon. Keep up…
    (taps head)
the emptiness up here, buddy boy.

BUTCHER I'm keeping you alive, Cass. Take your hand away
from that rock.

CASS After you.

    (They tense together again until Cass eventually snorts)

CASS Pathetic.
    (then)
Like I was saying, Butcher… that no-tomorrow, it's like that light of
yours there. It… throws light on things, wouldn't you say? But if
that bit of the jigsaw puzzle of no-tomorrow isn't there sudden-like…
like your light, Butcher… well, it's not normal, right? Not Butcher's
normal. But, you see, you dummy, it *is* normal. It's not-there
normal, see. That's what those synapses running around that mush up
there of yours can't twig onto, Butcher. And what does that say about
you and old Bunting there? It goes you got the wrong victim, mate.
That no-tomorrow possibility makes you the real victim of little old
Butcher, Butcher. You got the wrong man, you dumb ox.

BUTCHER Speak for yourself, ice-picker. You can spout all the
shit you want, but I said you're gone this time, bloody Cass, and I
mean it.

    *(Butcher makes a show of putting his rock down, but Cass
    doesn't trust him and doesn't follow suit)*

BUTCHER Getting the shits up, is the great Cass? Afraid of
Butcher and so it comes out. About Bunting.. Maybe he was pegging
out anyway. What do I know? Maybe he was trying to take us with
him. I don't know. Maybe… nobody'll ask.

CASS Maybe somebody will ask.

BUTCHER Maybe. Maybe not. What I'm trying to do here, Cass, is calling a truce.

CASS Maybe you are. Maybe you aren't.

BUTCHER Bunting… might be he's not worth it. Just saying maybe, Cass.

CASS I hear you.

BUTCHER Funny how Bunting got it so bad, going off his tit like that. Cats. Chrissalmighty. Okay, I'm not saying here and I'm not saying there… but all I'm going on about is maybe they'll look at it as a case of either Bunting or us.

CASS (craftily) Could be.

BUTCHER Yeah. Maybe. I dunno.

> *(Butcher makes a show of going back to his tapping but he is still watching Cass out of the corner of his eye and Cass is of course aware of it. Nevertheless, this gives them both a welcome respite)*

CASS You say a few words over him, Butcher?

BUTCHER Come off it.

CASS I can't remember any of those Christian lines. 'The Lord is My Shepherd'… how corny insulting would that be. Anything in the bible about cats, Butcher?

BUTCHER Knock it off.

CASS (but cynically) No, straight up. An antsy bastard like me ought to remember what he's being ungod done down over, right? I ought to be able to say, right Butcher you go to church religiously so you won't know a fucking thing… you don't even *have* to know…

but me, now I ought to know what to say about me not having any faith in Big Huey when I'm face-to-face with Big Huey. That's what I reckon, Butcher.

BUTCHER   What're you shitting on about now?

CASS   Jesus, Butcher, hawk up a gorbie and make it as the most imaginative you're going to be today. Bunting being remembered, Butcher. You going to go out hating my guts and me hating yours. That makes us something at least. We deserve something at least. Same with Bunting, is all I saying. Deserves something. Something that rounds off Bunting. Try a thought, Butcher, other than straining over the shit hole. Both of us try.

> *(Butcher grudgingly nods. Their 'requiem' for Bunting is callous, yet factual, even perhaps truthful, especially since neither was very close to the older man. They also use it as a thankful diversion)*

BUTCHER   Bunting, he was always just a poor old bastard, far as I could see. He was always getting it in the neck, even the kids having a go at his hump. But walking on. You'd say that much about him. Never drank or smoked, they say.

CASS   No wonder he went silly in the head…

BUTCHER   Always talking about nothing. Never heard anything about him and cats. The word goes he never once swore. How can a real man live like that?

CASS   Dunno?

BUTCHER   Dunno.

CASS   (taking it up) Bunting. Bloody old Bunting. They called him Humpy, you're right. Or the Hunchback of Knotty Pine, or something. Always mumbling away to himself; maybe he was always spruiking on about cats, but nobody knew. Poofie? Who knows? Before she left him, they reckon his wife used to ride his hump to get a bit. No, she died. Maybe left and died, both. With Bunting, who knows. Who's Bunting?

460

BUTCHER He stank like water never touched him. Long as I can remember, he was always old. If I'm not wrong, once I heard tell he sexed on with a cat, straight up.

CASS (jokishly) Male or female cat?

BUTCHER (ditto) Female. There was nothing queer about Bunting. There was this rumour he used to sometimes sleep down here to save the effort of going up and coming back down again.

CASS Bunting. What a lad.

BUTCHER Yeah.

(Pause)

CASS Anything else?

BUTCHER (bright thought) I was one of the little pricks who used to throw rocks at him. He shouldn't retired years ago. Wouldn't lay down.

CASS Stubborn.

BUTCHER Stubborn.

CASS Sub borned stub born, shouldn't have been sprayed up against the fence and picked up by his mother. Wife gone, rellies all gone, cats gone. Bye bye, Baby Bunting; you've been...
    (throws it out)
BUTCHERED!

(Butcher reacts. They face up to each other again. An open fight to the death is only avoided when Cass has another spasm of pain, has to fight to hold it in)

BUTCHER (sotto voce) That what you're going to tell 'em, junkie?

CASS What... else?

BUTCHER   And you reckon they'll believe you?

CASS   Before you, Butcher. The trouble is there's going to be nobody to tell.

BUTCHER   They'll get here, and when they do, you've *gone* this time.

CASS   (openly in pain again) Nobody, Butcher. Not even a nod out of Godgob Himself. Nix. Nil. The big fat zero. See, Butcher... whatever might have happened, no Lazarus type revenge for Bunting. All it'll be is if you're still living you grazed better than Bunting, full stop, end of...
     (doubling up)
So who's... going to tell Bunting that? You... or... me?

> *(Is overwhelmed momentarily. Butcher sees his chance and comes on with his rock but he has hesitated too long and Cass is able to pick his own rock up and fling it at the helmet. It's a good enough hit to smash the light.*
>
> *Blackout.*

23.

(In the intervening darkness, clear signs of the two men fighting grotesquely without being able to see each other. This is frighteningly claustrophobic, punctuated by their catching breaths and grunts as they grope around, lunging)

24.

(Lighting for the audience, as previously. Cass and Butcher are performing a danse macabre... groping, moving cautiously, stopping to listen, swinging their rocks about themselves. All they know is the other man is dangerously close by; it is a horror for both... the guesses, the wrong ways, the wild swings, touching and the repugnance of the blackness more

overwhelming than the need to come out best.

Cass might be hurting but the impenetrable blackness evens up the situation.

Then comes the next rumble. This is much stronger than the earlier ones and the resulting rock fall more approximate. Their duel becomes comparatively minor. Their fear is reflected in how both literally try to burrow themselves out of harm's way when the tremor reaches its climax.

Blackout)

25.

(The tremor passes)

CASS   DAMN YOU, SHITHEAD!

BUTCHER   DIE, PRICK!

(Pause)

BUTCHER   You didn't have to do that to the old guy.

CASS   I'm too had it to tangle with you anymore, pal.

BUTCHER   You smashed the light. It was my light.
   (then)
YOU THINK YOU'RE GOD HIMSELF?

(They are lying back from each other. The danger from the other has momentarily passed, but they keep their rocks close to hand and they remain wary of any sudden sound of movement.

Butcher has been really set back having lost his light. It makes Cass now more aggressive, and knowing it)

CASS   Butcher, I am a voice. Holus bolus, all that's left of me. I am floating, Butcher. I am around you everywhere. I am *the rock.*

BUTCHER   I'll see you in hell.

(He goes back to tapping but is hampered in listening for any reply and listening for any attack from Cass)

CASS   So my Carol was your One'n'only, eh? You should've told me. I would've pissed myself laughing. Hey, I could have told her and she could have blamed getting knocked up on you. You didn't knock up my wife, did you, Butcher. Sneaky, creeping in between her legs. No, I don't reckon. You always did plough in behind me, didn't you, loser?

BUTCHER   It near killed her when she lost that baby, but what'd you care. This time I win, Cass.

CASS   Ah, the razor-blade race for life now, is it? You won't win. You could never win anything.

BUTCHER   Big junkhead world beater.

CASS   (not unremorsefully) I didn't know why I left her that time, Butcher, and that's a fact. I don't even know if there was any reason or not now. Someone I forget just came along and I guess I thought that's where life went for me. I don't mean your type of 'living', dumbo, not your charge accounts and the back-seat leather smell of your new bombs… Butcher's goodies, right?... I don't mean that. I mean the I-can-have. Something about potential, like all those hundreds of thousands of coaches kept spouting about. I should have listened more. I admit that. But that's not the point.
     (listens)
Keep tapping, Butcher, so I know where you are.

BUTCHER   I'll tap your head, big shot.

(Pause)

BUTCHER   She never came back home again. I was waiting for her, Cass.

CASS   Not the point, mate. Point is, I got the notion to flow on and she was left standing and I was sorry. I guess I was sorry. I'm not sorry now, is the point.

BUTCHER   Suck on this, Cass.

CASS   (calmly) Would you really kill me too, Butcher?

BUTCHER   I could ask you the same, bastard.

CASS   Listen, Butcher.

BUTCHER   What?

CASS   Wouldn't it be beautiful just to be able to lie back right now and go blank?

BUTCHER   (thinks, before:) Yeah.

> *(Another fire from spontaneous combustion breaks out.*
>
> *Butcher, more able, gets to it first. He scrambles to get the rubble aside so he can put it out, when he realises he is now clearly seen against the flame, whereas Cass remains in the shadows unseen. Butcher scrambles to get away from the light)*

CASS   *Put it out, fool!*

> *(Butcher scrambles back and covers the fire. As soon as he does so, he gets hurriedly back to his place, resumes tapping with an urgency brought on by shock)*

CASS   You check to see if there was any, Butcher?

BUTCHER   What now?

CASS   Wood lying about. Wood could've made a torch.

BUTCHER   Shit!

CASS (real put down) Don't be so thick, Butcher. Never change, will you?
  (then)
You should've seen your face when you realized you were a sitting duck against that fire.

BUTCHER They're up there and they're gonna see you get yours, Cass.

CASS You don't sound too sure anymore, Butcher.

BUTCHER I want them to see what you really are, Cass.

CASS You know, Butcher, I'll go. Gladly. Jesus, let it come. *Chrissakes*!
  (gets a hold of himself)
Okay. But not by a self-starting fire, mate. Or smoke. Or gas. Monoxide, okay, but not by a blower. Not by a seam of coal, Butcher. Not burning or choking a man off and not…

BUTCHER (outcry) LET THE BASTARD FALL!

  (Pause)

CASS Frachet.

BUTCHER What?

CASS Frachet, mate. Like in frachetty. Or ratshit. Okay, you go, you go and there's that…
  (spasm of pain)
Logic. 'Kay. Burning or choking. The longest linger, but what I mean is that's not going out. That's *dying* before you going out. I hate that! That's being killed not being allowed to pass on. But to die… clawing at yourself, Butcher…

BUTCHER Oh, God, man.

CASS Keep tapping, son.

BUTCHER Get knotted.

CASS   Wouldn't mind getting knotted one last time, mate.

BUTCHER   (thankful for release) Not half.

CASS   (ditto) You take the top half; I'll take the bottom half.
   (sing song)
'I'll be in scrotum afore ye…'

   *(But any camaraderie ends there at this time. Each goes back
   to his thoughts)*

CASS   (only starting off slowly) Son, you go in and come out of that
church of yours smiling, so what's with being made in your Big
Huey's image when there's more dying than being dead? No, I mean
it. What goes with the suffering for years… the pain and the
humiliations, like… before you can get to peg out? That thing up on
the Cross, that supposed to be a shining example to us all? That was
fucking awful, Butcher. That was agony itself, like this is what all
you guys'n'gals can ever expect. Where's the nice-and-softly time
and then breathing a sigh bye-bye, full stop?

BUTCHER   Don't go even more whacko on a man, Cass.

CASS   No, I want to know… that the Grand Design you go for?
Jesus wept. Why not a big light switch in the sky and one flick and
lights-out; you're outa here no sweat, sayonara? Nothing in between
life and death, Butcher. No qualifying event called *dying*. What's
this *dying*, Butcher. That Huey's Grand Plan? *Suffer* the little
chil'run the only thing He ever no-bulled about? That's just treating
us like animals, son. Maybe animals are what we are to your Huey,
Butcher. They say animals don't know what's going on, so that's
what it looks like to me… being treated like animals. Not human,
Butcher. Negative on the dignity befitting one of your ribs. Animals.
That the message you've been getting all along from your church but
you haven't twigged it, because you haven't lamped onto the animal
hooves beneath the robes? Butcher, give me a big light switch in the
sky any day. One flick and you're gone.

BUTCHER   Yeah, with you, some hope.

CASS (near outright panic) I don't want to go out choking on smoke. I don't want to be struggling under water to breathe. I don't want to be screaming in pain under a shit load of rock. I don't want to be gasping towards my last breath a half an hour away. Fuck this *dying* caper. Who said we had to go out *dying* anyway?
    (letting go)
Butcher, listen, Butcher…!

BUTCHER I'm listening, mad man.

CASS I'll go, I'll go but… *this ain't right, Butcher!*

BUTCHER Hey, it's bad enough for me too.

   (There is another quietening, gathering moment)

CASS You know, Butcher. A little high here or there made it come back easy enough… even going through the lock-up now'n'again… but coming back here… like, back down here to my old Dad's tunnels… it's where I think I've been coming all my life.

BUTCHER So what? Half of us.

CASS No, what I'm sprigging on about is maybe this's the only thing I've really understood all my born days, Butcher. Here. Now.

BUTCHER Yeah, and I'll say again… so w…
    (stops up short, stunned)
I hear them!
    (confirms)
I can bloody hear them!

CASS YES!

   (They both exult and then frantically go at the knocking on the rock faces, now careless of any danger from the other man.

   But almost simultaneously they come back to their reality that they would be murderous to each other and also the problem they have with Bunting's death.

They move apart again, face up to each other)

BUTCHER   Don't get any ideas, Cass.

CASS   Speak for yourself, idiot.

> *(Of the two, Butcher is the more confident now. Despite the danger he feels from Cass, he is positively exuberant and goes back to his tapping with gusto as a show of superiority.*
>
> *Cass, on the other hand, quickly seems down and uncaring. He is drifting off in fits and starts again, even starting to shake again)*

BUTCHER   (to up above) Yeah, come on, you big beautiful bastards.

CASS   Who cares, Butcher?

BUTCHER   You care, big achiever, you care.

CASS   I'm hurt, Butcher.

BUTCHER   Keep going on about it, and I might believe you, junkie.

CASS   You mightn't have any trouble getting over your bullshit about Bunting and me after all, Butcher.

BUTCHER   You bet your booties, pal.

CASS   (warning) Don't try anything, Butcher.

> *(Bunting resumes his tapping again, still hearing the rescuers. His exhilaration makes him so full of feeling he has to stop and spout what for him is a long introspection)*

BUTCHER   You know what I know now, Cass? I've beaten you, mug. This time it's my turn. Always bloody Cass out ahead of me, but not now. I gave ten times the guts you gave, bloody Cass. I stuck it out. I stayed around and slugged it out, because I never had it easy like bloody shining-light fucking Cass. Prick! When you weren't pussyfooting around here getting all the glory, I stuck and I won. I was the top operator around here and don't you forget it.

(to Cass's reaction to that)

You can snigger, shithead. Big champ. World beater. You wouldn't know what real *sticking* meant. Me, I had to sweat my tit off all the way. Then you come back.. A fucking junkie, a jailbird, a total bloody failure. A deadbeat. And they reckon the sun still shines out of your arse like I was nothing! But, yeah, just so you remember it, I'll say it again, flunk-off... I've beaten you this time.

CASS   A fact?

BUTCHER   A fact, bastard. And they're coming and gonna see what you did and how Cass ain't fit enough to lick my boots, mug.

CASS   (softly) I never said I was, Butcher. I just said you're as meaningless as me.

BUTCHER   (after stopping to think on that) I almost feel sorry for you, Cass.

CASS   I feel sorry for you, Butcher.

BUTCHER   I mean that, Cass.

CASS   Butcher, so do I.

> *(They pause to peer hard in each other's direction. It is as though they are re-assessing the other man. When Butcher goes on, it is markedly more conciliatory...)*

BUTCHER   What'll be going on up there? The alarm. That. Did you ever hear it? I did once. My Mum froze on the spot. Her face went white. All night standing around. Waiting. Dead still. The cold white breaths. The TV and all the outsiders. Sure. Hey, Cass, we'll be on Nine's news for sure.

(stops on thought)

Who'll they show up there waiting? For Bunting, not a red fig. For you, Cass, who?

(Cass doesn't answer because they'd be no one either)

Big man, bit zero. For me? All me mates, my mob, me back-up?

470

CASS   Maybe for ten minutes and then into the pub.

BUTCHER   (quiet acquiescence) Yeah.

CASS   You know something Butcher?

BUTCHER   Yeah?

CASS   You can come and get me now, melonhead. What do you want me to do? Bleep while you home in?

> *(Butcher contemplates that only for a moment before he throws his rock away)*

BUTCHER   Take it easy.

CASS   Come on then.

BUTCHER   Up yours.

> *(They lean back. This is a precious moment of relaxation.*
>
> *Then Butcher resumes his tapping and listening. But he pulls up abruptly. Taps harder, listens more intensely. Then...)*

BUTCHER   (disbelief) I think they're gone again, Cass.
    (frantically taps)
They're not answering. Cass?
    (then)
WHY?!

26.

> *(Through the darkness we hear Butcher madly backing his rock against the rock face. He has to give up momentarily through exhaustion of having little air*
>
> *The 'audience' lighting returns)*

CASS   Steady, son.

BUTCHER   No, mate, no…

CASS   You've got it.

BUTCHER   I keep telling you don't talk to me like a fucking child, shithead.

CASS   That's it, Butcher.

BUTCHER   What's fucking it?

CASS   See, how it all comes back to the beginning? Butcher?

BUTCHER   Up yours with the butter knife.

   (Now they hear why the return-tapping has ceased)

BUTCHER   (surprisingly tonelessly) You hear that?

CASS   I hear it.

   (A very deep rumble then tremor from seemingly the bowels of the earth. There is no doubt about the finality of it. It is frightening oncoming wave rises to full pitch as a background to:)

BUTCHER   Cass.

CASS   Butcher.

BUTCHER   CHRIST!

CASS   CHRIST!

BUTCHER   Where are you, Cass?

CASS   Over here.

   (They grope for each other, touch, stay besides one another.

They are now starting to get thrown around.

Cass moves particularly)

BUTCHER   *What are you doing?*

CASS   Waving my dick, Butcher.

BUTCHER   What?

CASS   Waving my dick.

(Pause)

BUTCHER   Ain't much of a dick, Cass.

CASS   Still beats yours by a mile.

BUTCHER   You wish, mate.

CASS   Any rate, what're you doing, Butcher?

BUTCHER   I'm waving; what else? A bloody flag, Cass!

CASS   Butcher, this dick here almost had it good…

BUTCHER   You're not kidding!

(They keep shouting defiance to encourage each other before they are drowned out. Their mouths are still moving when

the final cave-in comes)

(End)

www.ingramcontent.com/pod-product-compliance
Lightning Source LLC
Chambersburg PA
CBHW080508090426
42734CB00015B/3004